CITY LINKAGE

Art and Culture Fostering
Urban Futures

Michael Ziehl
Carsten Rabe
Till Haupt (eds.)

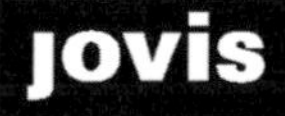

Black-out curtain 3 by Camilla Rasborg at Viktoria Kaserne (fux eG)

Thanks

We would like to thank all who contributed to *City Linkage* and to the City Link Festival. This goes first of all to the authors, the contributing artists and cultural producers as well as the Cultural Office of Hamburg—especially to Ruth Bäßler, who made both, this book and the festival possible.

4

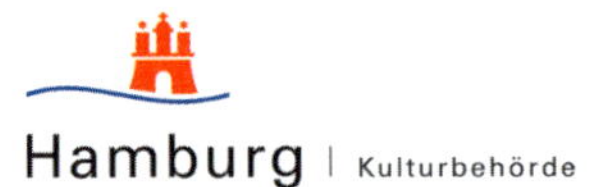

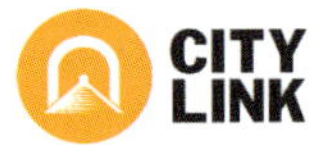

Content

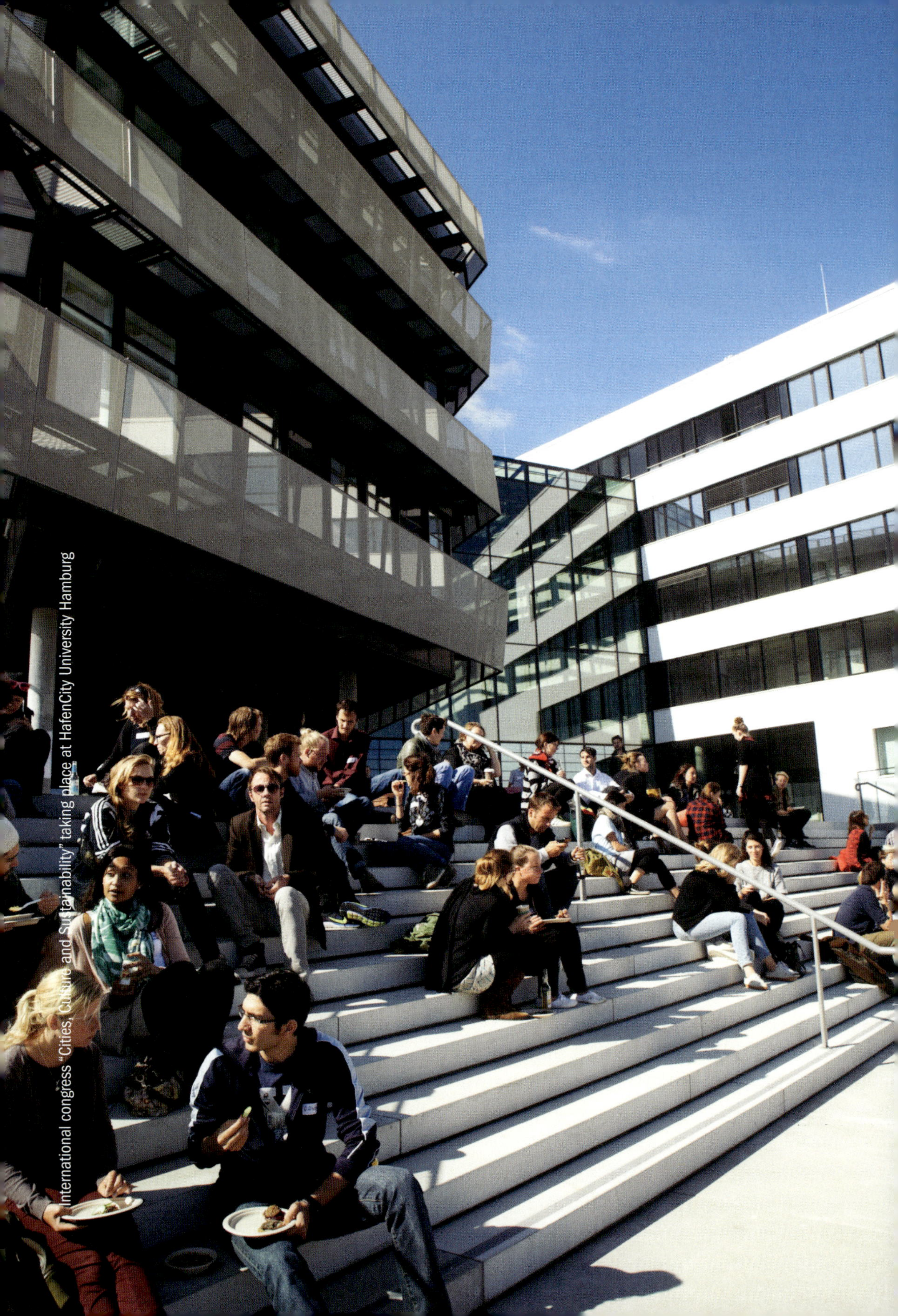

International congress "Cities, Culture and Sustainability" taking place at HafenCity University Hamburg

City Linkage: Introduction

Michael Ziehl, Carsten Rabe, Till Haupt

Arts and culture professionals increasingly involve themselves in questions of urban development: How do we want to live together? How can citizens directly participate in city politics? How can we shape cities so that they are liveable? Given the current processes of transformation, these questions are more relevant than ever. Through climate change, globalization, and neo-liberalization, the rapid changes of our cities often bring negative consequences for the city dwellers. In the search for solutions to the city of the future, it is clear that self-organized places of artistic and cultural production play an important role. *City Linkage* is concerned with their contributions to a sustainable city.

The contents of the publication date back to the City Link Festival Hamburg in Autumn 2014. During the nine-day festival, artists and cultural practitioners from Hamburg and Copenhagen showed contemporary art, organized exhibitions, and gave performances and concerts. Eleven artist-run spaces and projects in Hamburg opened their doors for these events. The audience was offered a unique insight into the self-organized art scene of the two cities. Actions in the public sphere made the festival a recreational and educational highlight in Hamburg. The international congress "Cities, Culture and Sustainability" opened a dialogue on sustainable cultural policy and the importance of art for the future of our cities. This effectively bridged the gap between creators, city activists, art lovers, and experts.

The festival was launched by the City Link network, which itself was initiated by the GivRum group from Copenhagen in 2012. Hamburg and Copenhagen should come closer together—not merely because of enhanced transport and commerce via the planned Fehmarn Belt Tunnel, but also in dialogue on art and culture. The initiators from Copenhagen and their partners in Hamburg organized exhibitions and group tours in both cities. Cultural workers visited each other and toured art and cultural projects. Furthermore, discussions and workshops were organized. It became clear that in these two cities art and cultural production is closely intertwined with respective urban development. The working conditions of artists and cultural workers are changing in the context of the urban environment. Production and exhibition venues have to compete in dynamic property markets. Additionally, in many cases urban austerity measures negatively impact the cultural sector. These factors contribute to both the precariousness and commodification of art and culture.

Those concerned have various reactions and see both problems as well as opportunities in these developments. Their reactions range from creative resistance to adaptation to the changing conditions. Thus they make a practical contribution to the sustainable transformation of our cities. They criticize the increasing commercialization and precariousness of life via public campaigns. They organize themselves collectively to tackle negative outcomes and demonstrate alternative living and working models—also for other stakeholders. In many cases they show solidarity with urban inhabitants and create learning environments for new models of cooperation between citizens and administration. Thus, they help to mitigate many of the negative consequences of urban transformation processes for themselves and other citizens and create visions of the future for the city.

City Linkage illustrates the particular importance of art and artists and of the places and projects that they have organized for sustainable urban development. There are contributions from artists, researchers, activists, and theorists in the publication. It is less about the connection between cities (City Link) as to what unites within cities (City Linkage). Hamburg and Copenhagen deliver many practical examples—and the City Link Festival is one of them. *City Linkage* shows images from selected festival moments and artworks. Contributing artist-run spaces and projects in Hamburg and Copenhagen present themselves. Lectures at the congress are represented by technical contributions. The authors look at self-organized art and cultural projects far beyond Hamburg and Copenhagen.

The first article attends to the manifold potentials and contradictions that arise when artists get involved in urban development. **Annabel Trautwein** utilizes theses that evolved from a discussion between artists, urban activists, and art experts from Hamburg and Copenhagen. The next contribution from **Sacha Kagan** is concerned with the chances of current transformative processes for the development of a "radical open citizenship." Artists and cultural workers play a special role for him, because they globally open up so-called "spaces of possibilities"—the cradles of resilient urban development. **Oleg Koefoed** deepens the concept of resilient development by describing cities as "Complex Adaptive Systems." For him, the many tensions, interactions, and dependencies between urban policy and cultural initiatives are both driving and inhibiting forces for transformative processes.

Elke Krasny illuminates practices of artists and activists that create self-sufficient organizations while facing the precariousness brought about by neoliberal processes of transformation. In this way they resist prevailing urban policy while simultaneously taking responsibility for themselves and their city. **Levente Polyák** shows that the professions of architects, designers, and artists are changing. Instead of designing physical products or buildings, their work is based on developing concepts in the context of managing resources resulting from experiences with crises and facilitating cooperation that leads to the implementation of their ideas.

Such a development project is described by **Michael Ziehl** in his contribution. The Gängeviertel in Hamburg was occupied in 2009 by an artists' initiative in the wake of the financial crisis. Subsequently, the city administration and the occupiers developed an alternative method of renovation. However, the cooperation is not working as well as it should due to a missing functional model for self-administration. The Copenhagen project PB43 turned out rather differently. After five years in the converted industrial premises, the self-organized cultural space has been pushed out by a more well-to-do investor. In order to preserve a future for the project, the City of Copenhagen offered them another property, as described by **Steen Andersen**.

In conclusion, twelve artist-run spaces and projects from Hamburg and Copenhagen will be presented. They show that Copenhagen has a flourishing young art scene. Visual art exhibits a spirit of optimism—as experienced in Hamburg at the turn of the millennium. The city is enlivened with new places for conceptual and minimal art, painting, drawing, and media art. Many artists cooperate across borders with creative professionals and even with the Hamburg art scene. Numerous joint exhibitions and exchange programs strengthen the contact and enrich the discourse of individual challenges and common solutions.

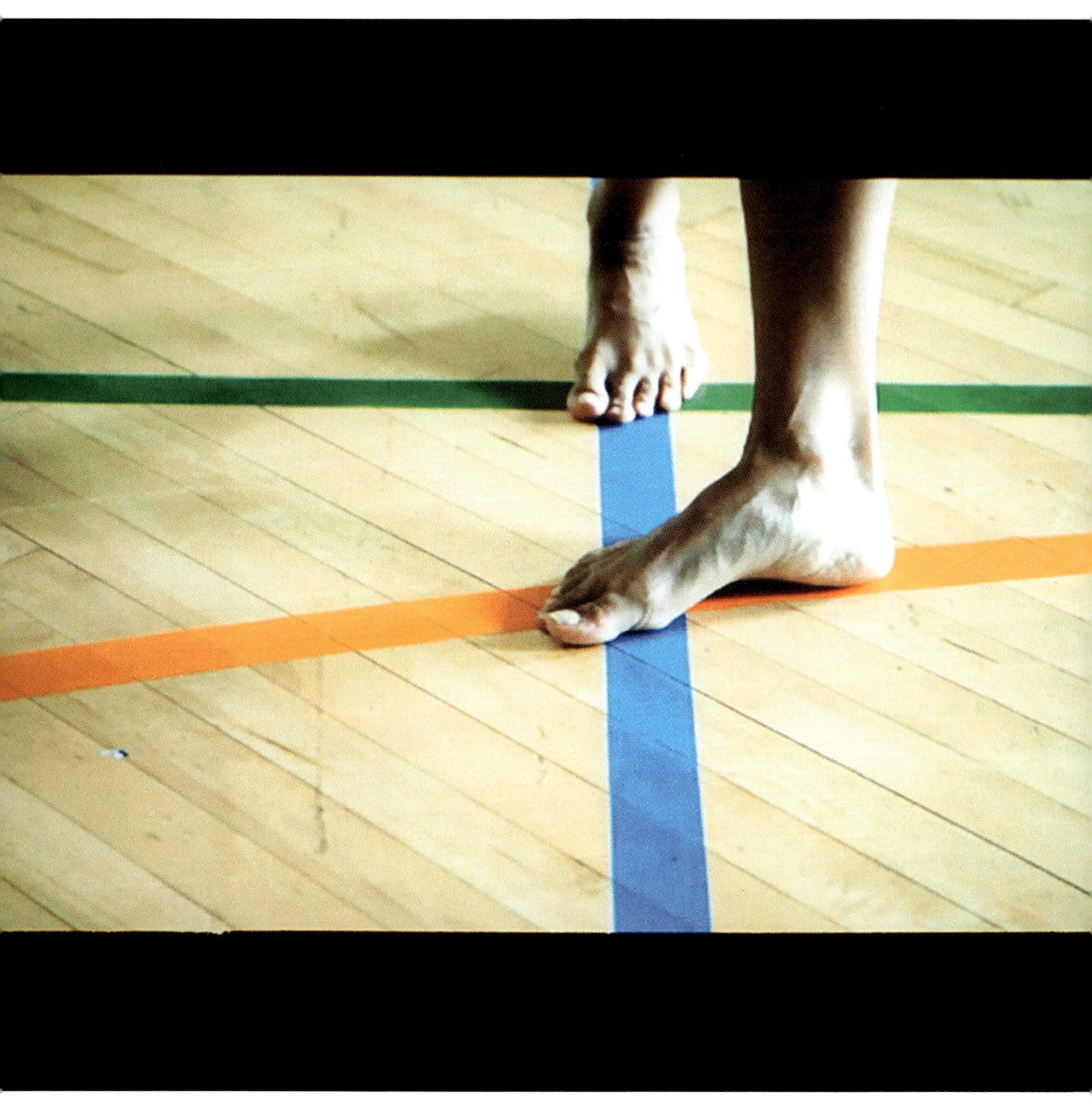

Video still, *Balancing Act* by Nina Mangalanayagam at Galerie Speckstraße

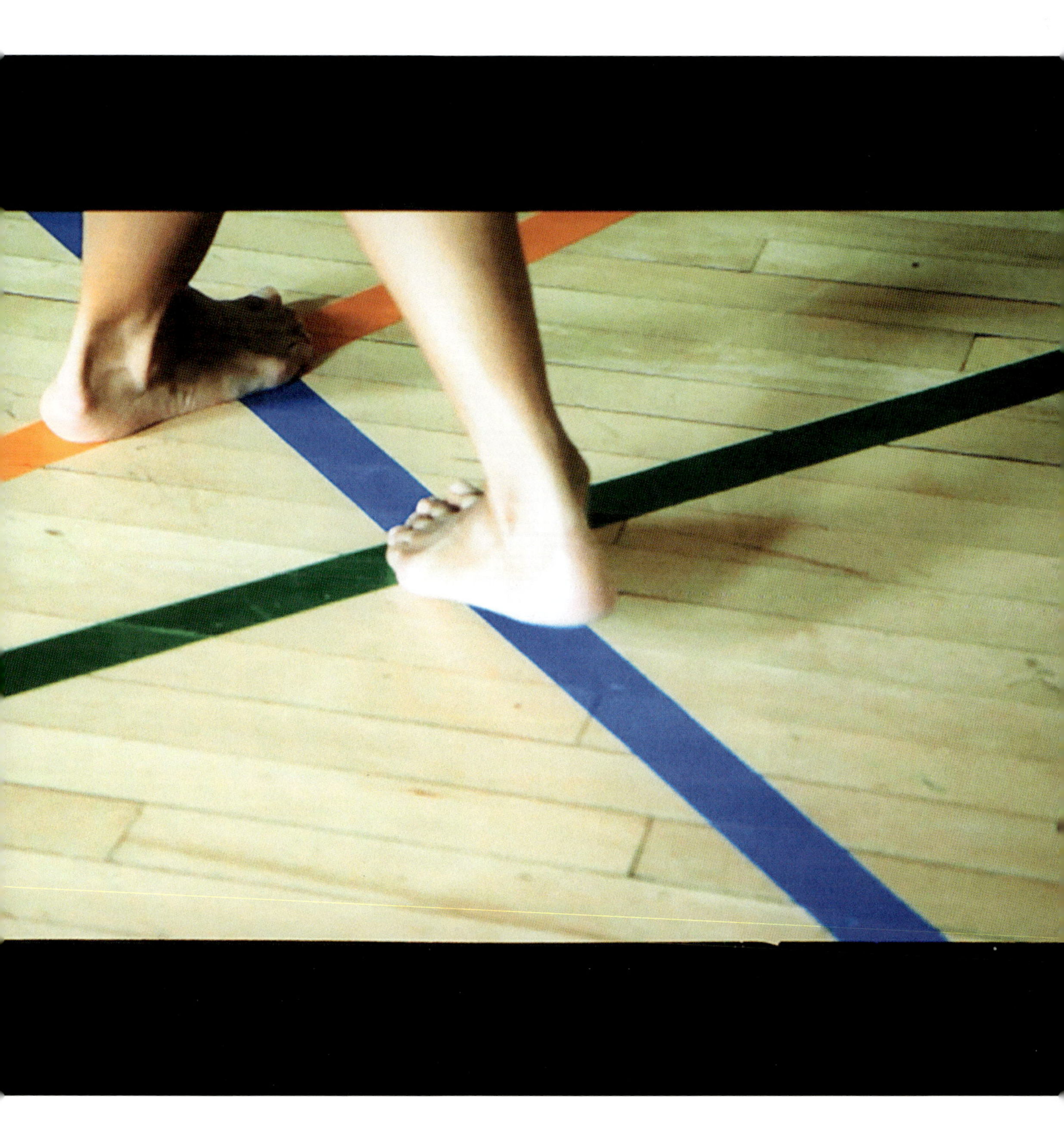

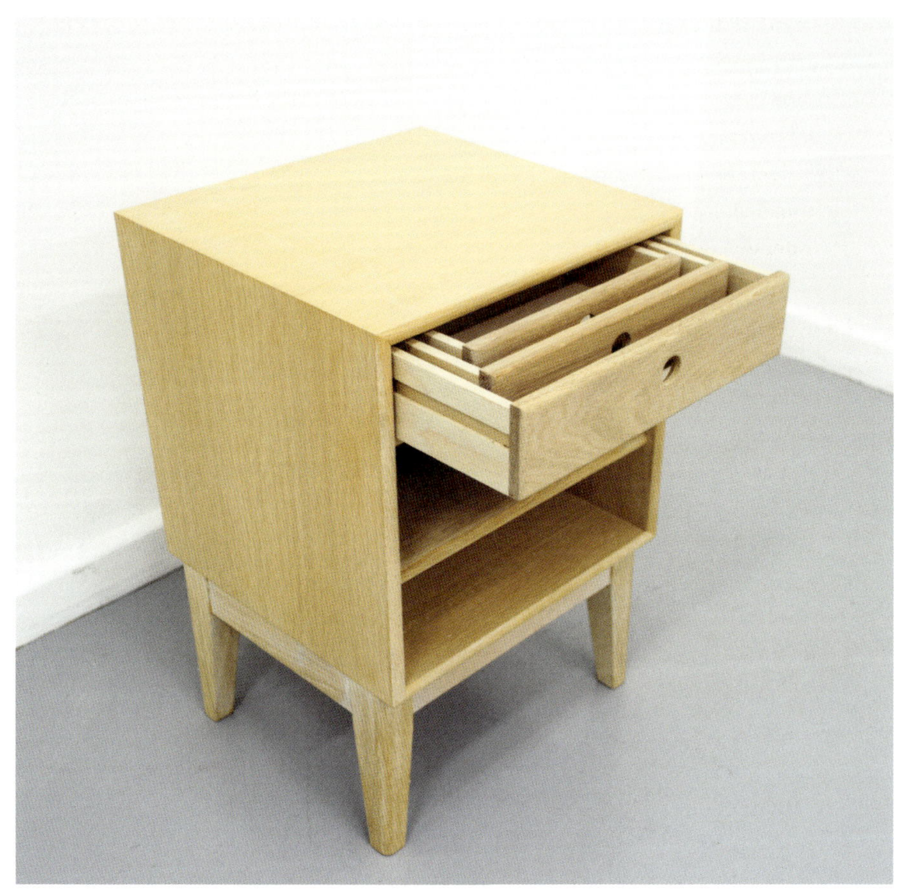

Rebus by Heidi Hove at Viktoria Kaserne (fux eG)

12

The City as Oeuvre: How Art Develops Urban Culture

Annabel Trautwein

The arts as a driving force for a culture of self-determined urban development—this is a goal central to the working methods of many artists. The aspiration to really change the city, however, calls forth opposition and skepticism from within the ranks of those involved. From artist and urban planner to theorist and activist, all argue about the identity, value, and efficacy of art in urban space. This text looks at statements and theses arising from a discussion between **Till F.E. Haupt, Christoph Schäfer, Michael Lingner, Steen Andersen,** and **Michael Ziehl.**

What can art contribute to the sustainability and livability of cities? For some theorists of the visual arts, the question seems rather inappropriate: art, they argue, urgently needs reform before it can credibly develop alternatives for other fields. Why toil on the foreign lands of urban development, especially since this is apparently occupied by the intentions of capitalist enterprises and the artist has virtually no opportunities to become involved in its development? If there must be a revolution, then it should first and foremost take place in one's own nest: the scholarship award committees and funding agencies; in advisory boards and academies. For many, this requirement is plainly obvious.

But some city activists confront the issue with skepticism: why should it be art that provides the solution? Many who are engaged in the free urban-culture scene do not consider themselves to be artists. Among them are journalists, artisans, scientists, architects, social workers, and students of different professions. Equally diverse is the motivation of their commitment—artistic creation is not necessarily high on their list of priorities.

Nevertheless, a glance to the dynamic and contested niches of the city shows that artists are often those responsible for opening new spaces and paving the way for new urban culture. They follow the impulse to create counter-proposals from a critique of existing conditions, to raise questions, and to independently develop solutions that are emancipated from politically and socially predetermined methods. Individual artists, heterogeneous interest groups, and sometimes even entire neighborhoods become the creators and authors of collective artworks that further develop the city according to their own ideas and needs. This genuine artistic logic seems to confirm an ideal picture: the artist as a self-determined subject who independently fashions life beyond the limits of standards and commerce.

In the context of this ideal, the importance of art for urban society goes far beyond the creation and exhibition of art works: it has become a lifestyle. Under the motto of the Creative Class theory, artistic intervention has become the imperative of our time—creativity is required not only in design studios and workshops, in ensembles and advertising agencies, but in all areas of work and life, both professionally and personally. We all should respond flexibly and creatively to the issues of our time, answers should be sought from within ourselves, new areas of action should be developed, and ways off the beaten path should be tread. We should become the artisans of our own lives.

Unfortunately, many professional artists fall disillusioned by the wayside. Instead of autonomy and emancipation, within their own sphere of activity they experience not only pressure to perform, but also the brutal constraints of selection and exploitation. A bitter realization follows: art that follows the predetermined logic of the art world and funding policy is prevented from being self-determined, emancipatory, and creative. On the contrary, agents within the "art operating system" permit foreign bodies such as policy and marketing to decide their chances of social impact, and in anticipatory obedience they even mentally allow themselves to participate in an exploitative system in which artistic creation loses its self-worth. To regain its emancipatory force, art would have to free itself from the conventional logic of acquisition and exploitation.

Urban Artistic Culture Creates Its Own Art Scene

Artists often encounter a very real problem when searching for a suitable studio. The choice of designated areas in the city is scarce, rents are often not affordable, and funded or allocated spaces often do not correspond to practical or ideological requirements. By contrast, many city quarters offer empty buildings and abandoned spaces that artists need for their work. These serve not only as studios, but also as a source of inspiration for an artistic confrontation with space and society itself—topics that for many artists are relevant and sexy in today's globalized society. The motto "think global act local" is also the subject of their own city and workspace. Urban space becomes a work of art.

However, the self-authorized design of urban space opens a new field of conflict for urban art: it contradicts the rules of administratively controlled urban development. Instead of selection in the struggle for scholarships, support programs, and the pressure of the commercial art world, artists are now faced with restrictions and obligations posed by officials and authorities. They are not alone in this conflict: even political initiatives, spontaneous citizen movements, and privately organized interest groups fight for space for their projects. Their original motivations, their respective self-image, and organizational structures may differ, but they have a common goal of successfully contending for working space in order to be creative in self-determined and emancipatory ways. Networks grow out of the gathering of lone wolves, the union of which creates places of collaborative culture, where activists gather knowledge, forces, and experiences in order to jointly develop new approaches in and for urban space. A new potential is visible: artists and creative activists working to create a culture of collaborative improvement and enrichment of the city for the people who use them.

It is a culture that follows its own artistic logic and has emancipated itself from the paradigms and mechanisms of commercial culture marketing. These self-created and self-managed places allow the artists to create and establish an alternative art scene beyond that of the academies and commercial galleries. Those who work in these places share an existential experience: there is another way to arrive at recognizable, high-quality art production than the one exclusively provided by the selection mechanisms of the institutionalized art world. At the same time urban artistic culture creates access and exchange above and beyond its original nucleus: between universities, self-managed cultural centers, and galleries as well as between established artists, ambitious amateurs, or an interested audience from various groups in society.

This alternative, low-threshold avenue to art creates new incentives that enable and encourage an urban culture of artistic production and reception. The value herein goes beyond the art scene and its social status and is increasingly relevant to the urban community as a whole, even if regulatory, managed urban development reluctantly responds: self-managed cultural places allow people to change and customize the city as they like. Their eccentricity and charisma makes one curious and demonstrates an artistic practice in public space, which is conceivable also for people who do not see themselves as professional artists.

Inclusive Culture as a Place for Learning in a Socially Tense City

Self-managed, urban culture is inclusive—and thus creates an answer to current challenges of the urban social fabric. Urban societies are changing faster than ever. People who are initially strangers meet each other spontaneously. Social movements are born and grow, are accelerated by digital communications, and then decay. Status attributions are relentlessly renegotiated. Such a flexible and mobile urban society calls for each and every individual to strive to create their own space in the sense of performing an artistic life. Here self-managed cultural places may be resting places and areas of experimentation: they offer opportunities to interact, to be productive, and to try out new forms of labor within different social structures.

The decisive factor is the openness of these places. Artistically working and thinking collectives develop social structures and manners that free them from the traditions and practices of companies and institutions. Their collaborative practice invites one to participate by bringing individual knowledge and skills and to be effective as an individual, regardless of status or position in the overall process. Preexisting hierarchies and structural limitations fade into the background. These structures and behaviors, operated under the umbrella of self-managed culture, are often welcoming to newcomers and offer great potential for making new connections: soup kitchens, free shops, bars, self-help workshops, and political groups are all places that may be a first address for foreign students or refugees, who might otherwise have difficulty being productive, exchanging knowledge, establishing relations, and participating in urban society. In this way, urban art and cultural places meet an urgent need that administratively controlled urban planning cannot: the need of interfaces for cultural exchange between different groups of urban society.

Artists Take Political and Institutional Responsibility

Just as art expands into urban space, one encounters a new understanding of urban development that aims at far more than the mere construction of housing, office buildings, and roads: urban development wants atmosphere, personality, and originality—values that are also one focus of artistic creation. Although both sides attach different qualities to these values in detail, art and urban development can communicate with each other on this basis. A common frame of reference is created, making a new exchange possible.

The fruits of such exchanges can already be seen in many places in the cityscape: formerly lifeless or shunned urban areas are being rediscovered as cultural areas and meeting places, which helps to revitalize entire neighborhoods. As the example of PB43 in Copenhagen shows, remote places that have been neglected by urban planning can be recovered for co-creative urban development when creative working collectives and municipal institutions begin trusting and cooperating with each other. By developing their own places, artists and creative city activists assume responsibility for parts of the city, up to and including institutional responsibility in administrative positions and seats in political working groups.

Away from Project Funding, Towards Urban Artistic Culture

The value of art for city development goes far beyond its role as a marketing tool; in professional discourse, this finding is consensus. However, a paradigm shift on the political and regulatory level is hesitant at best. Even if artists defend themselves against their exploitation and compete for recognition of their services for a sustainably better city, they risk being recognized reflexively for a market-optimized city image and political instrumentalization: criticism is provided as a feature of the city's diversity and thereby effectively muzzled. Although an externally visible and vibrant artistic and creative scene are like items on the checklist for the city's image-controlling, original artistic, self-managed culture is domesticated by temporary subsidies and related conditions. Instead of the arts existing as the foundation of civilization and coexistence, they are still limited to objects or events, marketable works, or reduced to productions focused on objects and their authors. As a result, politicians and municipal administrations exacerbate the struggle for recognition and resources, while the emancipatory and literally creative aspects of urban art simply fade into the background.

Cities need to learn to conceive of art and creativity as a culture that thrives in the long term and permanently bears fruit, not merely as a culture in the form of individual projects that need resources in certain places during limited funding periods. Even today, self-managed art spaces show the value that such a culture of creative, self-managed use of space can have for urban society. They also demonstrate that examination and innovation need not topple existing structures, but actually supplement them with important factors. Positive reactions to the City Link Festival in Hamburg give hope that a thriving arts scene can receive more and more recognition in politics and administration as an enrichment for the whole of urban society.

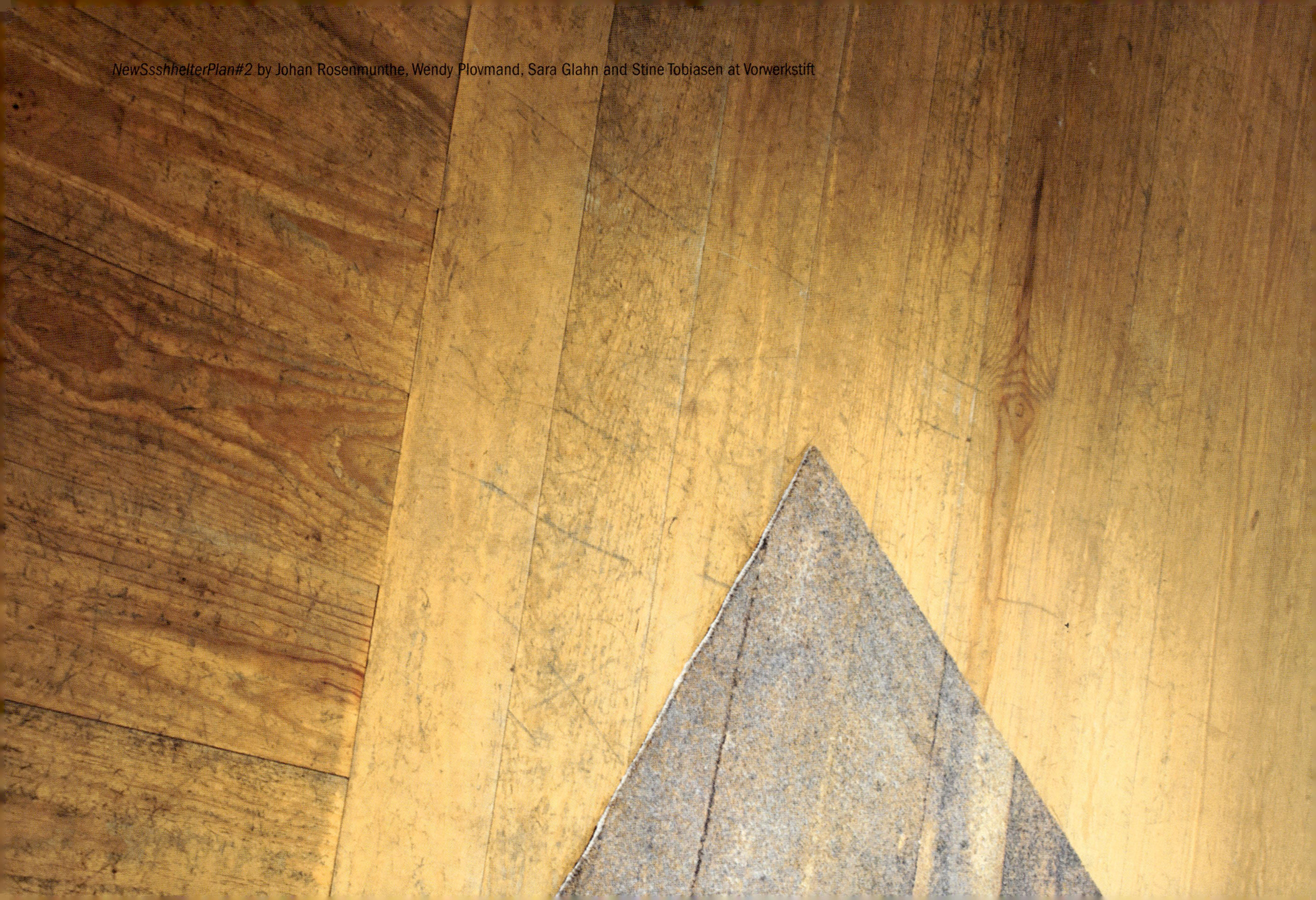

NewSsshhelterPlan#2 by Johan Rosenmunthe, Wendy Plovmand, Sara Glahn and Stine Tobiasen at Vorwerkstift

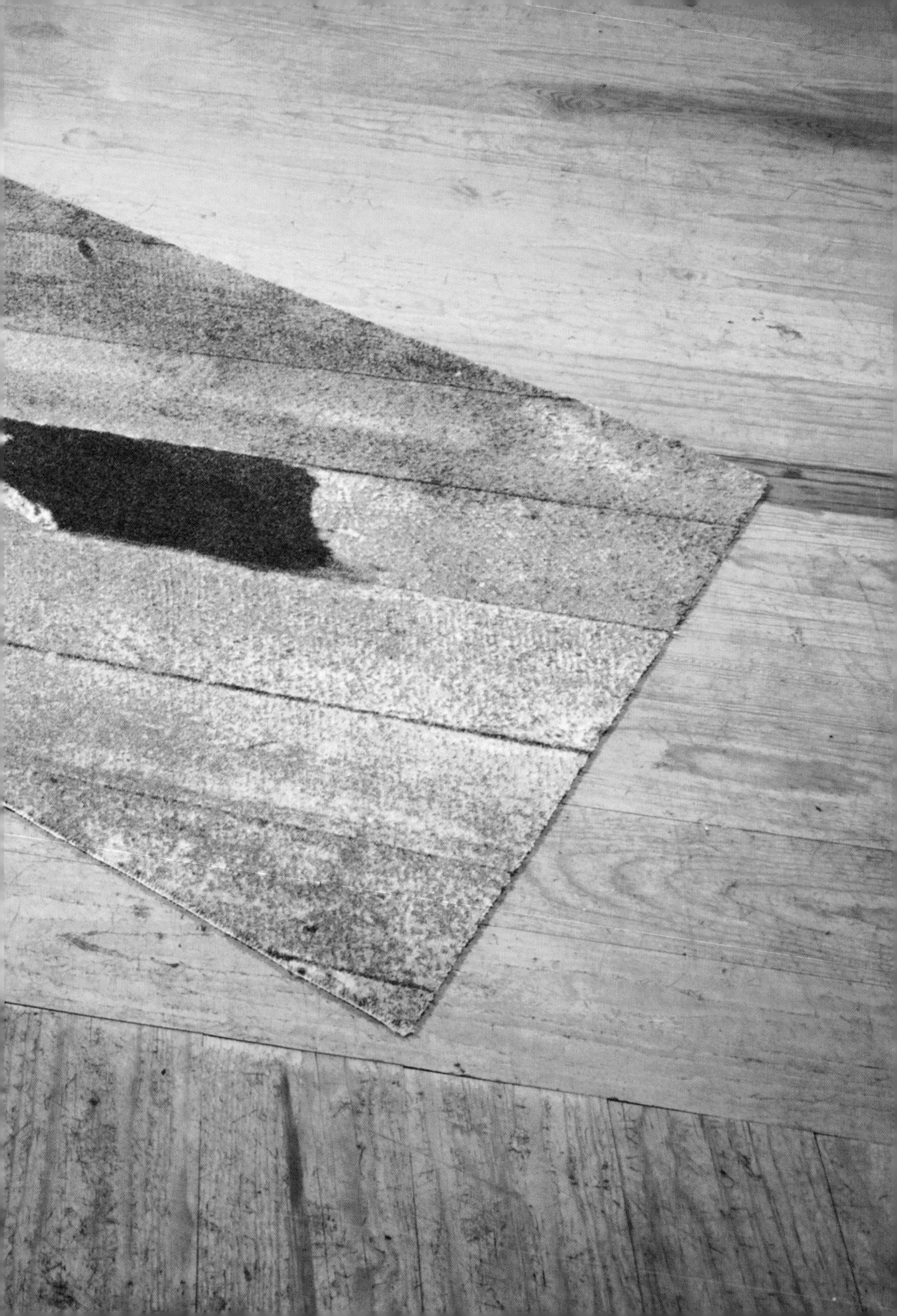

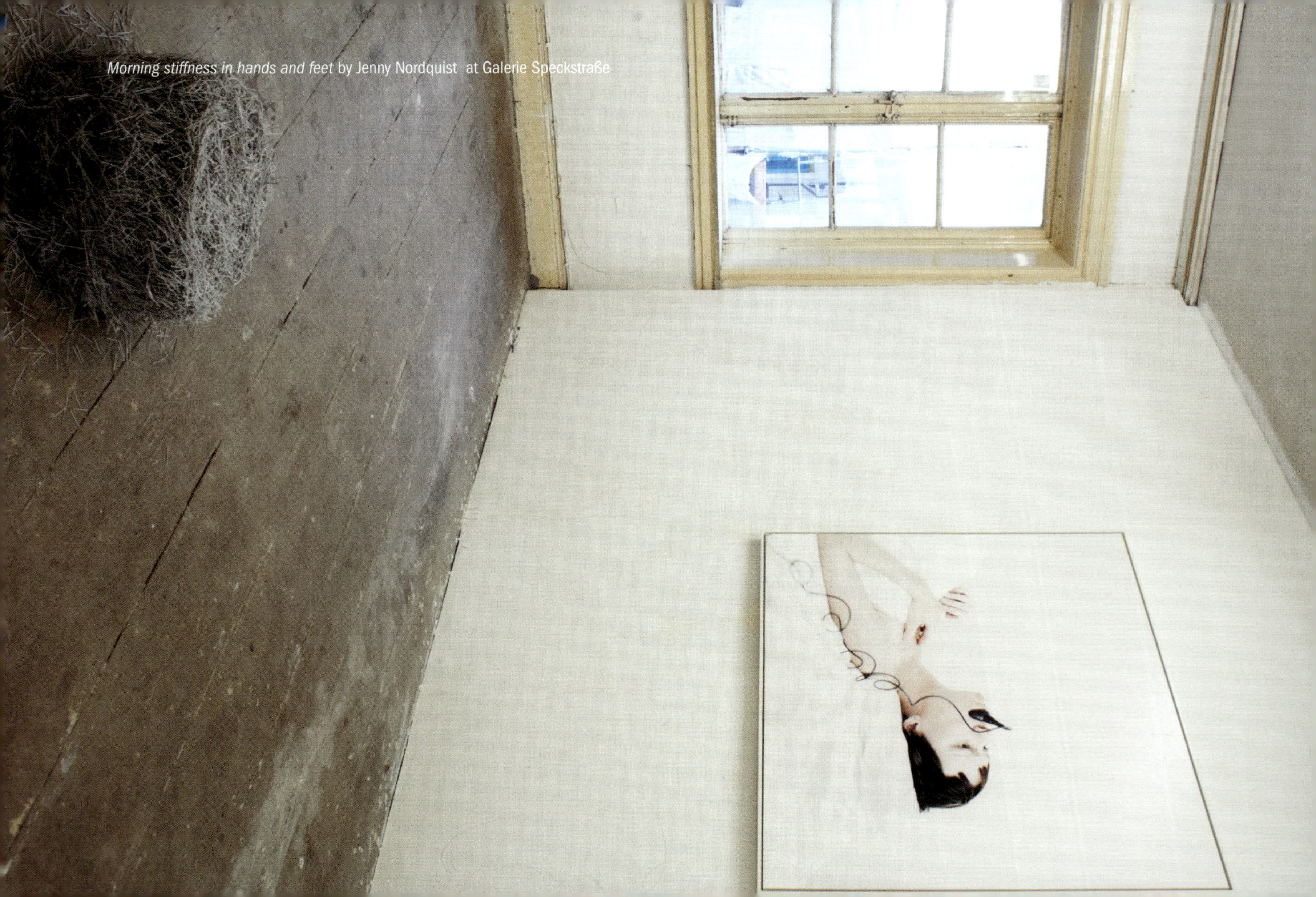

Morning stiffness in hands and feet by Jenny Nordquist at Galerie Speckstraße

The Emergence of Creative Sustainable Cities

Sacha Kagan

Are the discourses and practices connected to the creative city, sustainable city, and to urban resilience bound to reinforce neoliberal urban development? Or can they instead point toward the emergence of a radical open citizenship through the emergence and eventual scaling-up of networks of spaces of possibilities? In the following pages, I have gathered some thoughts on the latter scenario.

Creative Sustainable Cities

The unsustainability of policies for creative cities as advocated by Richard Florida's "Creative Class" discourse has already been discussed by many researchers and professionals in cultural and social fields over the past years. I too have been involved in such critical discourse, always retaining space for the consideration of alternatives as related to the concepts of "sustainability" and "resilience" in urban contexts (Kagan and Hahn 2011, Kirchberg and Kagan 2013). I wish to expand upon this facet of the topic by discussing alternative models that are being sought after and experimented with by artists and other creative cultural agents engaged with issues of sustainability in urban development. I will be looking at approaches to the relations between city, culture, and sustainability that are diverging from the neoliberal "creative city" model by working toward the emergence of what might hopefully become a "creative sustainable city."

In 2010, I organized a workshop in Brussels in collaboration with Masayuki Sasaki (Osaka City University). We were invited by the Asia Europe Foundation (ASEF) as part of the 4th "Connecting Civil Societies" Conference by ASEF in preparation for the 8th ASEM Summit (Asia Europe Meeting). Thanks to the gathering of artists, social scientists, and cultural professionals engaged in the search process of sustainability in cities, this workshop allowed for an in-depth exploration and formulation of key desired features regarding the question "What is a sustainable creative city?" We summarized our responses as follows: "A Sustainable Creative City should embrace participatory, bottom-up, intergenerational approaches where 'trial and error' (i.e. iterative) experiments are fostered. In such a city, long-term developments and processes are regarded as important, rather than products. The whole city is mobilizing creative potential to 're-invent' the 'logic of the house' or 'oikos logos.' Viewed as living organisms, sustainable creative cities build on their capacities and resources to create tangible and intangible values for the present and the future. Bio-cultural diversity should be a basis for urban resilience," (Kagan and Verstraete 2011, n.p.).

Given that we are operating on a symbolic level where different hegemonic and counter-hegemonic discourses make their claims (Laclau and Mouffe 1985), the exact formulations of expressions play an important role, also as regarding the order of words and associated emotional weights. This is why I prefer to speak of "creative sustainable cities" rather than of "sustainable creative cities": the aim is not to merely bring superficial ecological, social, and cultural updates to the neoliberal program of the "creative city" (by adding the adjective "sustainable" in front of it), but rather to contribute and add to the social-ecological discourses on "sustainable cities" by stressing some functions, properties, and priorities related to culture and the arts (by bringing the adjective "creative" to the front of the phrase).

Urban Resilience

The concept of resilience has risen in popularity over recent years; even starting to overshadow the concept of sustainability in many circles. As a consequence, the term of resilience itself is experiencing increasing re-articulation by hegemonic forces for the justification of neoliberal programs. Recently, a British comedian reportedly argued that "people don't need to be resilient, they just need to stop being fucking oppressed." This gut reaction begs for two elements of response: first of all, the meaning of resilience should be carefully considered—and I will try to contribute a few elements in this direction in the following paragraphs; secondly, I want to stress that the semantic and political struggle over concepts, once they rise to attention, is an unavoidable and normal aspect of the political realm. Words in political use necessarily receive different discursive and emotional valuation through communicative processes that are (notwithstanding Habermassian fairy tales of communicative action) bound to push and pull meanings in different and sometimes irreconcilable directions. This is true of "resilience" as much as it is true of "sustainability" or "creativity." Rather than taking a perpetual flight, I concur with Mouffe's agonistics as a plea for us to engage in (counter-) hegemonic claims, acknowledging political processes and one's own footing in their healthily-muddy waters (Mouffe 2013). In passing, a third element of response is still due, regarding the "fucking oppressed": Mouffian agonistics also reminds us that the idea of a supposedly communist society, free of all forms of antagonism and hence finally free of all elements of oppression, entails a dangerously totalitarian concept of consensual, pacified society. It is an idea that, when put into practice, entails deeply oppressive consequences.

Therefore, in the search for "creative sustainable cities," let's "get on with" resilience as well. Resilience is about the capacity of evolving through serious crises. It is neither merely resistance, nor mere adaptation. It integrates some elements of both, resistance and adaptation, without losing sight of the ethical goals of sustainability—as they were set in the "Manifeste Convivialiste" (Les Convivialistes 2013). Within sustainability science, and among climate change researchers, resilience is assumed to become a more and more relevant approach over the next few decades when the trusted approaches that fueled urban development will be severely tested (John and Kagan 2014).

The concept of "resilience" comes from the scientific study of the ways in which natural and social systems, have (or have not) managed to survive in the past by evolving in the face of changing contexts.[1] Three characteristics are shared by the species, ecosystems and societies that have proved able to survive and evolve through extreme crises. The first characteristic of resilience is "redundancy," which means being able to take multiple approaches for arriving at the same goal. To use a food metaphor, the body has numerous ways other than the symptoms of hypoglycemia for instructing itself to eat. Redundancy is severely reduced by efficiency. Efficiently organized societies will generally have less redundancy, thereby threatening their resilience. If the human body was a super-efficient machine, and hypoglycemia was the only way to motivate the body to consume food, human beings would be a non-viable species. In the arena of urban concerns, one potential threat to redundancy in cities lies in the obsession with efficiency associated with the development of "smart cities." The second characteristic of resilience is diversity, which means having diverse options available; such as a variety of ways of seeing the world and expressing oneself, as well as multiple ways of learning from experience and transmitting knowledge. Both cultural diversity and biological diversity should be preserved and, where possible, even increased. Following the thoughts of authors investigating resilience (discussed in John and Kagan 2014), I need to stress that paramount to resilient urbanity are diverse modes of learning that result from diverse modes of knowing the reality around us. This implies provincializing logico-deductive thinking as only one of several emotional learning modes (and not as hierarchically superior to emotional, experiential, and embodied ways of learning). In short, if we seriously dig into the "diversity" characteristic of resilience, we soon enter a deeper discussion about epistemic issues and transdisciplinarity beyond the scope of the issue treated in this essay. The third characteristic of resilience is "self-organization": the communities, neighborhoods, and groups of people constituting the city need to gain the capacity of self-organization and self-determination of their responses to crises. This contradicts not only the common expectation of always being passed down assistance and direction from a helping hand at the top, but also goes against the naive expectation that "natural" market laws would spontaneously solve any and all problems without some form of collective management.

[1] Beware: I am not using the term "evolution" in the neo-Darwinian, sociobiological sense. Much rather, in Tim Ingold's sense.

Urban resilience requires the realization of these three sets of characteristics throughout the different layers of the city's fabric. One possible way for cities to develop these qualities of resilience, which I am looking into in my current research, is through art (i.e., art in a wide sense, including all sorts of creative cultural practices, and inheriting the discourses of Allan Kaprow, Joseph Beuys, Helen and Newton Harrison, Wochenklausur, Isabelle Frémeaux and John Jordan, and several others). My hypothesis is not that urban resilience will be enhanced through just any form of artistic production. Rather, I mean specific forms of artistic practice that bring artists (and other creative practitioners not explicitly labeled as "artists") together with other urban subjects in processes of urban development to help them collaboratively "un-plan" our cities, make urban questions more interesting, queer our conceptions of urban development, and "plan" cities in more participatory, creative, and emergence-friendly ways while becoming less "control-freaky."

Resilience, as I understand it, is a creative process. But the resilient city is not the usual money-making "creative city." The kind of creativity it needs is not that "Kreativitäts-dispositiv" (creativity dispositive) that Andreas Reckwitz criticized in his critique of creativity (Reckwitz 2012), but rather that other kind of creativity that Reckwitz sketchily (and timidly?) pointed at at the very end of his work: a creativity that grows from and fuels everyday life. It is a creativity for which the activists at Gängeviertel and among the "Recht auf Stadt" ("Right to the City") network in Hamburg have given a name: "Möglichkeitsräume" ("Spaces of Possibility"). These "Spaces of Possibility" have also been called other things: for example, Hans Dieleman in Mexico calls them "Spaces of Imagination and Experimentation" (Dieleman 2012). These are indeed spaces where imagination, experimentation, and—I would add, not just any experience, but more critically, challenging experiences—open up future-oriented questions and perspectives. And these are training grounds for experimental developments that may contribute to urban resilience. These are also spaces (both physical, geographic spaces as well as spaces in our minds) where social conventions are reflected, unfrozen, and challenged; and where imaginative and experimental practices unfold thanks to lessened conventional constraints (see also Kagan 2012).

Radical Open Citizenship

What are the political consequences of looking at climate change from the perspective of the need for resilience? Droughts, floods, and other natural catastrophes related to climate change will, sooner or later, have tremendous impact on the economy and productivity of settlements, on social cohesion, on political institutions, and other institutions. An increasing instability of established structures can be expected (including

State structures as well as global markets). In simple words: if we do not want to end up
with tragic situations and new forms of totalitarian regimes, the so-called "civil society"
must become prepared and immediately begin enhancing the resilience of human
communities. Especially in the so-called Global North, we need to re-learn, through
practice, qualities of self-organization. We can look at inspiration from the Global
South: for example, Argentinian Horizontalidad, which was a great inspiration for the
Occupy movement. These two movements are characterized by open learning processes
that allow a radically innovative development of new types of knowledge and flexibility—
a key feature of resilience.

However, this does not mean that in preparing for such eventualities, resilience thinking
is necessarily a strategy that (1) reinforces the neoliberal agenda of a withdrawal from
the welfare state and/or (2) partakes in the politically toothless strategy of "Exodus"
from institutional politics, which according to Chantal Mouffe (2013) would be a historical mistake advocated by Hardt & Negri and practiced by the Occupy movement. I
want here to stress again that resilience points to the value of redundancy, and redundancy should also concern the different mechanisms of the unfolding of political and
urban processes of development. In simpler words, enhancing self-organization should
not preclude further critical engagement with institutions of urban policy-making.
Besides, in the nearer future, the city-government of Hamburg is probably not going to
collapse or radically change overnight. The activists at Gängeviertel in Hamburg realized this long ago and do not follow an either/or dichotomous type of thinking in this
matter. They pursue self-organization, concertations, negotiation and critical dialogue
with the city government.

Now, and pragmatically, in a city like Hamburg, when aiming to foster the emergence,
development and eventual scaling-up of "Spaces of Possibility", one crucial question is:
how to organize these spaces as a commons, given each city's specific political, administrative, economic situation? This is a question that has been raised by many activists
and cultural actors during meetings I have held with them over the past few years: not
only in Germany (where the debate on the commons is especially visible and supported
by institutional agents such as the Heinrich Böll Foundation), but also in other places
facing a diversity of specific challenges in e.g., Latin-Ame-
rican or Asian cities.[2] Here, I am thankful to be able to follow the practices and reflections of the Hamburg practitioners (from the Gängeviertel and more widely from the
Hamburg "Right to the City" network). For example, as is
now well-known thanks to the works of Elinor Ostrom and
those following her (e.g., Silke Helfrich in Germany), the

[2] I noticed (during my empirical explorations in
Asian cities such as Bangalore, Seoul or Singapore) that some artists and activists from these
cities place a locally-specific stress on the exploration of the "commons" (and use a discourse
referring to commons, i.e., not only to "public
space").

commons imply the existence of non-market sets of economic relationships that puts emphasis upon sharing, gifting, caring, and collective managing, which have to find ways to co-exist with other forms of economic logic (such as market logic and the logic of state financing). In concrete terms, urban social-cultural centers such as the Centro Sociale and Gängeviertel's Fabrique in Hamburg should not, for example, be asked to pay rent to the city for their usage of their respective buildings.

It is an especially complex issue of finding a working balance between this imperative (and the important alternative culture it fosters) and the dissonant logic of City Hall and of other urban actors, as is being faced by the Gängeviertel at this very moment. Hence, managing the commons requires bold new ways of collaborating with diverse stakeholders, including the city government, in order to find such balance within an agonistic dialogue, rather than being limited by the predictable outcomes of antagonistic confrontation.

Movements, Networks and Creative Spaces

Above, I mentioned the movements Horizontalidad ("horizontalism") and Occupy. There are several more movements that should be considered and critically discussed, but going into detail is unfortunately beyond the scope of this text. Among the relevant movements and networks are Transition Towns, groupings related to notions of Buen Vivir, "degrowth," intercultural gardens, and of course the "Right to the City" network which is strong in Hamburg but also in some other cities around the world. Recently, a large group of French-speaking intellectuals proposed some common traits uniting all these movements, in a text called the "Manifeste Convivialiste" (Les Convivialistes 2013). All these movements use networked organizations, rather than remaining isolated and scattered or relying on hierarchical structures. This encourages both diversity and partial redundancy which "allow[s] for people to collectively coordinate multiple and divergent courses of action and produce multiple solutions to a problem" (Maeckelbergh 2013: 78). Furthermore, it catalyzes a synergy between different areas of alternative organization, "placing them in a larger dynamic of transition" (Rumpala 2013: 17). As Rumpala (2013) suggests, further networking of these initiatives would be a prerequisite to a wider transition to sustainability. Other than this networking, I should also stress the importance of creative dimensions in spaces of challenging imagination and experimentation. As an art sociologist, I am biased towards paying attention to these aspects as I am especially interested in the different roles and forms of agencies that a diversity of artists (and more generally, of creative practitioners from a variety of professions and personal backgrounds) bring into the creation and development of such spaces. My attention is also focused on the relations of these creative agents to urban social movements and to urban policy developments.

The latter is the focus of my current empirical research, which is in an early stage. Therefore, I will not present any "conclusions" here, but merely sketch a few preliminary considerations on initiatives I am pursuing in different cities around the world. The following is therefore no more than a collection of hunches, guesswork and initial observations based on fragmentary early impressions from the field, gathered from 2014 onward—in other words, no conclusive statements:

In Oslo (Norway), I took part in the official founding of CAN (Concerned Artists Norway). I visited Oslo twice, each time for several weeks and interviewed a diversity of artists, researchers, and others.[3] In Cluj-Napoca (Rumania) I heard from different actors from arts organizations as well as social scientists about diverse initiatives in the city that included the protest movement against "Rosia Montana," which culminated in 2013. In Singapore I learned from the artists-duo "Post-Museum" about their artistic research documenting current developments at the site of "Bukit Brown," and from several other artists and organizations about their relationships to urban developments on the island-city-state.[4] These three cases appear to show, albeit in different ways and within different contexts, the emergence of creative initiatives that develop spaces for active civic engagement; by and large in the form of creative variations of protest cultures. These forms of creative initiatives entail a strong dimension of protest, are helpful, and probably indispensable in their respective contexts. They probably are also building the foundation for further developments. However, my first impression is that they may not be fully realizing the potential of "Spaces of Possibility" as discussed above.

In New York City, I visited several ecological artists, including for example the "Waterwash ABC" project site (in the South Bronx), initiated by the artist Lillian Ball (with several partnering organizations and individuals, e.g., the South Bronx NGO "Rock the Boat").[5] This project combined ecological site remediation, educational and intercultural social practice, and elements of participatory urban development. My students and I also interviewed Wendy Brawer at the headquarters for the "Green Maps" organization in Manhattan, which supports various grassroots green initiatives in NYC and other cities around the world.

In Cologne (Germany), the German Cultura21 network is supporting a local event, the "Tag des guten Lebens" ("Day of the Good Life"), which is carried out by a local coalition

[3] I want to thank CAN, PNEK and the individual artists who generously hosted me at their places in Oslo, for their support, and thank PNEK and The Telemark University College for covering my travel costs to Norway.

[4] I thank the URA (Urban Redevelopment Authority) and Ong & Ong Architects, for their invitation to Singapore, generously supporting me to stay a few days longer for an exploratory research on my own, as well as their invitation to take part at a symposium and art festival.

[5] I wholeheartedly thank the ecological artist, and transdisciplinary researcher Aviva Rahmani, for not only hosting me over that whole period of time, but also for taking me to relevant events in NYC and organizing and hosting a gathering with leading ecological artists, and engaging me in in-depth research exchanges on practices and discourses of ecological artists. This short text does not (yet) allow me to do justice to the many insights I (and my students) gained from meeting New York-based ecological artists during that couple of weeks.

of over a hundred organizations known as the "Agora Köln." The event is a cultural format for a "car-free Sunday," in which newfound urban spaces are used not only for sustainability initiatives to introduce themselves to each other and the public, but also for local communities, individuals, and neighborhood groups and activities to connect, share, have fun, and creatively re-appropriate the cultural commons of the streets and other outdoor spaces without cars disturbing them.[6] In its first iteration in 2013, the event saw the participation of over 100,000 persons (according to the police). In Hanover (Germany) several artists and cultural initiatives are actively developing sustainability-related projects.[7]

There is, for example, the "Kultur des Wandels" ("KdW—Culture of Change") festival: an annual event that takes over a public square for several days in order to bring together sustainability initiatives and cultural actors from the city into a situation where public space, private space, and the commons are staged to joyfully mingle, interact with one another, and where networking is facilitated. I need not describe the details by which the Gängeviertel in Hamburg (founded in 2009) implemented the strategic roles of "art" and "design" in the early phase of the occupation (directed towards media and policy-makers). The Gängeviertel initiators sought an embedded role for art in the further development of their place as part of experimenting with resilient urban lifestyles, alternative economic systems, et cetera.

I see several qualities present in the cross-section of these examples. Predominantly in the German cases mentioned above (and to some extent in the networking of different initiatives in New York City), I see the emergence of diverse forms of "Spaces of Possibility" that go beyond mere protest movements, awareness raising, or individual project-based initiatives, and are aiming to inspire experiments of transformations in the everyday lives of urban subjects. Despite the limitations and challenges faced by these initiatives, this is where I find the most promising grounds for hope in the emergence of "Creative Sustainable Cities."

[6] See www.tagdesgutenlebens.de

[7] My research activity in Hanover is part of the research project "City as Space of Possibility" at the Leuphana University, from 2015 to 2018, supported by "Niedersächsisches Vorab" funding for "science for sustainable development" from the State of Lower Saxony. See www.leuphana.de/sam

References

- Les Convivialistes (2013): *Manifeste Convivialiste: Déclaration d'interdépendance.* Lormont: Le bord de l'eau.
- Dieleman, H. (2012), "Transdisciplinary Artful Doing in Spaces of Experimentation and Imagination." In: *Transdisciplinary Journal of Engineering and Science,* 3: 44–57.
- John, B. and S. Kagan (2014): "Extreme Climate Events as Opportunities for Radical Open Citizenship." In: *Open Citizenship,* vol. 5 (1): 60–75.
- Kagan, S. (2012): *Toward Global (Environ)Mental Change: Transformative Art and Cultures of Sustainability.* Berlin: Heinrich Boell Stiftung.
- Kagan, S. and J. Hahn (2011): "Creative Cities and (Un)Sustainability: From Creative Class to Sustainable Creative Cities." In: Culture and Local Governance / Culture et gouvernance locale, vol. 3,(1–2).
- Kagan S. and K. Verstraete (2011): "Sustainable Creative Cities: the role of the arts in globalised urban contexts." In: *Extended report from workshop 3 at the ASEF CCS4 Conference.* Singapore, Lüneburg: Asia-Europe Foundation, Leuphana Universität Lüneburg.
- Kirchberg, V. and S. Kagan (2013): "The roles of artists in the emergence of creative sustainable cities: Theoretical clues and empirical illustrations." In: *City, Culture and Society* 4(3): 137–152.
- Laclau, E. and C. Mouffe (1985): *Hegemony and Socialist Strategy.* Verso.
- Maeckelbergh, M. (2013): "What comes after democracy?" In: *Open Citizenship* 4(1): 74–79.
- Mouffe C., Agonistics (2013): *Thinking the World Politically.* Verso.
- Reckwitz A (2012): *Die Erfindung der Kreativität – Zum Prozess gesellschaftlicher Ästhetisierung.* Suhrkamp.
- Rumpala, Y. (2013): "Degrowth as transition: An exploration of prospects of realization and conditions of possibility." Paper presented at the European Sociological Association 11th Conference (28–31 August 2013, Torino).

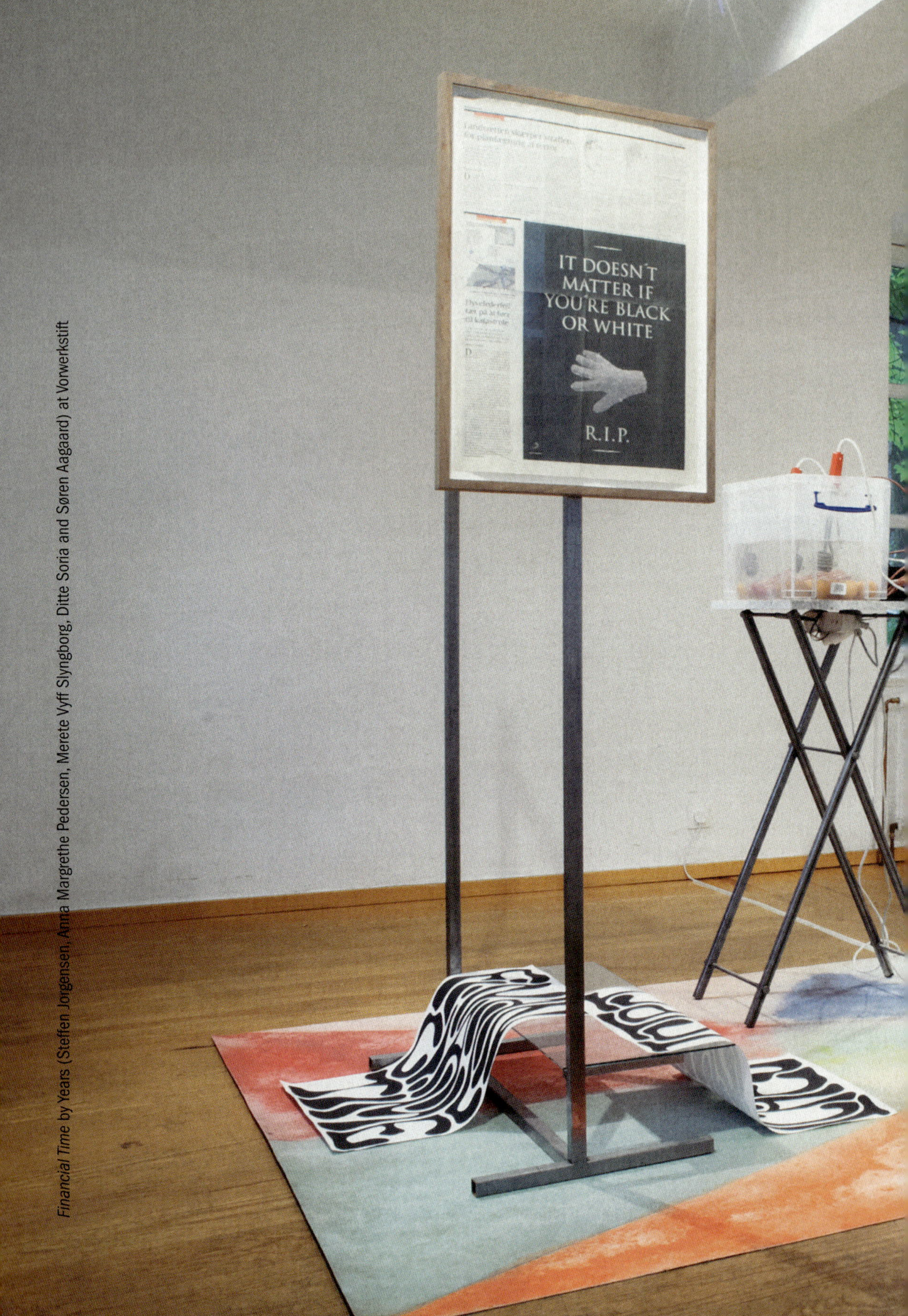

Financial Time by Years (Steffen Jørgensen, Anna Margrethe Pedersen, Merete Vyff Slyngborg, Ditte Soria and Søren Aagaard) at Vorwerkstift

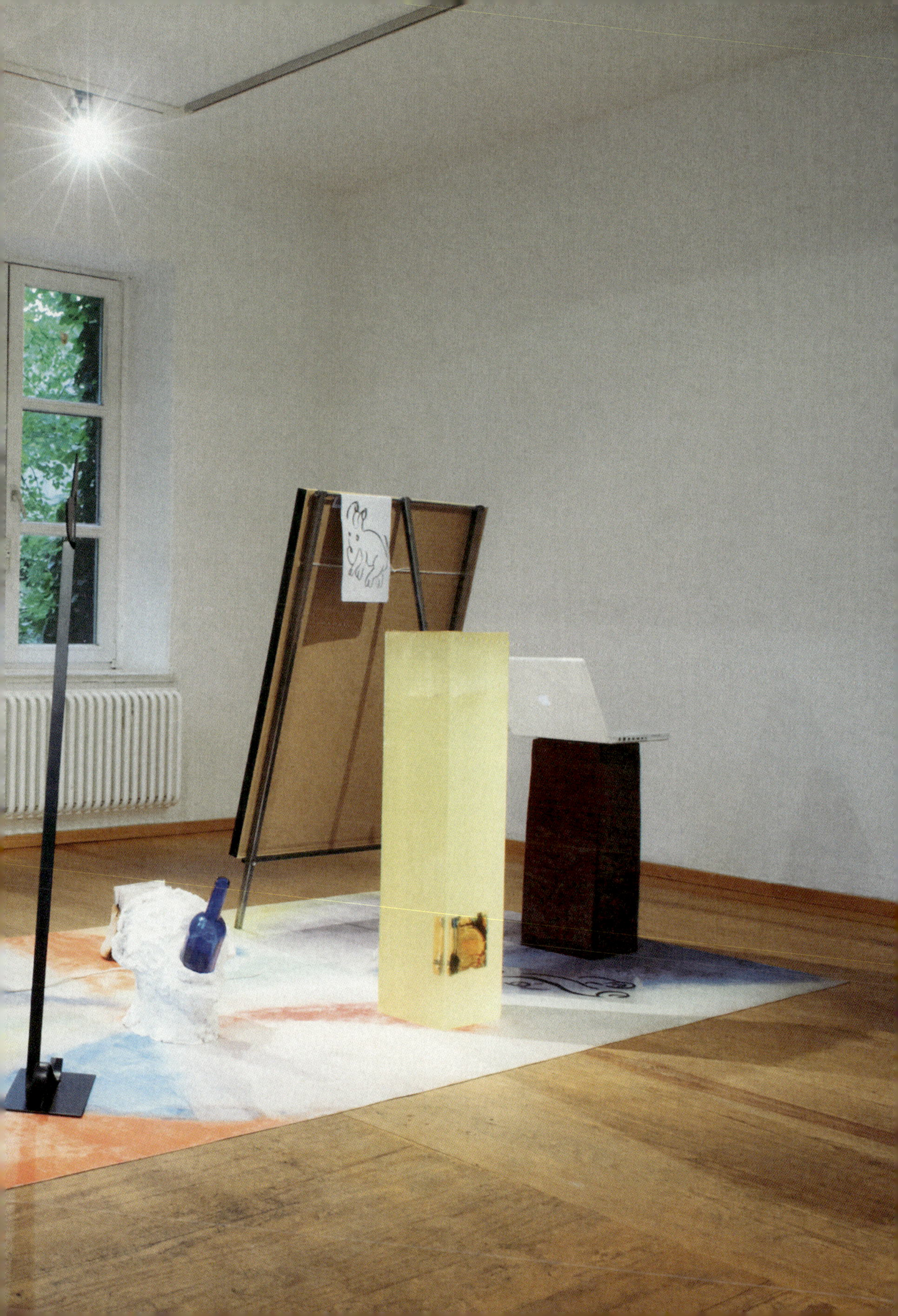

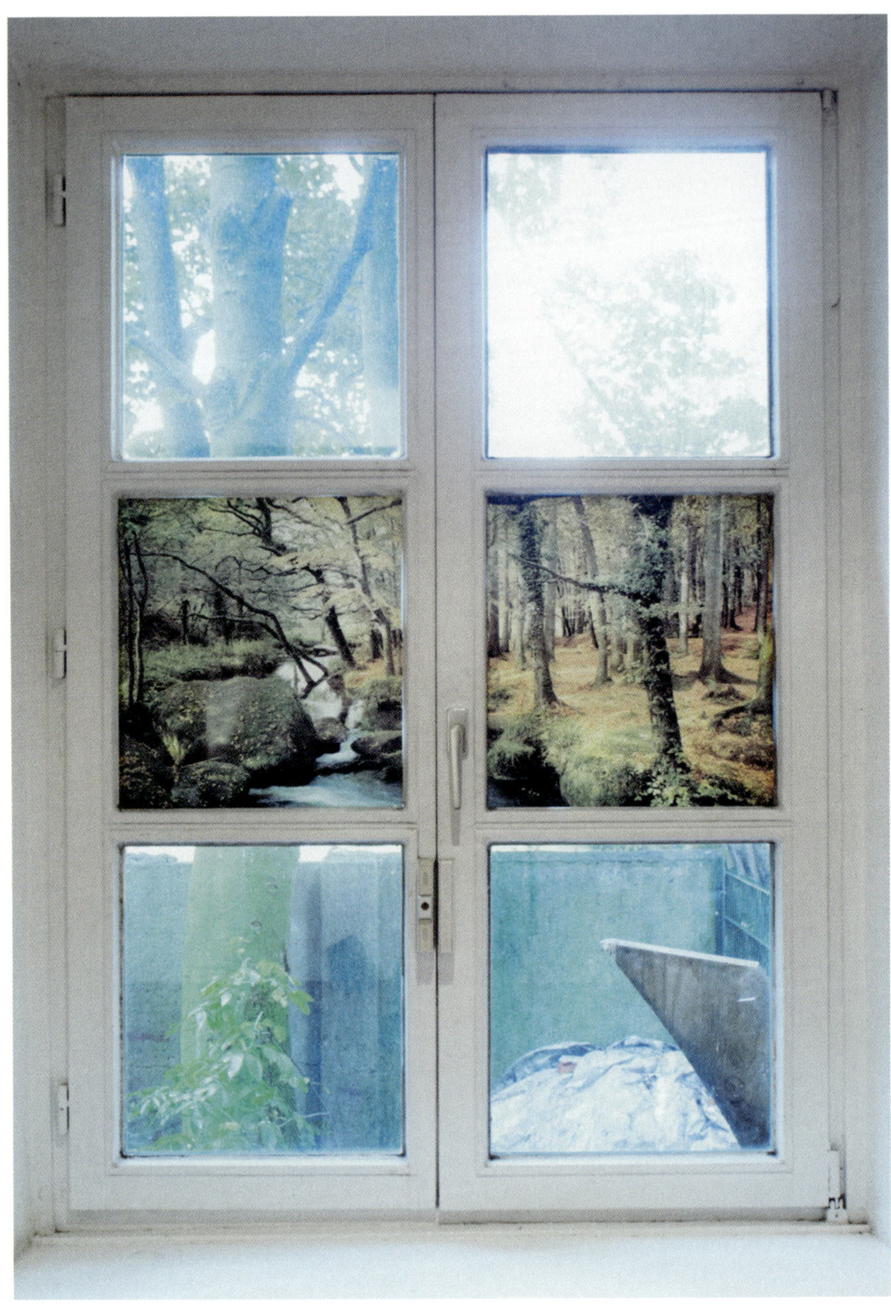

NewSsshhelterPlan#2 by Johan Rosenmunthe, Wendy Plovmand, Sara Glahn and
Stine Tobiasen at Vorwerkstift

Into the Fringe: On Cultural Interventions for Sustainability and Resilience

Oleg Koefoed

This essay looks at the role of cultural intervention in the pursuit of urban sustainability and resilience in Copenhagen. It sets off from a theoretical backdrop of Complex Adaptive Systems, a semantic understanding of narratives of bio-cultural ecosystems and tensions as a guiding concept. It then reflects on the relation between Copenhagen as Green Capital in 2014, and a couple of culturally rooted events that took place during the title year. The reflection unfolds a series of tensions, between explicit intentions, organizing implementation, new forms of partnerships, formats of events, and the nature of the actors between entrepreneur and grassroots; as well as the tensions built into the events themselves, the environment, and the participants. Finally, it raises the issue of engagement, community, innovation, and transformation; and how cultural interventions work within such contexts. Do we preserve systems beyond their assumed tipping point or do we push them towards transformation?

The Role of Culture in a Transforming World

"Culture is an essential component of sustainable development; represents a source of identity, innovation and creativity for the individual and community; and is an important factor in building social inclusion and eradicating poverty, providing for economic growth, and ownership of development processes" (UN 2014).

The UN says it: culture is diversity. It is innovation. It is creative economy. It is a receptor for tendencies to change, and a receptacle for the preservation of societies in the face of major threats. Culture will be a lever of sustainable development. We know it: culture is highly dynamic and increasingly complex flows and networks, adding hectic speed of recirculation and intertwining of everything to Geertz' "webs of meaning" (Geertz 1973) and Williams' "ways of life" (Williams, 1989/1958). Culture is the holder of the narratives we live by and the ontologies by which we organize our world. It expresses the way we perceive the world and sets the frame for how we understand the way we organize work and institutions (Clammer 2012, Kuecker 2011). It consists of practices and institutions, materializes in bodies and infrastructures, and works its way back again to living creatures and communities. In the wake of waves of complexity, culture invents technologies that amplify and modify our communication and practices. Culture creates and shares artifacts that we use to share the epistemology and ontology of our time. Culture is the field of tension in which all artifacts and narratives rise and move; narratives that are seemingly beyond our control and increasingly powerful in their effect on decision-making. And so far, the narratives fail to really challenge the issues of ownership on a deeper level, while technology mainly increases inequality.

A recent research project (Dessein, Soini et al. 2015) sums up three major roles of culture with regards to sustainability: Culture *in* sustainability, in which the role of culture is mainly to adopt the logic of sustainable solutions and try to apply them, working as a "fourth pillar" of sustainable development; culture *for* sustainability, in which culture works through art, communication, et cetera in order to enhance awareness around the issues of sustainable development by trying to promote them; and culture *as* sustainability, in which culture is the very heart of sustainable development, and the pivotal agents around which the processes of transformation will succeed or fail. In the last case, sustainability is no longer a question, but becomes the order of the day and the paradigm guiding our minds and bodies. These three definitions are aspects of the relation of culture to sustainability, rather than separate forms of acting. Culture *in*, *for*, and *as* sustainability. Culture is embedded in the very systems that (some of it) is calling to transform.

Cultural Interventions for Sustainability in Copenhagen

I. Tipping Points and Resilience: The City as a Complex Adaptive System

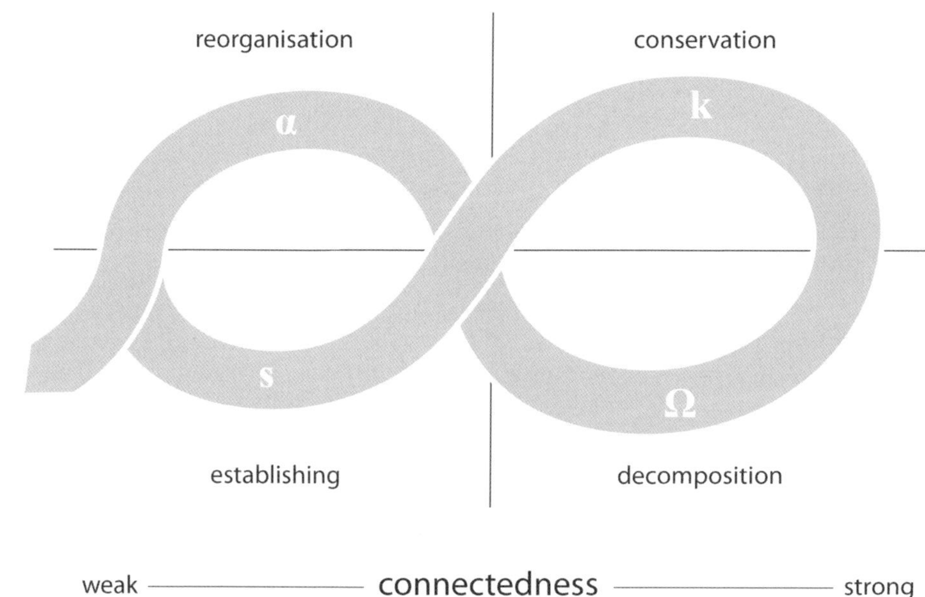

The Adaptive Cycle after Gunderson & Holling (2002)

The city can be seen as thousands of Complex Adaptive Systems, woven into one another to form a multitude. According to the theory of complex adaptive systems, it follows an adaptive cycle in four phases: establishing or use (s), conservation (k), decomposition (Ω) and reorganization or reconstruction (α) (or transition to new systemic regime). The different phases may overlap more or less, or stand out more clearly. In this movement, a system will be leaving its conservative strategy and begin to search for ways to reinvent itself, while its internal structure and order fall apart. Any system will be seeking to stay in an exploiting mode—but the processes of evolution tend to move towards decomposition, letting go of the system once it moves beyond its tipping point.

In the urban system, encounters lead to creations of new meshworks and networks, forming new tensions and patterns. Planners create physical or structural frameworks in time to harness the unpredictable moves of the meshworks and agents. Companies and actors in civil society try to keep up their ability to move as freely as possible, while trying to exploit the conservative tendencies of bureaucracy. But regimes such as capitalist potentialization and sustainability oriented transformation change the rules of this game (Koefoed and Frøslev 2015). To continue to exploit the system, the ruling regime must challenge the self-preserving identity mechanisms. To keep moving towards an always more resilient new system, the emerging regime must create new systems that improve conditions for new life forms to take over the capacity of the dying ones (Gunderson and Holling 2002: 401). To do this, it must draw on the cohesive trust-making element of existing communities. Forces draw in all directions at the same time. The results are an ever greater complexity and tensions on many different levels.

Resilience is normally defined as how much pressure the system can take before moving from K to Ω. From a classical growth perspective, resilience has to be managed as a way to exploit the border between K and Ω, accumulating capital and exploiting community cohesion. However, cities are increasingly complex and they move in more than one direction and more than one phase at a time. The overall movement is neither linear nor one-directional. All systems contain their own disappearance as part of their fabric. If we take that possibility into account, we might have a new definition of resilience. It could be rethought as "the capacity to contain change by passing on the capacity to live from one organism or one system to another, while the existing one moves past the tipping point and into decomposition?" (Koefoed 2013).

II. Cultural Innovation in Copenhagen

Copenhagen has invested heavily in becoming a venue for major cultural events (World Cycling Championships, Eurovision Song Contest et cetera). The city also hosts a number of spaces for young cultural sustainable startups across the city, and makes some areas accessible for temporary use. The spotlight is on swimming facilities at the harbor, the *Copenhagen Street Food* hall and Eurovision, rather than entrepreneurial projects like PB43, KPH, Byhøst, or Bolsjefabrikken. Still others remain largely invisible, below the threshold of city branding.

The story of cultural and creative industries in Copenhagen is similar to many other cities in Europe. Appreciation for the creativity, innovation, and growing employment of the sector is very high, including the ability of innovation to spread to other sectors (CKO 2011, CreativeSPIN 2015). Most cultural actors, however, are SMEs (small and medium entrepreneurs) or non-governmental organizations with little direct economic or political power. City departments and large companies in Copenhagen approach culture from a highly instrumental perspective. They seek to attract citizens, employees, and investment; or to increase the sense of well-being of those who live or work in the city. They seek to add flavor to their environmental agenda by using cultural events to promote their goals and programs. They invite cultural agents to find ingenious ways of making the environmental agenda more attractive, but in reality use only a fraction of these ideas. The field is dominated by a "creative city" approach and by a cultural/public sector still largely stuck in disciplinary silos.

In this saturated field of cultural events, a few initiatives apply culture to social innovation and sustainable development. To a great degree, their influence depends on the occurrence of public or public-private events such as *COP15* or *Sharing Copenhagen*, and of both the willingness of sponsors as well as the application of precarious labor. The role of culture for transformation towards a resilient and sustainable city is not negligible, but it suffers under a lack of mainstream visibility and a lack of collaborative efforts with a strong agenda. Innovative events like *CO2penhagen* in 2009 are rare and remain hard to finance. Activities such as *SustainFestival* struggle to stay afloat and must reinvent themselves to combine innovation with mainstream appeal.

And audiences? One could claim that most of those Danes living in Copenhagen are motivated for social and environmental causes and either caught up in seeing the world and acting pretty much as if it were the 1980's—mourning the loss of the safe and carefree old days yet not knowing what to do about it; roosting with others in objection of the loss; or trying to look collaboratively at new options (Cultura21 2014). This discourse sees the world as a fairy tale in which we either still believe in the princess, mourn the loss of her innocence, or protest with our friends against her violation. Strong narratives of a future in which we are handling the waves we face are largely unknown. Such narratives would enforce resilience, open up to transformation, release, decomposition, and reconstruction of a new system. But audiences, institutions, and cultural agents seem to largely lack the capacity to see a different world beyond the present crises.

III: Climate Change Strategies

"Copenhagen as a livable, innovative, sustainable and democratic city with a political will to lead the way in the battle for an improved quality of life for the citizen" (Copenhagen 2011).

"Copenhageners should be able to live safely in their city, also when the rain falls in massive amounts. (…) With a common effort, we and the future generations of Copenhageners will still be able to live safely and invest in Copenhagen" (Copenhagen 2012).

In 2011, Copenhagen witnessed some of the most serious rainfalls it had seen in many years. Since then, the forecasts speak of still more rain. In a country in which the rising sea causes no major panic and the cities are flat, the threat comes from the sky. Massive rainfalls flood roads, not to mention cellars full of things, memories, and histories. These conditions have led to a change in city planning. Copenhagen has taken on a multi-billion-kroner plan to integrate rainfall adaptation into general redesigns of urban infrastructure. It is continuously carrying out a number of infrastructural projects improving (e.g., cycling conditions) in a long-term strategy aiming to make the city CO2 neutral by 2050. There is a firmly established vision of Copenhagen as a city that acts to temper climate change, while providing a clean, green city for its citizens.

The political strategy seeks to maintain comfortable, everyday livability for its citizens, while gently preparing for threats to resilience in the classical understanding. This is also the core of the city's branding. At the same time, real estate development works across these strategies. For the first time in the history of the city, dozens of high-rises are appearing in the city. The face of the city is changing. Over the last decades, many spaces were left undeveloped and accessible for temporary use, lending their use to inexpensive spaces for cultural entrepreneurs. Today, these areas are disappearing; gradually being expelled by the real estate market (BOP Consulting 2015). At some point, all the minor systems in the city, as well as the city as a mega-system, will probably break down and decompose. This is even inscribed as a common challenge in the latest plans for the city.

Changes in infrastructure influence culture as life forms, but planning excludes culture in the experimental sense of the word. Planning serves as a conscious strategy to attract and please both citizens and direct investment from foreigners. The dominating disciplines behind these strategies are engineering and economics. Culture plays neither a strong role in the planning of strategies, nor in their execution. The strategy of the city as such is not about change or transformation. No old system is really being challenged. Thus, the official role of culture is mainly one of subservience to an existing regime.

IV: Sharing Copenhagen

"That we can now call ourselves the green capital of Europe, is a great encouragement to all citizens of Copenhagen as well as to the green enterprises [...]" (head mayor Frank Jensen 2013).

It was logical for Copenhagen to run for the title of European Green Capital. That it received the award is hardly surprising. However, the city appropriated very little budget and even less strategy.[1] The project would be run as partnerships, calling for sponsors and partners that would enter with financial instruments as well as other forms of support. The strategy for the title year as green capital would partly follow the overall method for Copenhagen as climate friendly city: showcasing and attracting investment. The core of Sharing Copenhagen is a communication partnership and co-branding model. The idea of public-private partnerships is of course not a new one. But inviting all partners big and small to crack down on the plan for the title year was new for the civil servants of Copenhagen and spelled out a set of tensions and impossibilities.

The first tension was about intentions: Copenhagen placed itself on the international stage as one of the more ambitious members of networks such as *C40*. This collaboration entails dialogues with mayors of big cities and aims at influencing big politics across the globe. It naturally entails partnerships with major companies which place Copenhagen in an important position of helping to pull industrial partners in a green direction. It was noticeable that there existed a great distance from this level of engagement to collaborating with small organizations or SME's in the field of culture and sustainability, and supporting partnerships with citizens, communities, and small collectives.

The second tension was innovation. Copenhagen aimed at combining the planning of technical and engineering innovation by creating a nexus of partnerships (Åkerstrøm 2013) in dialogue with citizens as well as with industries and local planning schemes like neighborhood revitalization to meet the need for a livable and inclusive city. Bauwens and Kostakis point out that our epoch is very much defined by what is shared and what is not. In a public-urban field, that which is rarely shared are the ways that the municipality is organi-

[1] Sharing Copenhagen partnership workshop, October 2013. In comparison, one of the winter swimming facilities at the harbor was recently promised 1.8 Million euro for the development of their construction.

zed and the ownership of the land. Where urban policy could appear to be "suspensions of power and responsibility from the public manager" (Torfing 2014), it could just as easily be discussed the degree to which the relation between the city and its civil society has become more open and democratic. It could also be discussed how resilience is played out in this context. *Sharing Copenhagen* supports the visibility of small start-ups and non-profits on the edge of the cultural field. However, this project has not become the place from which truly innovative models grow for collaboration between a large public partner and a multiplicity of small change agents in the layers of the city's civil society and SME's. The *Sharing Copenhagen* strategy leaves a problem unsolved: the blindness of the city departments toward unexpected innovation from the fields and layers outside of their focus of attention. This is precisely the cradle from which many ideas lead to greater innovation.

Is there Innovation? Two Cases for Self-Reflection

"City-dwellers have gradually become aware not only of the importance of nature in the urban setting but also of the environmental issues arising from the damages caused by human activities, locally and globally. This [...] has gradually produced a change in the shaping of the city and has contributed to the creation of a new urban aesthetic [especially visible in eco-neighborhoods and other such experiments]" (Blanc 2013).

It is not easy to identify the impact of culturally innovative practices or concepts on (trans)forming culture (seen as the way we live). I will consider two actions that are characterized by using culture as a medium. They work through collective actions, through social events bringing people together, and using different tools and media. Their direct goal is to enhance or strengthen a cultural indicator. Two questions are interesting here: How do the actions try to reach their goals? And do they transform and innovate?

Vild Festival—Eating the Commons

The annual *Vild Festival*, was initiated by the urban foraging collective *Byhøst* in 2013. The festival brings out citizens into the commons. It connects citizens/consumers with volunteer and semi-commercial actors by using food gathered in the "urban wild." The event highlights the accessibility of natural ingredients, of which a great multitude can be found on the vast area of Amager Fælled. *Byhøst* has been communicating the ease of using urban nature for supplies over the past five years. Via an online map for sharing the location of mint or horseradish in the city, they have developed into an event organizer playing off of a hedonist atmosphere and the hipster culture. *Vild Festival* is a small urban event that takes place in the middle of the commons, about 500 meters from the nearest road. It attracts 3,000 participants coming to play with crabs, collect weeds or fruit, talk about wild gardens, eat, drink, and socialize. The event is economically supported by the *Sharing Copenhagen* program and local councils. It is run like a town fair through partnerships between the actors and the organizer and between the organizer and the city. The core of the event is about being green and living in pact with urban nature. It resonates well with the style of the new generation of eco-actions: it is positive, simple, and about having a good time together. Its innovative character is gentle and embracing, and it could be argued that the whole positive feel-good setting in itself leads to inspiration and gives birth to other innovations.

Eco Island Amager—slow innovation

Eco Island is an artistic/cultural research concept developed by the non-profit organization Cultura21. The concept was born as a series of actions on the island of Amager, where our offices and homes are located. We were curious to see to what extent we could get a picture of the ecosystems and flows of the island. The explorations took their point of departure in stating that Amager already was an eco-island. We aimed at developing connections between people working on the island with issues of sustainability, hoping this might lead the way into new ideas for collaboration, projects, services, products, et cetera.

The project draws on tools for cultural mapping, walking, and drawing; and is designed as a participatory innovation process. It works site-specifically, with tools designed especially for the sites. A lab brought forth sketches of new ideas and possible common projects and formed bottom-up alliances of prototyping. *Eco Island* is a slow approach, creating a series of detours in order to make connections blossom while retaining sensitivity to the place. It is an open-ended process, leaving many doors open to interpretation by participants and partners. Its main criteria for success are an increased awareness, openness towards new projects, and increased cultural glue around sustainable solutions. This needs strong roots in the local arena in order to offer meaningful solutions. Another criterion for success is the dialogue with groups such as urban planners, architects, and sustainability civil servants in order to garner support for new knowledge or urban cultural planning.

Cultural Interventions: Innovation or Preservation?

"The challenge, then, is not simply that we need to spend a lot of money and change a lot of policies; it's that we need to think differently, radically differently, for those changes to be remotely possible. Right now, the triumph of market logic, with its ethos of domination and fierce competition, is paralyzing almost all serious efforts to respond to climate change" (Klein 2014: 23).

At this point, there are several issues at stake:
1. A lack of experience with connecting iterative processes with proofs of concept (*Eco Island*);
2. A lack of visibility of strong and simple concepts (*Vild Festival*);
3. A general epistemological challenge blocking the way for stronger projects and collaborations (both);
4. The majority of citizens of Copenhagen continue living like they are used to, which arises from a lack of a real sense of urgency on one side, and the absence of strong future narratives on the other. Taking engagement beyond a small part of the population will require changing the mainstream narrative by which we understand our everyday life and our directions.

The *Sharing Copenhagen* concept was sufficiently successful for the city to hold on to it—but with a reduced team. Some of the interesting elements of cross-disciplinary collaboration were never realized. What could have been a strong example for future co-creative processes ended up as a series of relatively standard events and marketing along the lines already clearly laid down by the major private partners.[2] One of the challenges of this future collaboration could be to establish stronger trans-disciplinary learning fields. Or even reconsidering how this platform could be the site of innovative, prototyping projects.

The French philosopher Natalie Blanc describes two forms of *disengagement.* The first has to do with the loss of "sensory features" of the city; the second with the closure and limiting of spaces, prohibiting movement and use by passers-by and pedestrians. My two examples seek to create contexts in which a re-engagement can take place. However, perhaps the events themselves may prevent a deeper engagement in transformation. Both events are at risk of promoting resilience towards a kind of survival within the existing regime. The presence of a sense of loss of connection to urban places leads to sorrow and disengagement. The first response of participants is to create communities around this very emotion. This is inscribed in the design of both projects. They support the forming of communities of sharing and innovating. Another understanding of success could involve registering engagement beyond the present, measuring investment, new partnerships, or derived innovative events.

[2] So far, no official evaluation has been published about the title year.

Using innovation as a method for approaching cultural-natural ecosystem issues implies that we have an aim from the outset, which is to do more than simply confirm our own presence. When applying "design thinking" to cultural-natural ecosystems, we also open ourselves to "prototyping": testing ideas and concepts in the field as a way of understanding both the field and the potentiality of the concept. Working from the perspective of an infinite number of possible futures, all collected into the openness of the present moment in which we work, demands a very high degree of focus on the process, material, and power/force; it demands a high degree of openness as to those with whom we work and where we work. Perhaps, rather than accommodating the needs of planners and other professionals, we should find new ways to invite them more continuously to engage in the "growing pathways" of discovering. This would also imply being able to move away from the extant, planned, and official intentions; and being able to break the molds if need be.

Breaking the Mold

"The world is arguably at a crossroads where the excesses, the fallacies, and the unsustainability of the current practices need to be recognized; appropriate regulatory changes have to be made where the usual recipes for confronting tensions fail; and conditions where production capital is put in control, greater social cohesion is achieved, and desperation and anger turn into creation, must be facilitated" (Bauwens & Kostakis 2014: 8).

Klein, Bauwens and Kostakis remind us of the challenges that we face. The role of culture is increasingly being addressed as part of the sustainability-oriented agenda (Dessein, Soïni et al, 2015). However, in the "Anthropocene" condition (Klein 2014), every single action might be a crucial player in influencing development. So rather than rejoice at the increased importance of culture, I suggest a self-critical look at the role that art, culture, and cultural agents are playing today; as a source of tensions as much as a source of solutions; and as a source of complacency as much as a source of innovation. We should remember, when reaching "into the fringes," to question the effects of our actions, and not let ourselves be satisfied with dancing together while the world moves into a clandestine neo-feudal economy.

We need to actively address the narratives that we work with. To look for stories of becoming what we could be. We must consider the goals that we serve: do we follow the conditions that are given to us, not always suited for innovation, or do we try to find ways to have a stronger voice towards transformation? An important challenge will be to actively address the possibility of transformation, and how we might create settings in which planners, officials, citizens, scientists, artists, and eco-entrepreneurs can embark on a common exploration and creation of a city that is both livable and economically healthy, while preparing for a shift of overall ecological regime (coming to us anyway). We need to explore ways of life that are alternatives to the kind of neo-feudal economy (and politics) that Bauwens and Kostakis describe. This demands insisting on Klein's new optimism, and for a more rigorous willingness to transform, including in cultural teams.

Cultural and art interventions recirculate or suspend value. A main function of cognitive capitalism is the appropriation of non-marketized value, transforming it into negotiable value for markets. Value that lies outside the market, or problems that point to potential solutions, are considered first of all as sources of virtual capital or potential innovation. At the same time as this movement accelerates, an alternative movement takes place. This movement consists in recirculating value back out of the commercial sphere, creating "suspended" chains of experience and experimentation on the fringe of the ubiquitous markets. However, this recirculation or reclaiming of streets, of time, matter, bodies, or knowledge is just as rapidly re-captured. This has led to a complex situation in which the lines between art, activism, creativity, commercialism, and politics are constantly being blurred. Temporary urban activism, "makerspaces", DIY/DIT communities et cetera, are turned into products and commercialized at the same rate as new ones appear. Political governing bodies of the city are on the hunt for innovative approaches to solve their problems, looking to tap from the same energy and vitality as the market. Cultural agents and public servants find themselves wrapped in flows and webs that are not at the service of a transformation toward cities that are more friendly to ecosystems and living structures. I suggest we focus on these movements as part of complex adaptive socio-bio-cultural ecosystems on their way from a tipping point towards collapse/release and potential reconstruction/restructuring. We are beyond the tipping point and in strong need of reinvention. But our very methods of increased sensitization, combined with the aloof absence of public partners from the flesh of the projects may actually be conserving the systems we should reinvent. We can only invite to participate in this journey if we are in transformation ourselves.

The rules of ownership and sharing stand as one of the most important keys to creating innovative solutions to the waves of complexity facing the world as we knew it. We should criticize the tendency to react to danger through control, secrecy, and isolation. Klein attacks the "ethos of domination and fierce competition," in which a competitive system is seen as the natural state of the world, and where risk is seen as a direct reason for identifying and seizing any challenge as an opportunity for more control. Bauwens and Kostakis identify the new systems of "neo-feudal cognitive capitalism," where ownership and economic value is kept under safeguard by new "sharing" hyper-companies (Uber, AirBnB et cetera). They give us reason to ask: Do our artistic practices and new forms of partnerships merely offer subtle forms of self-satisfaction upholding a sense of living the good life, as the new order grows around us? Do they offer ways to handle the waves? In Copenhagen, the city is "sharing" and the cultural agents create communities in a livable city. But the projects fold into much more complex contexts, and connect to structures and orders, as well as to possible structural transformations. The obstacles may be built into the very fabric of our own action designs. We may be part of the problem.

References

- Åkerstrøm, N. (2013): *Managing Intensity and Play at Work. Transient Relationships.* Monograph Books.
- Bauwens, M. and V. Kostakis (2014): *Network Society and Future Scenarios for a Collaborative Economy.* Palgrave.
- Blanc, N. (2013): Aesthetic Engagement in the City. Published online as: http://www.contempaesthetics.org/newvolume/pages/article.php?articleID=683
- BOP Consulting (2015): *Transformational Cultural Projects Report.* BOP.
- Clammer, John (2012): *Culture, Development and Social Theory: Towards an Integrated Social Development.* Zed Books.
- City of Copenhagen (2011): *Good, Better, Best – the City of Copenhagen's Bicycle Strategy 2011-2025.*
- City of Copenhagen (2012): *The City of Copenhagen Cloudburst Management Plan 2012.*
- Dessein, J. & K. Soïni et al (2015): *Culture in, for, and as Sustainable Development. Conclusions from the COST action IS1017 Investigating Cultural Sustainability.* COST.
- Geertz, Clifford (1973): *The Interpretation of Cultures.* Basic Books.
- Gunderson, L.S. & C.S. Holling (2002): *Panarchy: Understanding Transformations in Human and Natural Systems.* Island Press.
- Kern, Phillipe (2015): *The Smart Guide to Creative Spill-overs to Assist Cities Implementing Creative Spill-overs.* Urbact/CreativeSPIN/KEA.
- Klein, N. (2014): *This Changes Everything: Capitalism vs the Climate.* Simon & Schuster Books.
- Koefoed, O (2013): "Tingenes teater. Om frivillig suspension af viljer og magt." In: Gørtz, K. & M. Mejlhede: *Frivillig ledelse - erfaringsbaserede refleksioner, psykologiske forhold og filosofiske synsvinkler.* DJØFs Forlag.
- Koefoed, Oleg et al (2014): *Study for MSF of Dane's Values and Attitudes Towards Humanitarian Donations.* (Unpublished) Cultura21, 2014.
- Koefoed, O. & A. Frøslev (2015): "Siteness. A new Regime for Education and Sustainability." In: Kemp, P. & Frølund, S: *Nature and Education,* vol 3. Philosophy of Education series, Institut International de Philosophie, Paris.
- Kuecker, Glen D. and Thomas D. Hall (2011): "Resilience and Community in the Age of World-System Collapse." In: *Nature and Culture* 6:1(Spring):18–40.
- Rosted, J. et al. (2011): *Det Kreative København.* Fora.
- Torfing, J & A.H. Krogh (2014): *Leading Collaborative Innovation.* Paper presented at the Policy and Politics Conference, Bristol.
- United Nations (2014): *Culture and Sustainable Development in the Post-2015 Development* Agenda. http://www.un.org/en/ga/president/68/pdf/culture_sd/Culture%20and%20SD%20Summary%20of%20Key%20Messages_FINAL%20rev.pdf (asp 23-2-16).
- Williams, Raymond (1989): *Resources of Hope*: Culture, Democracy, Socialism. Verso. (Originally published in 1958).

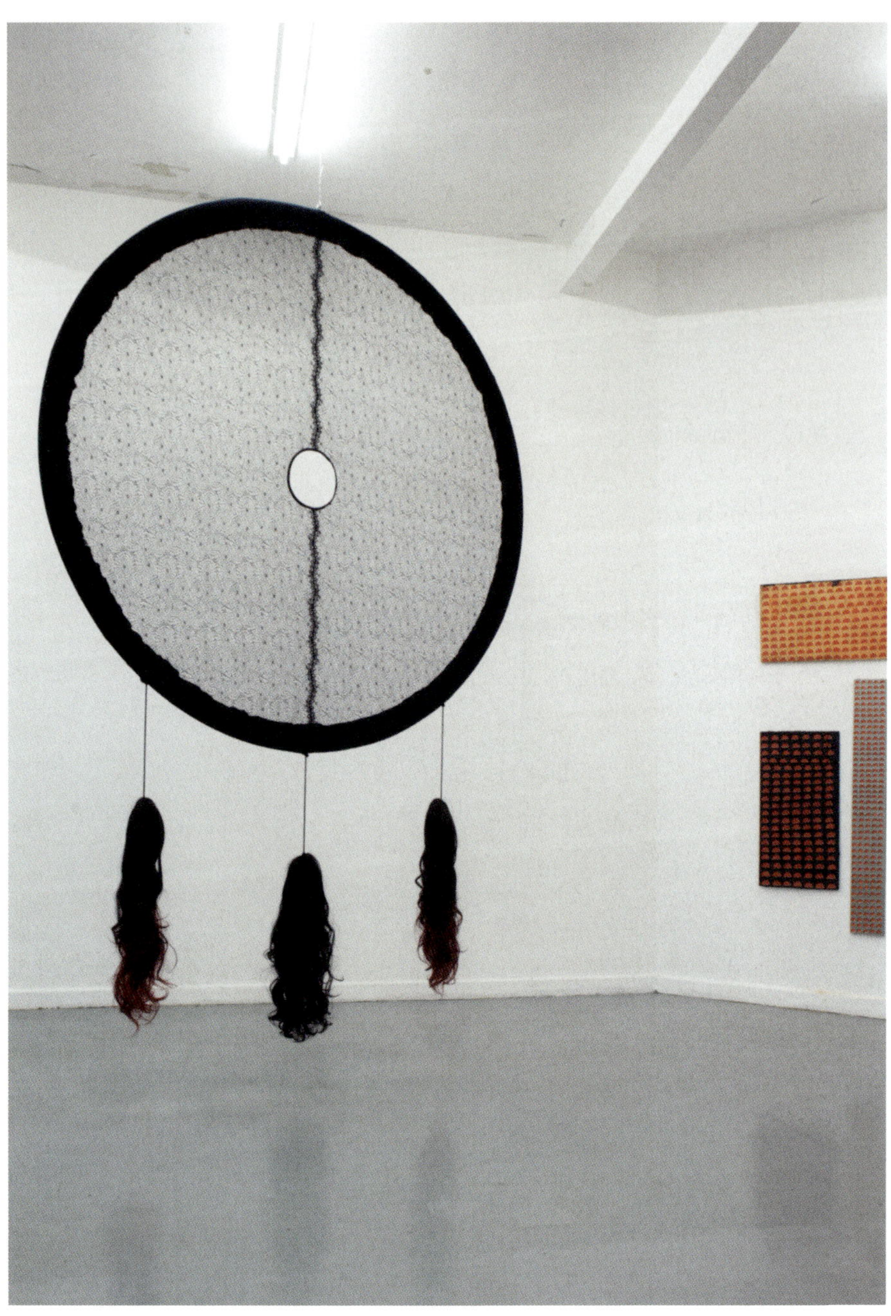

Artworks from Katja Windau and Nina Wengel at Viktoria Kaserne (fux eG)

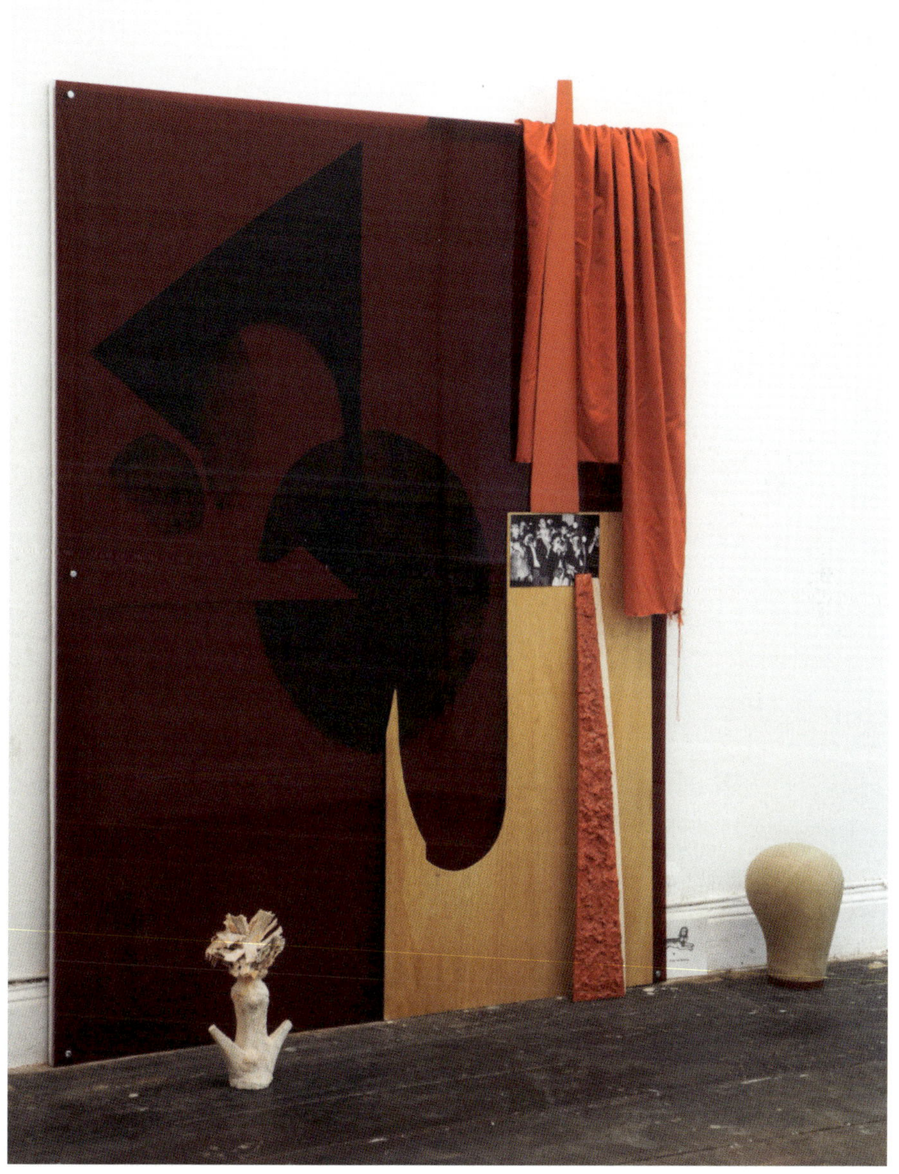

Installation Based on the Color Red by Sian Kristoffersen at Galerie Speckstraße

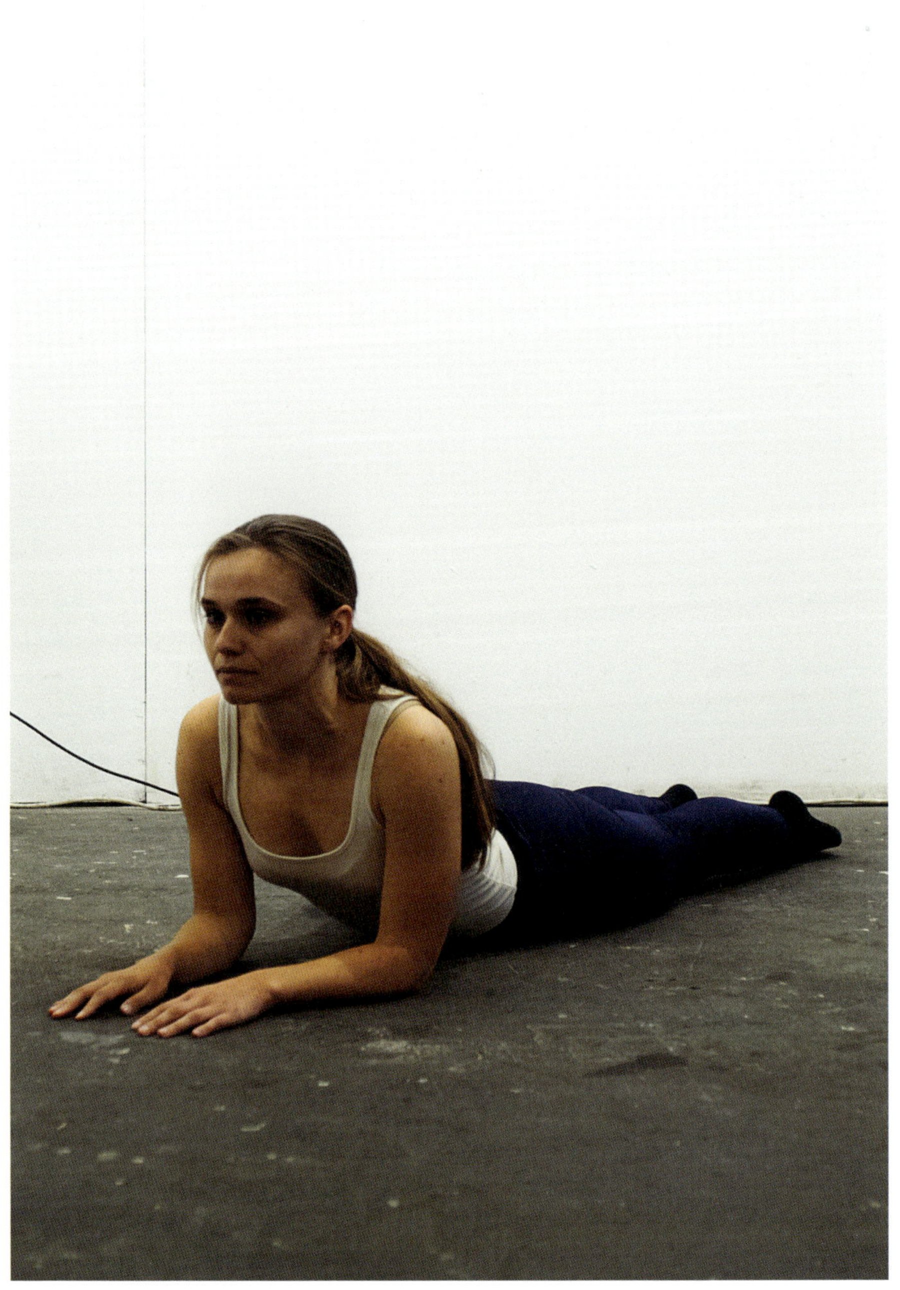

48

Work in Progress by Marie Torp at 2025

Hands-On: Contemporary Urban Subjects

Elke Krasny

Twenty-first century cities worldwide are the sites of deep urban transformation processes resulting in the systemic acceleration of economic, political, social, and spatial inequality and injustice. The economic changes wrought by neoliberalism govern urban subjects and impact on the scale of daily urban life, not only on the scale of policy and infrastructural measures. The precarization of bodies, space, and labor is far reaching. Prevailing logics of accumulation as well as predatory, and profit-driven, urbanization result in crises on both global and local scales. Such a dynamic not only effects fierce competition between cities but equally fierce competition within cities: between neighborhoods and even within neighborhoods. Ultimately, competition renders cities divided. This division that is caused by uneven growth is expressed in spatial, economic, social, and cultural terms. This leads to large parts of urban populations struggling with austerity, eviction, dispossession, expulsion, and precarization.[1] Inter-urban as well as intra-urban competition plays out on the level of everyday life of urban subjects. They are required to compete for jobs, housing, education and mobility as well as access to urban resources and infrastructures in general. In short, they have to compete for urban life. Extensive spatial and social division combined with fierce competition reinforces existing fault lines and establishes new ones between gendered and racialized subjects.

These transformations profoundly reshape and reorient people's lives. The politics of location and the specifics of situation impact on urban subjects. I experience these transformations as I live through the dissolution of the European welfare state, and as I witness how racist and xenophobic politics target immigrants, asylum seekers, and refugees. While I am finishing this text, the refugee crisis rages. On August 27, 2015 the Financial Times reports that "up to 50 migrants were found dead [...] in a Hungarian registered lorry abandoned on an Austrian motorway" (Byrne 2015). The same article states that "late in the day came reports of several hundred people caught on board a boat that sank off the Libyan coast" (ibid.). Reality instills political depression. Reality instills social despair. "Political depression is pervasive within recent histories of decolonization, civil rights, socialism and labor politics, and attention to affective politics is a way of trying to come to terms with disappointment, failure, and the slowness of change" (Cvetkovich 2012). One has to constantly remind oneself and others that the twenty-first century city is also the site where urban subjects struggle not to give up and not to give in. Despite the far-reaching processes of centrification, gentrification, consumption-driven massification, touristification, structural exploitation, racialisation, and gendering, urban subjects seek to find ways of mutual support and cooperation.

[1] On austerity see: Mendoza 2015, on eviction see: Deutsch: 1996, on dispossession see: Butler 2013, on expulsion see: Saskia Sassen 2014, on precarization see: Lorey 2015.

I would now like to connect the question of contemporaneity and global urban subject formation to the question of modernity and modern subject formation. Even though the scope of such an exploration would warrant an entire book, I take the risk to raise such a complex issue here in the context of a short essay. I do so in order to draw attention to the fact that what is said here is part of a much larger project connecting philosophies of subject formation, political thought, economy, and urban transformation. Modern subject formation as well as global subject formation are co-implicated in urban transformation processes. The modern subject and the modern city share a common history. The same can be said for the global subject. The global subject and the global city share a common presence, and in the future, will have shared a common history.

In historical terms, modern Western subject formation and its progress-centric orientation was closely linked with the projects of capitalism, colonialism, imperialism, and the modern city. These processes were rife with conflict. They were competitive and brutal. At the same time, they created new forms of mutual support, cooperation, and solidarity. They made possible alignments across lines of class, gender, and race. In contemporary terms, global subject formation is closely linked with the projects of neoliberalism, neocolonialism, globalization, and urban transformation. Contemporary global subject formation is based upon notions of independence, flexibility, and mobility, and the capacities to navigate knowledge, social and media relations, digital technologies, and all kinds of global and local networks. The historical modern subject as well as the contemporary global subject is constituted as urban subject. Again, it is of importance to not forget that such processes are never monolithic. Many other subjects were raised, historically. Many other subjects are raised, today. It is of importance to arrive at imagining urban subjects that seek to (re)claim their agency in co-dependence. Isabell Lorey states her interest "in developing a political and social theoretical perspective that starts from connectedness with others and takes different dimensions of the precarious into consideration. […] Understanding social relationality as primary does not mean starting from something that is equally common to all. Recognizing social relationality can only be the beginning of an entry process of becoming-common, involving discussions of possible common interests in the differences of the precarious, in order to invent with others new forms of organizing and new orders that break with the existing forms of governing in a refusal of obedience" (Lorey 2015).

It is equally crucial to conceive of urban subjects connected with each other in dimensions of what I want to call urban care. Turning to the work of feminist political theorist Joan Tronto I want to broaden extensively the understanding of care that is commonly described as domestic labor, child care, or health care. Following Tronto, caring is a way of being in/being with the world. Tronto understands caring as "a species activity that includes everything that we do to maintain, continue, and repair our 'world' so that we can live as well as possible. That world includes our bodies, our selves, and our environment, all of which we seek to interweave in a complex, life-sustaining web." (Tronto 1993) I now want to join Tronto's "complex interweaving" with Lorey's "social relationality." I argue here that care work is very much needed for producing such interweaving and making it useful for "social relationality." By no means do I want to disregard or in any way diminish the importance of what is commonly understood as care work, but I want to conceptually connect the dimension of ontological connectedness with the dimension of social connectedness. The gap that opens up between these two dimensions has to be filled with care work. This gap is filled with precarization. The more disenfranchised sociability, conviviality, and possibilities for testing and practicing connectedness become, the less time there is to fill this empty space with care (work). This results in a widening of this gap that profoundly puts any forging of social relationality at risk. The widening of this gap is therefore not accidental, but very much strategic and intrinsic to structural injustices of neoliberalization and precarization. The care work necessary to become social and political cannot take place due to the effective neoliberalisation, fracture, and precarization of time, place, and bodies.

In light of this, it is crucial to search, in practical as well as in theoretical terms, for urban 51 subject formations conducive to co-dependence and social relationality. In search of modern and global subject formations resistant to hegemonic demands of modernization and globalization, knowledge on histories of urban care are key. My research-based exhibition "Hands-On Urbanism: The Right to Green" sought to explore urban subjects within the history of the modern as well as the global city that took defining urbanism into their own hands. Through the lens of urban agriculture, subsistence, and urban gardening I traced transhistorical examples of urban care, cooperation, mutual support, and self-organization. In order to cover the period from mid nineteenth-century industrial modernization to contemporary globalization, the curatorial work for the exhibition involved both archival and field research.

I want to connect now the scale of modern and global subject formation and the modern and global city with the concrete details and examples of resistant and caring urban subjects. In what follows I will share the results of the research process in Ma Po Po Farm in Ma Shi Po Village in Hong Kong's New Territories. Ma Po Po Farm is one out of the twenty case studies included in the "Hands-On Urbanism: The Right to Green" exhibition. I will use the format of a curator's lecture to write about the Ma Po Po Farm case study.

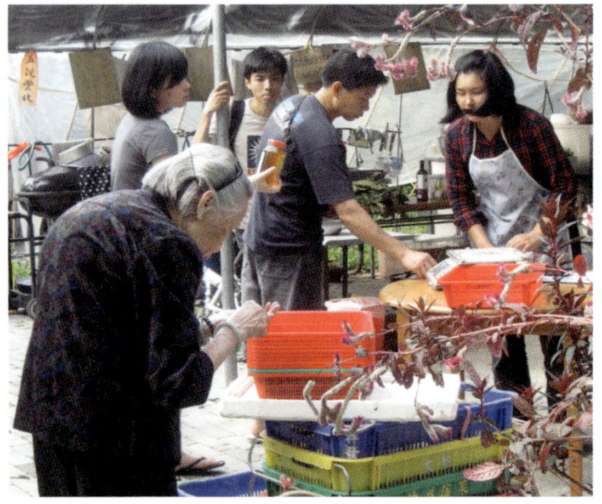

1. Becky Au and her grandmother

Image 1 shows Becky Au and her grandmother in Ma Shi Po Village in 2011. This image takes us back to the time of my field research. Ma Po Po Village is located in the new territories in Hong Kong. I would like to draw your attention to two people in this image. In the background we see Becky Au, the initiator of the resistant village community of the newly founded Ma Shi Po Farm and in the front we see Becky Au's grandmother who lives in one of the so-called informal farm houses.

Images 2 and 3 are aerial photographs demonstrating the urban transformation processes over time. There is much conflict in the village of Ma Shi Po. The political and economic power structures of Hong Kong's New Territories are reflected in the built environment, informal architecture, land use, and land rights of this village. The families who lived here prior to the 1898 occupation by the British Empire are considered natives, and, by law, can never be forced to sell their land. After the Second World War, the conflict between the Communist Party and the Kuomintang caused waves of refugees to flee from Mainland China. Many settled here, leasing land from the natives, who gradually migrated into the center of Hong Kong, or even the United Kingdom and beyond to other Commonwealth countries, but retained ownership of their land. The settlers built squatter houses on their rented land. In 1980, this type of informal settlement was pro-

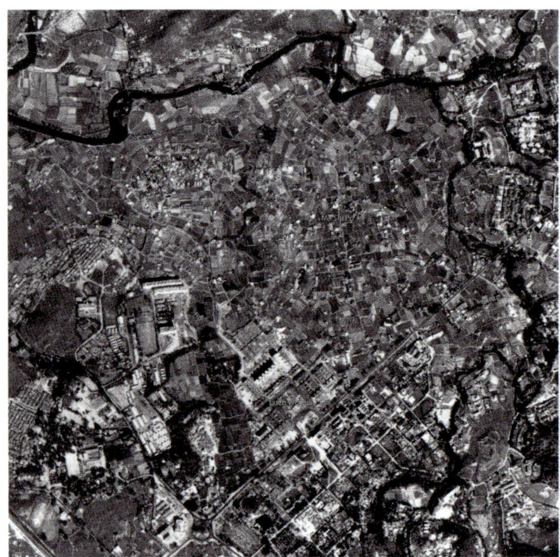

2. Aerial Photographs, Ma Shi Po, survey 1964

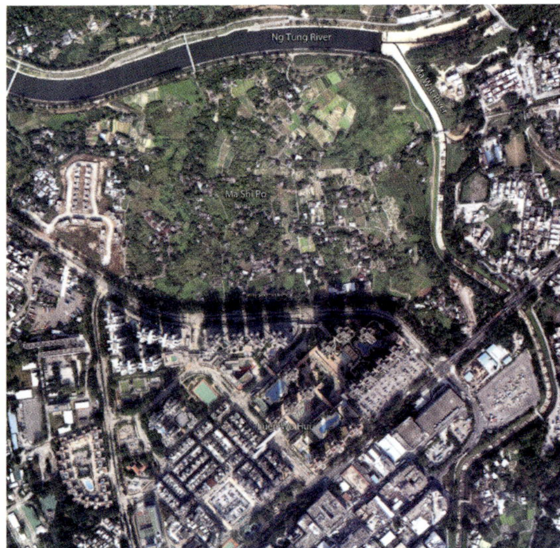

3. Aerial Photographs, Ma Shi Po, survey 2009

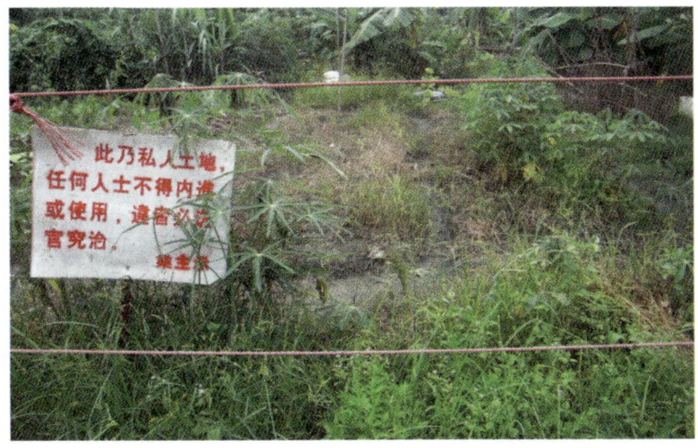

4. Abandoned farm land

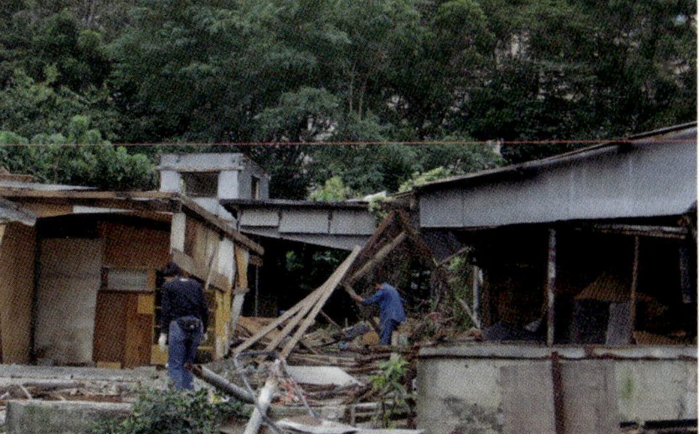

5. Demolition of farm houses

hibited. In 1982, and then again in 1984–85, all unofficially built homes in Hong Kong were registered by the Squatter Control and Clearance Office. Now, the city's official urban development plan moves toward the urbanization and densification of the New Territories, designating the area as residential and industrial, and no longer agricultural.

Images 4 and 5 show some of the already abandoned farm land and the demolition of farm houses. The continued existence of traditional green areas, farms, fishponds, and rice fields is under threat. Ma Shi Po's very existence is at risk due to the pressure from developers. The development magnate Henderson has already purchased 80% of the land from the descendants of natives; the people living and working on the land receive no compensation.

Image 6 shows one of the educational tours to raise consciousness for the villagers' continued resistance. Becky Au returned back home from her successful career in downtown Hong Kong to Ma Shi Po village and initiated a community farm based on the principles of permaculture. Together with other villagers, Hong Kong activists, artists, and local schools, she is trying to create a resistance movement to save the village. Led by Becky Au, the group has worked closely with elderly villagers in particular, but also with activists from Hong Kong, who participated in workshops on urban agriculture, permaculture, soap making, and bread baking. Dedicated to the preservation of the village, a group of thirty activists decided to work as part-time farmers. Educational activities with schools and public consultations with local government officials are organised by Ma Po Po Farm. Self-organization is key. Not only has the group relied wholly on self-management and self-organization, they also focus on tending to the land together and transferring knowledge between farming,

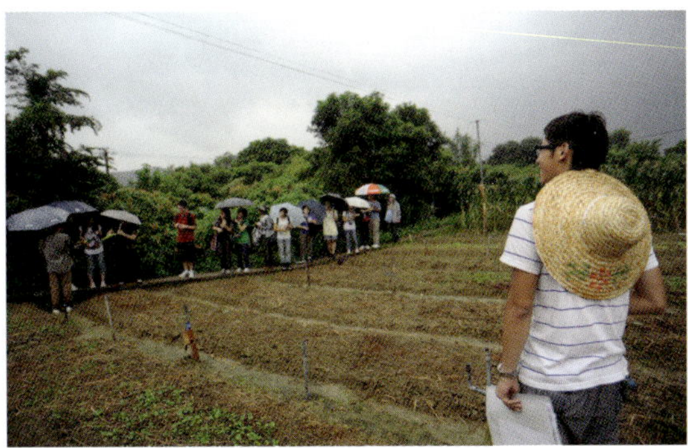

6. Educational Tours

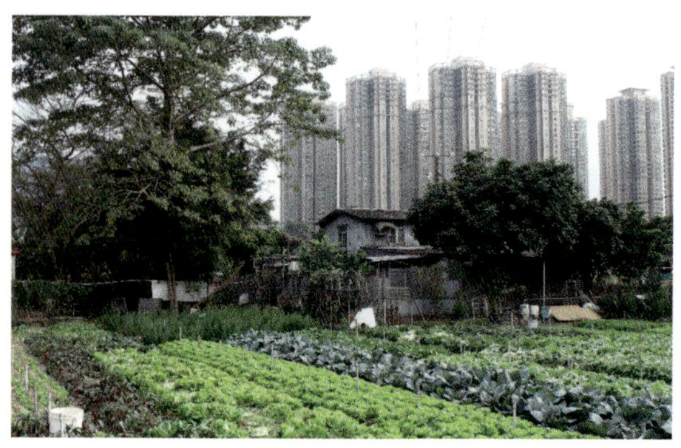

7. Ma Po Po Farm

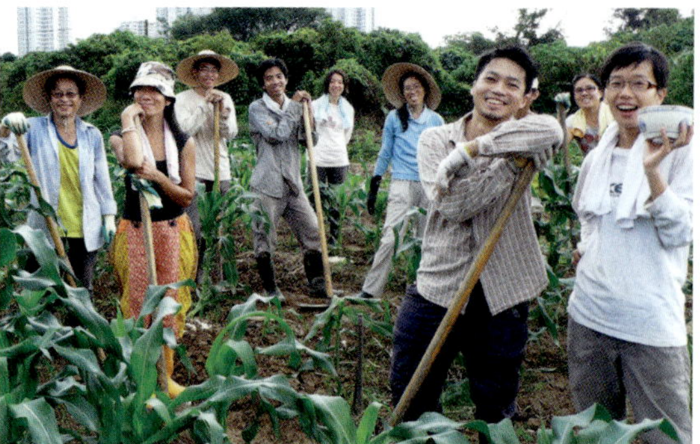

8. Ma Po Po Farming Graduates

the arts, sustainability, and community organizing to make the village culture part of the contemporary urban landscape. They introduced a knowledge transfer between traditional farmers, permaculture experts, and neo-farmers, who refer to themselves as part-time farmers; they also organize community consultations with the local municipality. The official urban development strategy is one of cooperating with the purely monetary interests of developers. The land is bought and the fields left fallow in order to then rezone the property from agricultural land to (much more profitable) building land. Residents are resettled or evicted. Even though the long-term perspective for Ma Po Po Farm and Ma Shi Po Village are bleak, ties of solidarity and a sense of belonging are created between the subjects of resistance and the landscape they tend. These ties attest to the villagers' continued practice of spatial justice and sustained affective labour. The "right to green" exerts the villagers' practice of their "right to the city."

Image 7 shows the complexities of urban realities: high-rise buildings, squatter houses, farmland. This is a chronopolitical image. The high-rise buildings we see in the background are commonly understood to represent future-oriented urban transformation processes, indicating first modernization and now globalization. The squatter houses and the agricultural land use we see in the foreground is commonly held to be of a rural past, which is only marginally and peripherally part of the urban. We have arrived today, as I would like to argue, in a fragile, vulnerable, and precarious equilibrium.[2] Many have come to understand that what we see in the foreground is as much part of the city's past as it is key for sustaining an urban future. Therefore, this image bears witness to a process of chronopolitical reorientation. The urban future is not decided yet. Now, the future still holds the potentiality of a co-existence of the urban and the rural. The struggles are still ongoing. Therefore, this is also the image that then became the key image for the exhibition, it is shown on the poster, on the invitation, and also on the cover of the book I edited on the occasion of the exhibition.

[2] Silvia Federici writes in her 2010 article *Feminism and the Politics of the Common in an Era of Primitive Accumulation* "Urban Gardens have opened the way to a 'rurbanization' process (…). They are centers of sociality, knowledge production, cultural and intergenerational exchange" (Federici 2012).

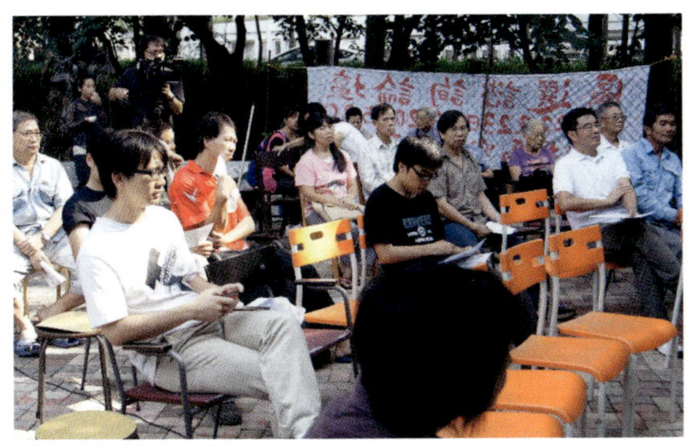
9. District Council Consultation

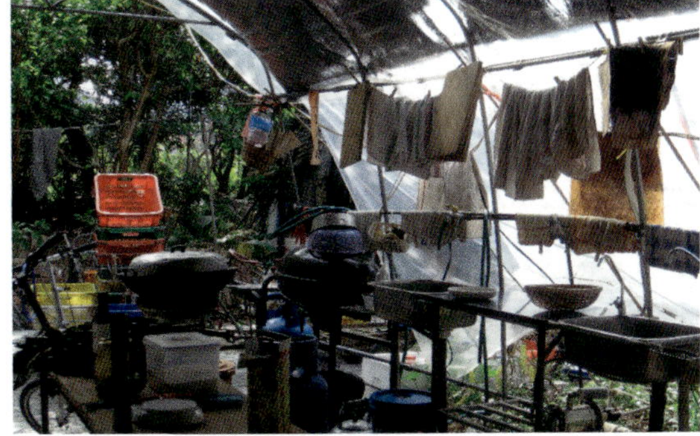
10. Ma Po Po's gathering place

Image 8 shows the graduation of new farmers. Young people from Hong Kong Central, many of them artists or designers, joined the villagers in their struggle and decided to become part-time farmers. Chi-Ho Chung is one of the farming graduates. He helped me with my research in Ma Po Po Village. I then invited him to Vienna to give a public talk in the Hands-On Urbanism exhibition at the Architecture Centre Vienna, where Chi-Ho Chung spoke about the strategies of self-organization and the ongoing struggle in Ma Po Po Village.

Image 9 shows a meeting with the local municipality. The assembly of chairs tells us about a process of participation that is initiated bottom-up, from the ground up, if you will. Today, very often participation is misused as a tool of governance. Participation by invitation from the administration or city officials leads to check lists, tick lists, and streamlined deliberation. This is far from open-ended conversation or critical practice. Many cities today, among them to give two examples, Berlin and Vienna, have written handbooks of participation. Looking at the chairs lined up in this image from Ma Po Po Village, they tell a different story. The villagers invited representatives of the local municipality to enter a process of discussing the future of the village. In this regard, I understand participation as such to be less a top-down strategy of governance, but rather an open-ended process based upon conversation.

Image 10 shows a piece of architecture and infrastructure that is key to the social and political life of Ma Po Po Village. The structure you see in this image is the most important piece of architecture in Ma Po Po Village as it serves as a space to congregate and have workshops. Political assembly, bread baking workshops, agricultural education, planning strategies for the farmers' market, sociability and conversation, all happen in this tent like structure.

Image 11 shows a contemporary urban farmer at work. Here, you see Becky Au again. One could argue that this image also holds a chronopolitical dimension. Contemporary urban farming critically points us to the fact that the chronopolitical split between the

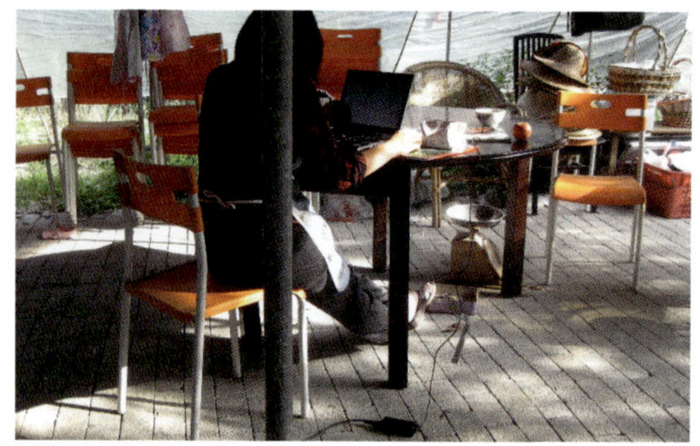

11. Becky Au, contemporary farmer and activist

rural and the urban, one conceived of as lagging behind, the other one understood as the avant garde of urbanization as modernization, have always already been skewed. The rural-urban divide is just as much a chronopolitical construction as the public-private divide. Becky Au embodies the practice of a contemporary urban farmer. She is both locally rooted and globally connected. She points to another concept of a global urban subject.

In concluding, I want to turn once more to the question of contemporary urban transformation processes and global urban subject formation. The prospects of global urban transformation are as bleak as they are dystopian. The sheer scale of transformation puts contemporary subject formation at risk. More and more, urban subjects become precarized subjects finding themselves with no time for self-chosen cooperation and conviviality with others, but rather with the need to compete with others at all times. It is under these conditions, that the global city witnesses new and emergent practices of cooperation, conviviality, resistance, and care. The global city becomes the test site for a chronopolitical reorientation and its fragile co-existence of the urban and the rural Ma Po Po Farm is proof that the right to the city entails a right to green. The community around Becky Au demonstrates that new forms of urban care based on subsistence perspectives, cooperation, mutual support, and resistance are possible. Artists and designers are amongst those who decided not only to become part-time farmers, but to invest themselves in community-organizing and equally in art-making in their self-chosen village context. Thus, supported by these global urban subjects, who chose to live and work differently caring for their rural-urban village, Hands-On Urbanism emerges as a lived and embodied practice within and under the conditions of contemporaneity and its structural urban transformation processes.

References

- Butler, J. and A. Athanasiou (2013): *Dispossession: The Performative in the Political.* Cambridge, UK and Malden, MA: Polity Press.
- Byrne, A. (2015): "Grim find on Austrian road shakes European migrant crisis talks." *Financial Times.* http://www.ft.com/intl/cms/s/0/83323a26-4cc0-11e5-9b5d-89a026fda5c9.html#axzz43Yd0B88g (asp 20-3-16).
- Cvetkovich, A. (2012): *Depression: a public feeling.* Durham and London: Duke University Press: 7.
- Deutsch, R. (1996): *Evictions: Art and Spatial Politics.* Cambridge, Massachusetts: MIT Press.
- Federici, S. (2012): "Feminism and the Politics of the Common in an Era of Primitive Accumulation." In: *Revolution at Point Zero. Housework, Reproduction, and Feminist Struggle.* Oakland: PM Press, Brooklyn: Common Notions, Brooklyn: Autonomomedia: 138–148.
- Lorey, I. (2015): *State of Insecurity: Government of the Precarious.* London and New York: Verso: 15.
- Mendoza, K.-A. (2015): *Austerity: The Demolition of the Welfare State and the Rise of Zombie Economy.* Oxford: New Internationalist.
- Saskia, S. (2014): *Expulsion: Brutality and Complexity in the Global Economy.* Cambridge, MA: Belknap Press.
- Tronto, J. (1993): *Moral Boundaries: A Political Argument for an Ethic of Care.* London and New York: Routledge: 103.

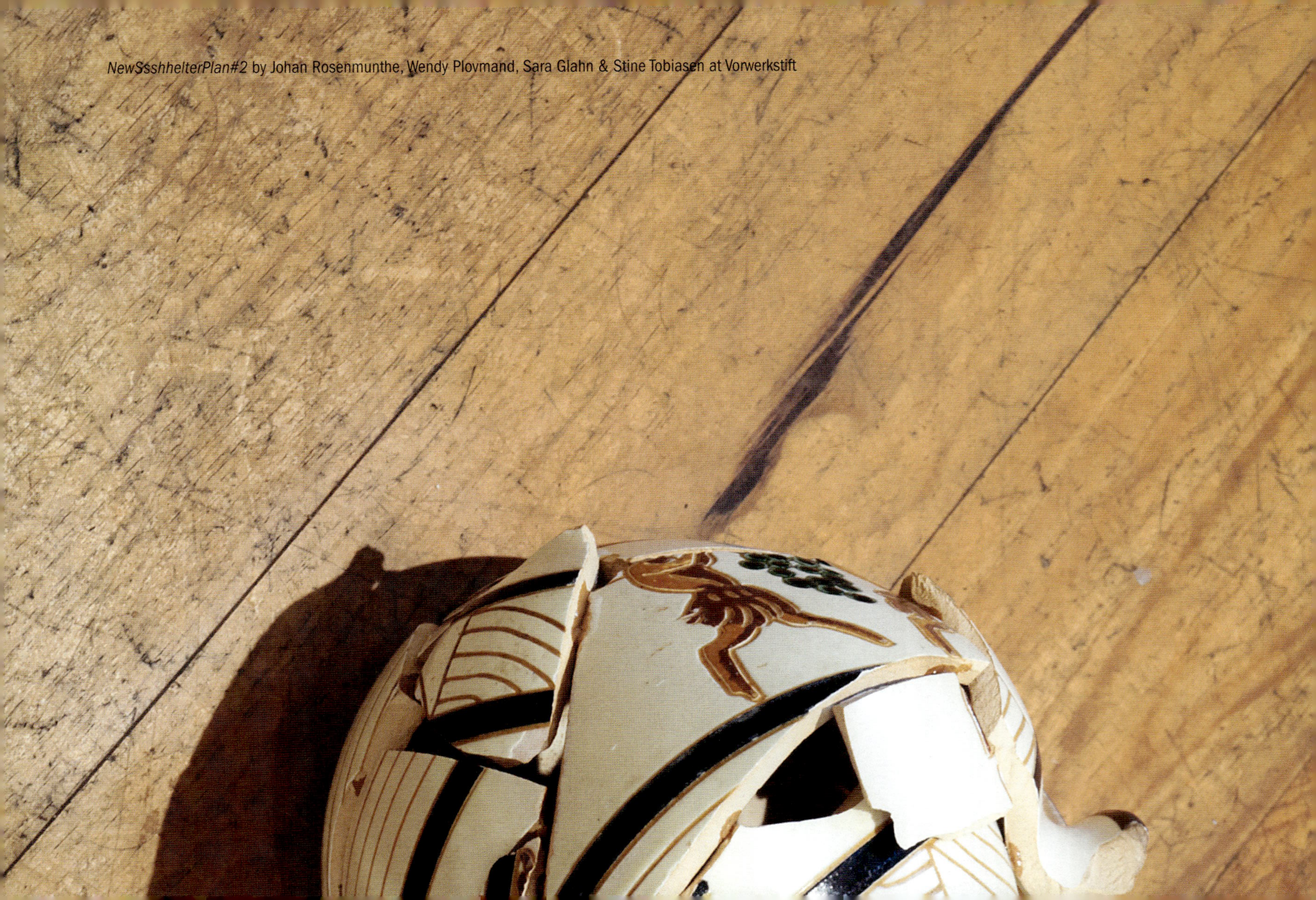

NewSsshhelterPlan#2 by Johan Rosenmunthe, Wendy Plovmand, Sara Glahn & Stine Tobiasen at Vorwerkstift

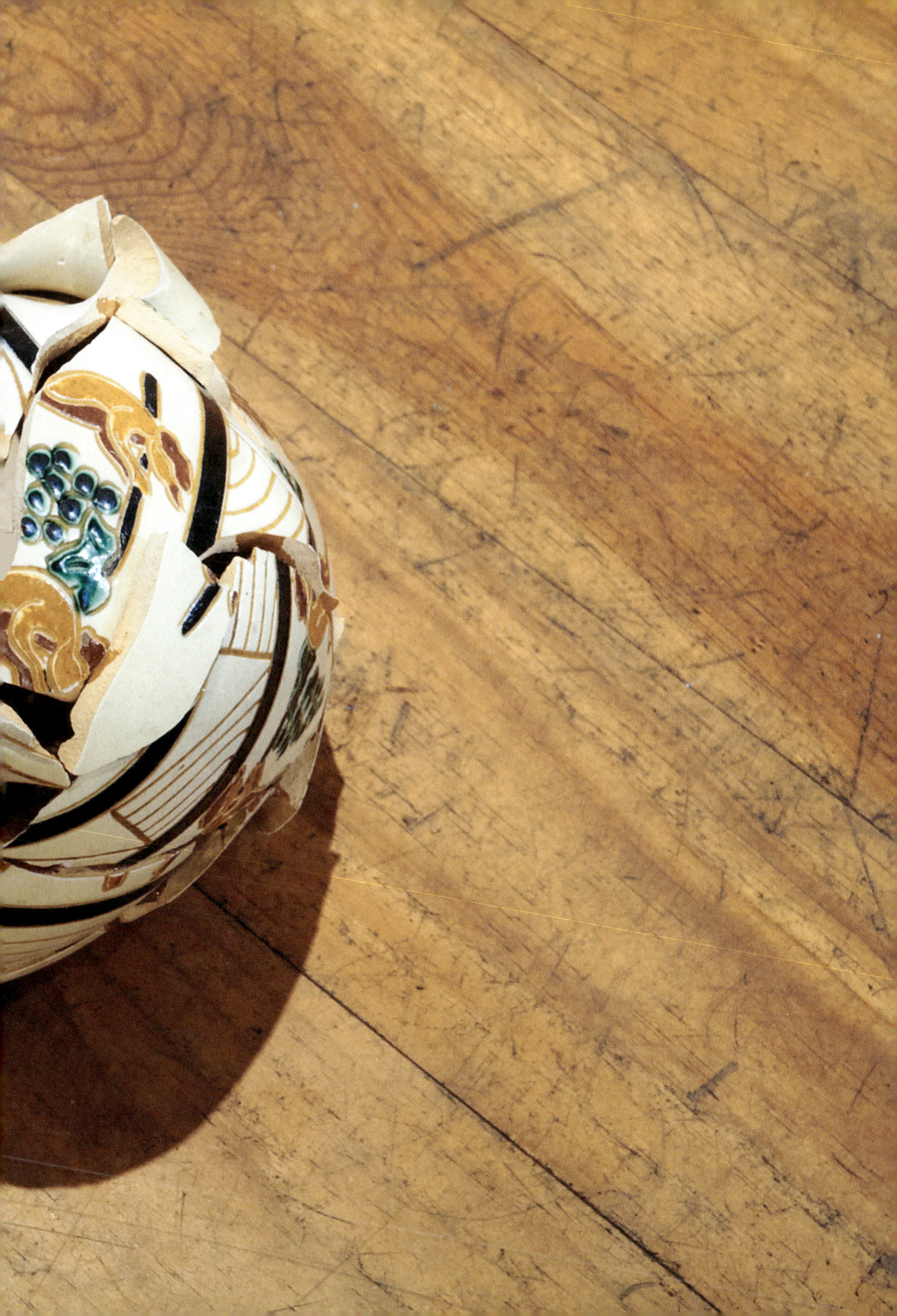

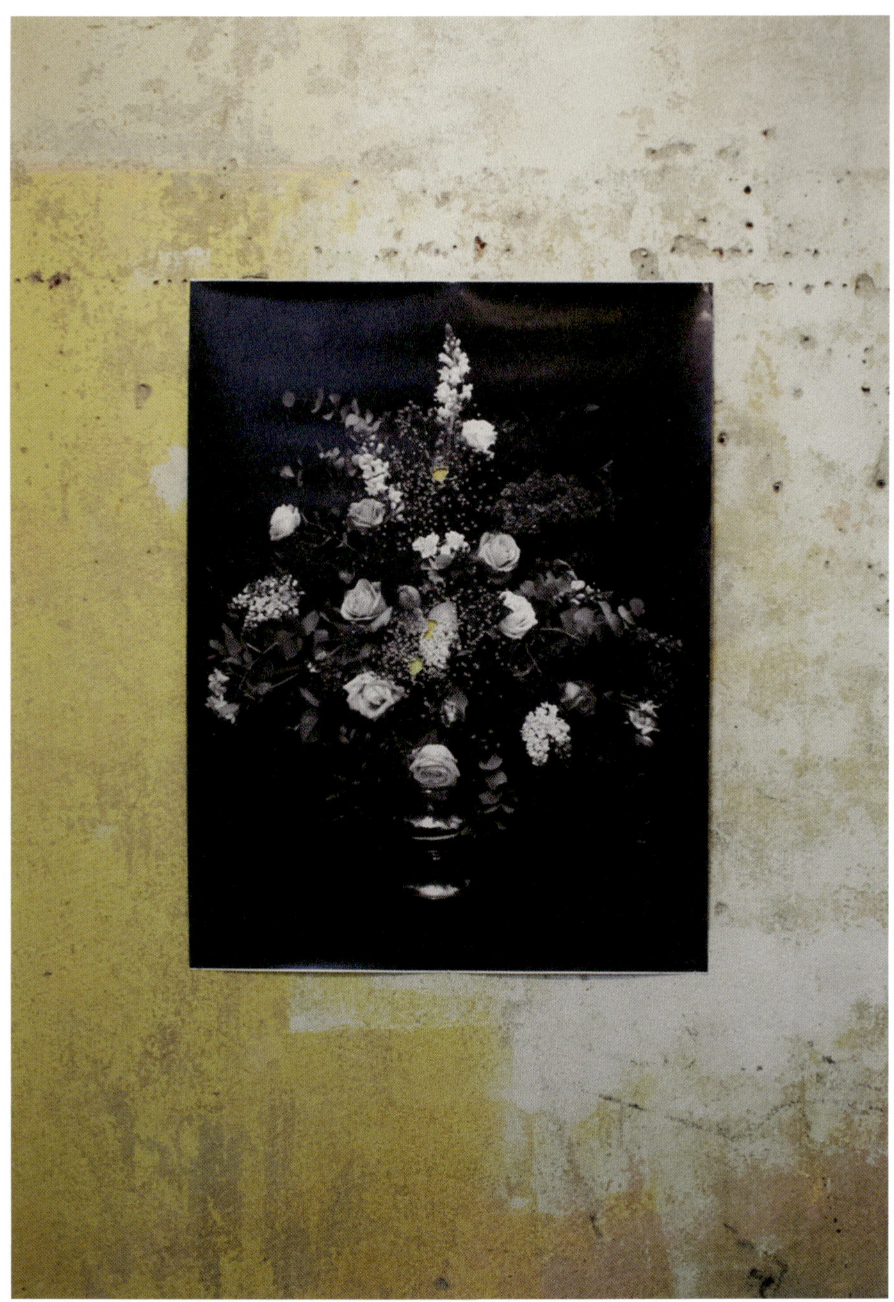

60

Still & Even by Alana Lake at Galerie Speckstraße

From Design to Mediation and Development: Emerging Urban Practices and Social Services in European Cities

Levente Polyák

European cities witnessed changing fortunes in the past decade: after the prosperous years of the early 2000s, the economic crisis resulting from over-development without necessary financial coverage reversed the economic benefits of growth-oriented development and pushed many municipalities close to bankruptcy. The economic breakdown, reinforced by various waves of political crises and austerity policies brought about the most recent crisis of European welfare states, prompting the public sector in many cities to withdraw from maintaining certain infrastructures and services related to culture, education, sports, health, and food provision, as well as to the maintenance of public and community spaces.

In many cities, citizen organizations and activist groups engaged in replacing the services dissolving from their communities: recognizing that traditional support structures and funding sources lost their capacity to feed community-oriented urban projects, they started elaborating alternative formats to help citizens access services and spaces. While in some cases the outsourcing of municipal services to communities happens through contractual agreements, in other cases it is a more conflicted process: often struggling with making their services recognized, many community organizations operate in semi-legality or illegality, running entirely on voluntary capacities.

Design and planning professionals had an ambiguous role in these processes: they were often stuck in pre-crisis organizational models and took time to adapt to the new circumstances and establish new positions in development processes. Recognizing the need for self-sustaining, alternative community infrastructures and services on one hand, and the direct social utility of their skills in community-initiated urban projects on the other, architects and planners began supporting community experiments, launching unsolicited projects, building frameworks for the involvement of different social groups, and introducing new development models in order to bring sense and life into dysfunctional elements of the built environment.

After outlining the process in which the financialization of urban development transformed architecture and austerity policies reshaped urban welfare and public services, this text will explore the transition to community-run services and spaces and look at the experience of various European cities by analyzing the role of design and planning professionals.

The Financialization of Architecture and the Economic Crisis

The 2007–08 economic crisis was in many ways connected to urban development: "The financial crash which found its origins in the property markets [demonstrated that] the built environment is not only incidental to global economic stability, it is instrumental" (Self & Bose 2014: 12). While the crisis was "originated in urban and suburban spaces," later it became a "state crisis with consequences for cities and subnational scales" (Donald, Glasmeier, Gray and Lobao 2014). The internationalization of mortgage markets, that is, the shift from "locally originated and locally held arrangements" to "locally originated but globally distributed" ones, led to the erosion of lending standards and "reversed red lining," turning low-income neighborhoods into targets for high-risk mortgages (Donald, Glasmeier, Gray and Lobao 2014). In turn, the easier access to mortgages provided by the relatively unrestrained financial markets prompted a boom in construction in and around European cities, resulting in vast areas of new housing and office units, conceived more as investment opportunities than as places to live or work.

This process brought along the financialization of urban development and planning, where buildings are "no longer something to use, but to own [with the hope of increased asset-value, rather than use-value, over time]" (de Graaf 2015). When the exchange-value of buildings gains prominence over their use-value, they lose all relationship with actual needs and begin acting "similarly to how financial products are being created and sold that have lost any connection with real production or a real economy" (Vanstiphout 2012: 94). Becoming targets of speculation, many former sites of welfare and cultural services (hospitals, schools, parks, theaters, and cinemas) become endangered species, calculated as potentially buildable square meters instead of potential contributions to life quality.

Architects have been complicit in this process: the financialization of urban development also profoundly transformed the practice of architecture. If modern architecture and planning were known as disciplines that engaged—sometimes devastatingly—in improving the quality of life in cities and their surroundings, contemporary architecture and planning kept very little of that ambition, losing their determining role in shaping the environment to "financial institutions which bankroll the developers who promote a sophisticated language of metrics targeted at increasing fiscal efficiency" (Self & Bose 2014: 10).

In his article, Reinier de Graaf takes Thomas Piketty's analysis of the evolution of capital in the past centuries and applies it to architecture: the late twentieth and early twenty-first centuries witnessed the return of the "primacy of wealth over work in economic benefits" where ownership again became an increasingly important part of wealth production, which led to the "built environment and particularly housing [acquiring] a fundamentally new role. From a means to provide shelter, it becomes a means to generate financial returns [...] The logic of a building no longer primarily reflects its intended use but instead serves mostly to promote a 'generic' desirability in economic terms. Judgment of architecture is deferred to the market. The 'architectural style' of buildings no longer conveys an ideological choice but a commercial one: architecture is worth whatever others are willing to pay for it [...] Once discovered as a form of capital, there is no choice for buildings but to operate according to the logic of capital" (de Graaf 2015).

Architecture's financial turn reduced the role of architects in urban development processes to "enticing investors with ingenious combinations of office floors guaranteed to generate money for the cultural facility located on the ground floor" (Vanstiphout 2014a: 59); or in general, to "performing an endless variation of style" and "inexpensively providing aesthetic form while the building and planning process is relegated to the developer" (Illner 2014: 54) and the "definition of the architect is replaced by that of the economist" (de Graaf 2015). The unleashed property markets that were at the origin of the financial crisis were among the fields hardest hit by it: the loosened rules of borrowing and lending made many homeowners incapable of paying back their mortgages and made many new developments obsolete before they were even finished. The disintegration of the construction industry that saw its profits evaporate in a few months' time directly affected the architecture profession: a large percentage of design jobs disappeared from the market, a situation made even more painful by the disappearance of public commissions in many cities. It also changed the image of architects: the devastating effect of the recession on the construction industry made them painfully aware of the unsustainability of previous concepts of funding mechanisms and development processes. Finding themselves in the midst of landscapes of unfinished constructions, vacant complexes and fragmented public spaces, a generation of designers and planners began to think critically about the speculation-based economy and to take into account the limitations of the shrunken market, starting to notice the opportunities of the urban areas neglected by the official planning mechanisms.

Austerity and the Changing Face of Urban Development

The changing role of architecture and planning in relation to finance was not the only significant impact on the logic of urban development. Municipal administrations, traditionally the main clients and managers of major urban works, have gradually lost their leading role, in some cases already in the years leading to the crisis. The increasing vulnerability of municipalities to financial markets was brought about by neoliberal policies, with which national governments, starting with the conservative revolution of the 1980's, forced cities to change their development patterns and priorities.

While the property boom of the early 2000s brought increasing wealth to cities, it also forced municipal administrations into a new kind of competition: responding to the "creative city" hype by aiming at attracting the "creative class" and especially the financial elite, municipalities tended to invest in iconic but risky developments, conceived as investments, and prioritized over maintaining crucial infrastructures and social services. The increasing vulnerability of municipalities revealed the general malaise of the welfare state, which was dependent upon constant growth and the increase of land values. With the growing insufficiency of regular tax revenues at carrying out basic tasks, municipal budgets became increasingly dependent on construction: "For staffing libraries and developing cultural programs, as well as for constructing and maintaining parks, boulevards, pavements and squares, municipalities relied upon revenues from land-development activities, some of which required risky investments" (Vanstiphout 2014a: 59).

The austerity measures introduced after the eruption of the crisis by national governments and European Institutions sought to reduce budget deficits by spending cuts, decreasing labor costs, privatization, the downsizing of local administrations and the reconfiguration of public services. These measures, which expanded the impact of neoliberal policies already in place, hit cities especially hard: with a fiscal tax base particularly vulnerable to the effects of financial instability and with many responsibilities rescaled from the central state to local governments, many cities struggled to pay back their debts and reached the limits of their ability to provide the necessary infrastructure to their residents. Obliged by national laws and financial creditors to keep debts at legal limits, municipalities carried out significant budget cuts in social and cultural services, and proceeded with the privatization of communal assets such as buildings and land. In the austerity logic, municipalities were "forced to become entrepreneurial in order to promote economic development, often resulting in service cuts to balance budgets," disproportionately impacting "the poor, the young, racialized communities, and the elderly leading to the intensification of socio-spatial segregation at the neighborhood, city, and inter-city levels" (Donald, Glasmeier, Gray and Lobao 2014).

In many cities, the financial collapse of many construction projects, the reduction of public services, and the successive waves of privatization brought about the decay or abandonment of important community facilities and public spaces. Besides frozen public development projects, many formerly public assets that were privatized for redevelopment for commercial and residential purposes have also been abandoned to decay. The unfinished residential complexes of Spain, the emptied and unsold educational complexes in Hungary, or the disaffected movie theaters, hospitals, and transportation buildings in Italy all bear witness to this process.

Building Parallel Infrastructures

While cities in Northwest Europe, often with more balanced budget sheets and the coordinated process of outsourcing municipal activities to other parties managed relatively well to weather the recession and outsource their services to communities in contractual forms, many cities in Southern and Eastern Europe, where the crisis hit national and local economies stronger, struggled to maintain even their most basic infrastructure. Many local communities in these cities, deeply affected by austerity measures, the reduction of services, and the loss of their spaces set it upon themselves to fill the vacuum left by municipalities and states. Although the act of counterbalancing cuts played out differently in different parts of Europe, there are nevertheless an observable convergence in the objectives of these initiatives: to create a parallel social and cultural infrastructure that is as independent from the authorities as possible.

In Spain, for instance, the crisis left many construction projects unfinished. Not only large housing estates at the peripheries of bigger cities, but also municipal projects have been abandoned since the economic downturn. One of the most spectacular stories of abandoned land is that of the Campo de Cebada, in Madrid's La Latina neighborhood. Until 1968, the square accommodated a market hall, half of which was later turned into a municipal sports center. Plans for demolishing and rebuilding the hall and the center were interrupted by the crisis that left the 5,000 square meter area unfinished and abandoned. A festival at the square in 2010 brought the French architecture collective exyzt, whose installation created a temporary swimming pool and a concert venue at the halted construction site. The installation helped locals to discover their unused spatial asset, and when the installation was dismantled after the festival, the community reclaimed the square and began to project their ideas into the space. As a result of the increasing number of people attending reunions and assemblies, the community formed an association and gave a formal proposal to the municipality. In accepting the proposal, the municipality signed a temporary agreement with the association that allowed the latter to begin managing the space in 2011, running it as a sports field, a meeting point, and an event venue for concerts and film screenings.

In Italy, the economic crisis began earlier and has been intensified by a permanent political crisis with a widening gap between the actions of public administrations and local challenges. In Rome, the incoherent policies of successive city administrations led to unequal urban development patterns, and the one-sided, developer-friendly crisis measures failed to provide solutions for social needs or help balance the city budget. Besides activist responses to the housing crisis, spaces of culture and education, such as cinemas, theaters or schools, and libraries have been equally taken over by self-organized communities, thereby addressing the lack of community services sustained by the city administration. Prompted by the failure of public services, local associations practically began "to take care of all that they need in a neighborhood, acting as the replacement of a service center or a public administration" (Cellamare 2014: 74).

There have been a number of noteworthy projects acting as important building blocks of the parallel infrastructure such as theater and cinema courses offered by a group of activists at Trastevere's abandoned Cinema America, the concerts organized at the occupied Cinema Palazzo, the community theater project proposed by the Fondazione Teatro Valle Bene Comune in a closed theater in Rome's historical center, the Museo dell'Altro e dell'Altrove (Museum of the Other and the Elsewhere) di Metropoliz established in an industrial complex occupied by migrant families, the Palestra Popolare (Community Gym), and educational activities offered by SCUP (Sport e Cultura Popolare) in an occupied school building. These undertakings have been inspired by and continue to inspire community projects in other European cities

Changing Roles for Design and Planning

Architects felt the shifting nature of urban development and services crawling under their own skin. In addition to the growing discontent that many architects felt about the architectural profession's dispossession of leadership and political roles, the economic crisis, which originated from the housing bubble and heavily affected the construction industries, led to a significant shrinking of the labor market for architects and planners. Finding themselves without commissions from public or private developers, designers and planners began to explore the possibilities of small-scale, often temporary interventions over extensive construction projects, responding to the needs of local communities instead of the requirements of speculation-driven investments.

Temporary and light structures have proved to be highly useful tools to unleash the potentials of sites, like in the case of exyzt's Campo de Cebada installation that acted as a catalyst in the area's re-appropriation by the local community. Acknowledging the achievements of the pioneers of temporary and mobile architecture decades ago, contemporary experimenters recognized that light structures are more responsive to the changes of the immediate environment than solid edifices, and they are more capable of bypassing regulations, thus allowing more space for experimentation and political messages. The installations of exyzt and like-minded collectives like Coloco, Ecosistema Urbano or raumlabor berlin all bear witness to the ways in which architecture evolves from "a static service—traditionally related to the slowness of urban construction and identity transformations—to that of a performance, i.e., a dynamic response to the accelerated needs of contemporary society" (Gadanho 2011).

Whether temporary or permanent, the construction of outdoor or indoor public spaces, festival installations or co-working space interiors, community gardens or sport fields constitutes the core of these practices. The need for designers to improve and establish spontaneous, emerging public spaces also contributes to the rise of a new genre of architecture offices. They function as collectives whose work focuses on the construction process rather than the final product or an architectural intervention. If collectives like raumlabor berlin or exyzt have become regular guests of temporary festivals all across the world, their interventions go beyond entertainment, as they often have empowering capacities to help participatory design processes unfold.

The restitution of designers' socio-political role required the progressive transformation of the architectural profession itself. In 2007, Michelle Provoost and Wouter Vanstiphout traced the first signs of this transformation by describing a new wave of architects and urban practitioners as the "Dutch School of Urban Design": "These practices don't wait for a client or a commission—they forge ahead on their own and find other ways to finance the project.... These offices, groups, and artists have abandoned the idea of the conventional architects' office or urban planning department and have blurred the boundaries between urban planning, urban design, art, and social work.... Their interventions can be physical objects but even then are more importantly tactical manipulations of political landscapes. By succeeding in building something, these groups change the political status quo in such a way that more things become thinkable and doable" (Provoost and Vanstiphout 2007: 38).

However, revisiting his article seven years later, Vanstiphout adjusted his impressions: accommodating originally subversive and community-oriented processes, commercial developers, housing corporations and municipalities instrumentalized "placemaking, urban farming, community architecture, and narrative design as integral parts of their methodology. Again the architects pushed into the role of pill sweeteners, grease on the wheels of much larger deals in which they have hardly any position" (Vanstiphout 2014b: 8). If the political and economic transformation of the past decade profoundly changed the architectural profession, it also raised many questions concerning the positions and roles of architects and designers: how can we arrive at a development process early enough to avoid its instrumentalization for distant objectives? How to ensure community involvement in controlling not only the built objects but also the destiny of spaces? How to become developers or financiers of community-built projects in order to reduce their exposure to commercial ambitions? How to "penetrate into mechanisms of power, money, policy-making, and knowledge that actually form the basis for the transformations of our cities and communities?" (Vanstiphout 2014b: 8).

New Models for Community-Led Development

The post-crisis years saw many actors recognize the fact that traditional funding and organizational models had lost their capacity to feed community-oriented urban projects. They started elaborating upon alternative formats to help citizens access services by aggregating their energies and becoming protagonists of urban development projects. At the same time, they avoided being instrumentalized by commercial or political objectives. Over the past decades, Britain witnessed the emergence of hundreds of community-led organizations looking for ways to aggregate their energies and resources to create spaces and services for their neighborhoods. This type of activity is particularly strong in London, where the rise of real estate prices risks pushing all non-commercial activities out of the city's more central boroughs. These organizations work on devolving power to a more local level by raising funds from communities to buy properties sold by municipalities or private owners, giving out shares to finance investments of community services and infrastructures, creating community centers, and building enterprises that return their profits to the neighborhood.

In Berlin, a new generation of cultural and social spaces are surfacing, resisting gentrification, and real estate speculation by creating access to cooperative ownership for communities. The ExRotaprint industrial complex, based in a former printing machine factory in the Northern Berlin neighborhood of Wedding, was bought from the Berlin municipality by its former tenants in 2009. This was undertaken with the help of two foundations interested in investing in sustainable, socially responsible community projects and in removing properties from the speculation cycle. The 10,000 square meter compound, once in danger of being sold to large developers, now accommodates a variety of social, cultural, and productive functions and is run in a cooperative model, creating enough profit to assure the buildings' gradual renovation. In many cases, the engines behind these projects are architects and planners who, on the one hand, acknowledged the importance of real estate or "land [that] frames the set called 'architecture' without itself becoming a member of that set" (Martin 2014), and on the other recognized that the "idea that we can dissociate architecture from the business model is the illusion of a seventeenth century Enlightenment model" (Johar 2012).

In Rotterdam, the architecture office Zones Urbaines Sensibles (ZUS) started to rent a space in a long-time abandoned office building (called Schieblock) at the center of the city. Ready to "engage with the main developments in society" and with a "critical awareness regarding commissions" (van Boxel and Koreman 2007: 36), in 2010 they convinced the building's owner to allow them to manage the whole building and bring in new tenants. The goal of ZUS was to prove the legitimacy of a step-by-step development model by filling the building with sustainable economic functions, re-establishing its connections with the surrounding urban fabric, and turning the Rotterdam downtown into an attractive, dynamic location. The core of the Schieblock's program is to pair and connect various functions in a mutually fecundating way, stimulating the exchange of competences and information, and creating links between different social groups. ZUS members call this development model "unsolicited architecture," where architects act as real estate developers by initiating projects instead of waiting for commissions. In addition to reusing and reconnecting empty buildings, this development model also offers an incubating process for NGOs, for social and cultural activities, and for start-up companies. Affordable space can be of great help in the establishment and maintenance of these types of organizations.

The Amsterdam-based architecture office space&matter chose another way to aggregate community capacities and resources in urban development projects. Recognizing that the design process is framed more by developers than architects, the architects decided to think with developers' logic. By getting in direct contact with investors, space&matter manages to provoke commissions and bring financial actors and developers into a game already prepared by the architects. In De Ceuvel, a new area in North Amsterdam, the architects collected discarded boats and turned them into temporary buildings for the site, thus radically reducing construction costs and compensating for the limited time period of the experiment. With platforms like CrowdBuilding and WeBuildHomes, space&matter created social networks to bring together future tenants and investors of a vacant building, helping designers and clients bypass real estate agents and large investors in the development process.

6B, a community art and office building in Saint-Denis, a northern suburb of Paris, has been born from the initiative of the architect (and exyzt collective-member) Julien Beller who began to rent an empty office building in 2010 for a limited period. The building, formerly used by the Alstrom company, was condemned to be demolished in order to give space for new buildings in a transforming neighborhood. However, the 7,000 square meter building, managed by an association created on-site, quickly filled with artists, designers, NGOs, and small companies, thus creating an important social and cultural hub in an area lacking similar services. With offices rented even by the

Ile-de-France region and plans by the association to buy the building, 6B has become part of the area's development plan.

Conclusions

As an effect of the economic crisis, political restructuring, and austerity policies, local administrations in many European cities have been struggling with maintaining social services and infrastructure. As a response to the crisis of the welfare state and the "welfare city," local communities, cultural groups, and citizen networks have emerged as new actors in urban development by helping to establish parallel social services and welfare systems. In this process, while addressing problems of community, participation, and ecology, many urban planners, architects, and community organizers borrowed the tools and instruments of developers, economists, and even law specialists to experiment with new models for funding urbanism and urban services. In these initiatives, aiming at replacing obsolete social infrastructures or filling the vacuum left by vanishing services, architecture has blended into a wider set of "citymaking" activities. No longer able to practice an autonomous discipline, the architect "emerges as detector of urban conditions to be improved as well as a connecting node between different professionals and experts" (Delicado 2014).

The experiments above, run by architects and planners or artists and community activists, signal the advent of a new urban economy that supports theories of the commons with sustainable development and management models. Besides the efforts of communities, and beyond the contribution of architects, planners, lawyers and economists, these processes also require meaningful cooperation with municipalities. While many new initiatives indicate the weakness of public administrations, they have the means to engage in making community experiments blossom. These initiatives are important resources for European cities but are often ignored or overlooked by decision-makers, and their potentials remain largely undiscovered. While some administrations have begun to cooperate with citizen initiatives, others have been indisposed to the recognition of their potentials. The 2016 Dutch presidency of the European Union focuses on a new European Urban Agenda. If all goes well, this Agenda will help decision-makers understand how administrations can accommodate and encourage these emerging practices in European cities.

References

- Cellamare, C. (2014): "Autorganizzazione e vita urbana". *Recinti Urbani. Roma e I luoghi dell'abitare*. Roma: Manifesto.
- de Graaf, R. (2015): "Architecture is now a tool of capital, complicit in a purpose antithetical to its social mission." *Architectural Review*. http://www.architectural-review.com/rethink/viewpoints/architecture-is-now-a-tool-of-capital-complicit-in-a-purpose-antithetical-to-its-social-mission/8681564.fullarticle (asp 23-2-16).
- Delicado, G. H. (2014): "Post World's End Architecture." http://www.designcurial.com/news/post-worlds-end-architecture-greece-4177054/ (asp 23-2-16).
- Donald, B., A. Glasmeier, M. Gray and L. Lobao (2014): "Austerity in the city: economic crisis and urban service decline?" *Cambridge Journal of Regions, Economy and Society*, 7: 3–15.
- Gadanho, P. (2014): "Back to the Streets: The Rise of Performance Architecture." http://www.domusweb.it/en/op-ed/2011/09/21/back-to-the-streets-the-rise-of-performance-architecture.html (asp 23-2-16).
- Illner, P. (2014): "For me, myself and I: Architecture in the age of self-reflexivity." *Real Estates*. London: Bedford Press: 51–56.
- Johar, I. (2012): "The Civic Entrepreneur". *Future Practice. Conversations from the Edge of Practice*. New York and London: Routledge.
- Martin, R. (2014): "Real Estate as Infrastructure as Architecture." https://placesjournal.org/article/fundamental-13/ (asp 23-2-16).
- Provoost, M. and W. Vanstiphout (2007): "Facts on the Ground. Urbanism from Mid-Road to Ditch." *Harvard Design Magazine*, 25: 36–42.
- Tonkiss, F. (2013): "Austerity urbanism and the makeshift city." *City: analysis of urban trends, culture, theory, policy, action*, 17 (3): 312–314.
- van Boxel, E. and K. Koreman (2007): *Re-public. Towards a New Spatial Politics*. Rotterdam: NAi Publishers.
- Vanstiphout, W. (2012): "The Historian of the Present." *Future Practice. Conversations from the Edge of Practice*. New York and London: Routledge.
- Vanstiphout, W. (2014): "The self-destruction machine." *Real Estates*. London: Bedford Press: 57–66.
- Vanstiphout, W. (2014): "Dark Matter. Ditch Urbanism Revisited." *Harvard Design Magazine*, 37: 6–11.

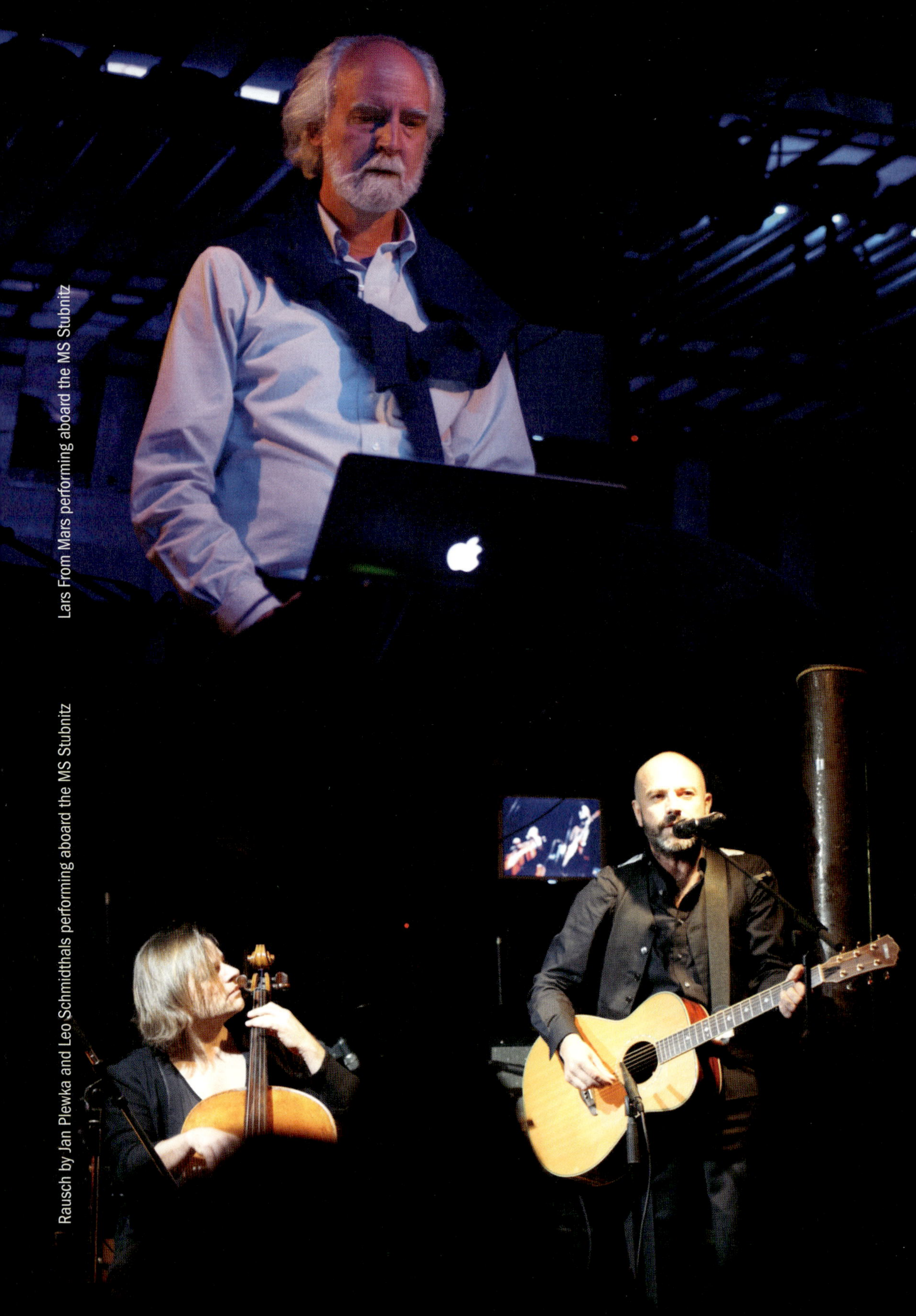

Lars From Mars performing aboard the MS Stubnitz
Rausch by Jan Plewka and Leo Schmidthals performing aboard the MS Stubnitz

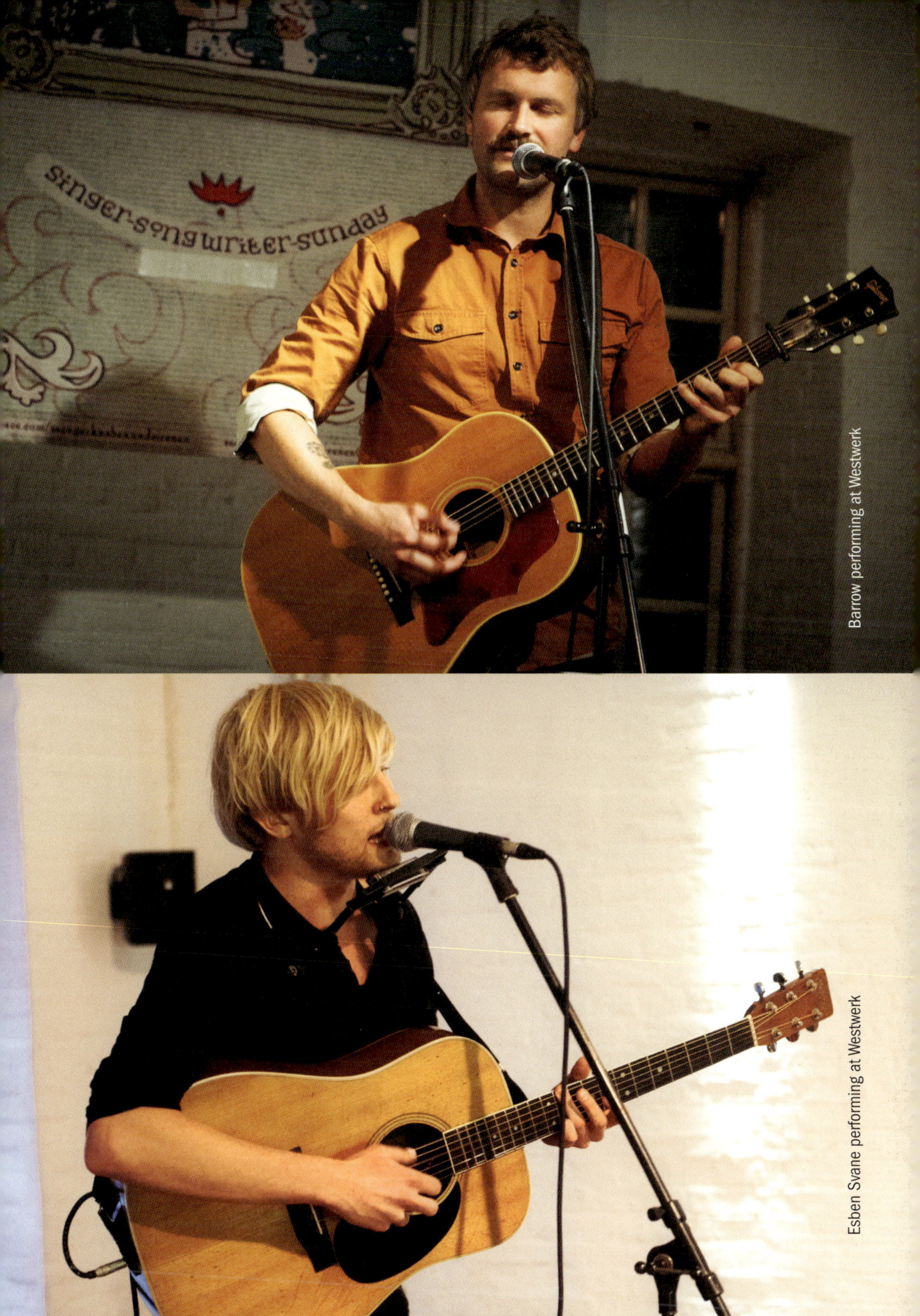

Barrow performing at Westwerk

Esben Svane performing at Westwerk

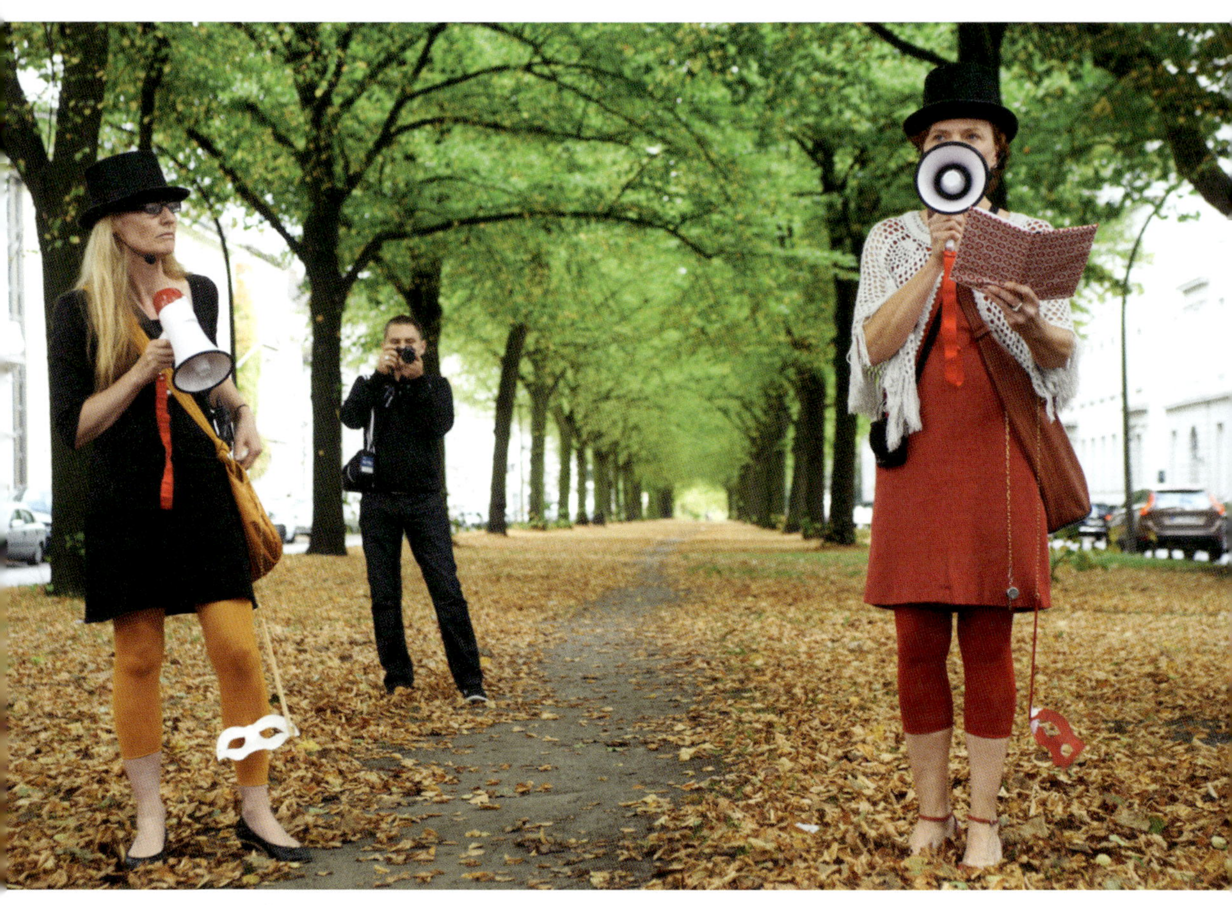

200 Years Danish Era in Altona by Urte Langrock and Anette Habel

Cooperation with Resistance: The Development of Gängeviertel in Hamburg

Michael Ziehl

After ten years of vacancy, the twelve buildings of the Gängeviertel were occupied by an artists' initiative and rescued from demolition. In the heart of Hamburg, the initiative created a non-commercial place for art, culture, and social affairs and campaigned for the authentic restoration of the buildings. Two years after the occupation, the City of Hamburg and the occupiers agreed upon a common development process. But the cooperation and renovation process are not progressing smoothly, because the cooperation partners are not working together effectively. At the moment solutions are being sought that will enable the Gängeviertel cooperative to successfully manage the properties. This will provide an opportunity to develop a new model for cooperation between citizens and municipalities, which is based on the needs of the residents and their capabilities and is less influenced by investor interests and financial capital.

Prehistory

The Gängeviertels characterized Hamburg for centuries. Beginning in the seventeenth century, ordinary workers lived in these city quarters that were defined by narrow streets, corridors, and courtyards. Even then, the population of Hamburg grew rapidly, so more and more people lived within the city walls. The Gängeviertels steadily became more densely occupied. It was primarily craftsmen and laborers that moved into the houses. The residents lived and worked in very confined spaces. Mid-nineteenth century, these extremely crowded living conditions became a public cause of worry due to the outbreak of a cholera epidemic. The gradual demolition of the old buildings began around this time. The Gängeviertels have been almost completely eliminated over the course of different phases of urban redevelopment. What is now called the "Gängeviertel," is the last ensemble where the structure of the historic working-class neighborhoods can still be witnessed. Between Valentinskamp, Caffamacherreihe, and Speckstrasse there remain twelve houses that bear witness to a bygone era, surrounded on all sides by multi-story office buildings made of steel and glass. Although this last remnant stood under the official protection of historic buildings and was owned by the City of Hamburg, it seemed likely to be demolished. After the Second World War, the city had barely taken care of the maintenance of the buildings. The residents gradually left as a result of systemic neglect, which caused the living conditions to get worse and worse. The abandoned flats were no longer rented out. The result was that the Gängeviertel was almost completely empty for over ten years and naturally continued to fall deeper into disrepair.

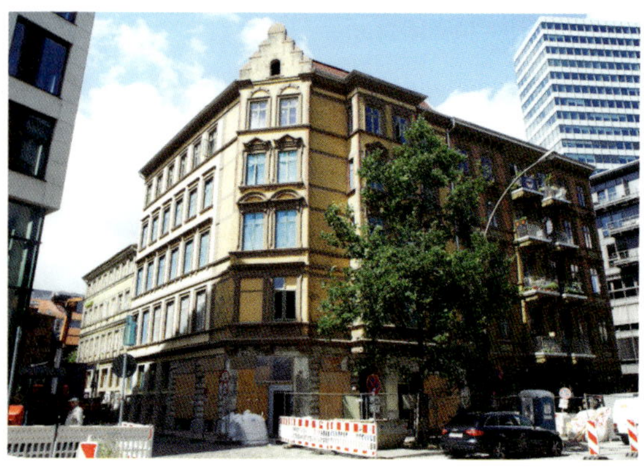
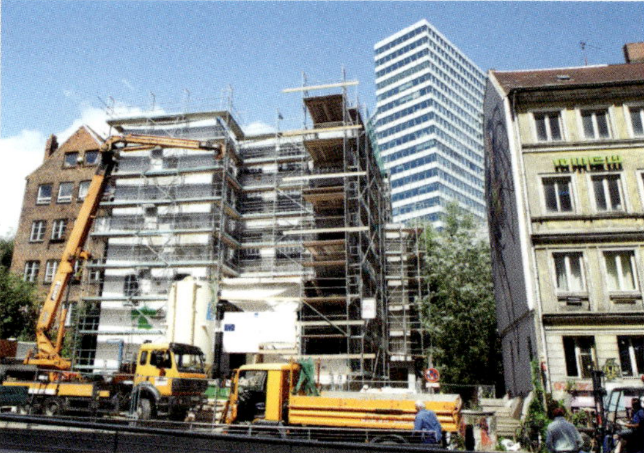

Renovation of the Jupi-Haus   Renovation of the Fabrique

In 2008 the City of Hamburg sold the Gängeviertel to the highest bidding investor, who wanted to build expensive apartments, offices and commercial space to the sum of fifty million euros. To enable this redevelopment, the City of Hamburg permitted the demolition of about eighty percent of the protected historic buildings. The demolition plans were justified on the basis of the ailing conditions of the houses and the high renovation costs associated with putting them back into shape. At this time, two experienced artists' collectives in an almost completely vacant Gängeviertel were using two storefronts respectively as a studio space and gallery. They heard about the sale and the demolition plans and some of them wanted to mobilize against this advancing "selling off of the city." They started to build a network of like-minded people. It was at the invitation of these first activists that artists, architects, urban planners, preservationists, political activists, and engaged citizens came together for a weekly meeting in the Gängeviertel in order to exchange knowledge and experience. Many of the participants were dissatisfied with the direction that Hamburg was taking. In many places across the city, old buildings had been sold and demolished. Mainly offices and expensive apartments were being built, although there was a lack of affordable housing and a great deal of office space stood empty. Everywhere rent was on the increase and the process of gentrification was shattering many neighborhoods. Urban niches for cultural and artistic work had been irrevocably lost. Instead of installing countermeasures, the city government spent taxpayers' money on image-building actions and flagship projects, presenting itself internationally as a tolerant city of culture, all of which helped the inflationary spiral to continually grow.

The activists wanted to use the Gängeviertel to make an example against these policies and approaches to market-based urbanism. They made a plan to occupy the Gängeviertel. They were motivated by the rumor that the investor had money problems arising from the pervasive financial crisis of 2008, which threatened to scuttle the development plans. The financial crisis also led to a critical attitude towards real estate speculation and investor projects. This opened up a window of opportunity for an alternative approach as envisioned by the activists. In other sectors, further opposition was formed against the extant urban development policy. In 2008, in the nearby district of St. Pauli, the "Action Network against Gentrification" was created. In parallel, a group began working on the establishment of an autonomous neighborhood meeting as a counterpoint to gentrification. In early summer 2009, the documentary film "Empire St. Pauli" was released. The film problematized the transformation of the district and has been shown more than fifty times in Hamburg alone. Via these channels, public attention was brought to subjects such as the increase of rent, the construction of luxury real estate, the changes to the cityscape, and the displacement of people. A few months later, about twenty urban policy initiatives founded the Hamburg network "Right to the City." Since then, the network has continually addressed issues such as housing, rent increases, displacement, privatization, and vacancy by organizing demonstrations and protests. Today around sixty initiatives collaborate in the "Right to the City" network. The success of the occupation of the Gängeviertel and the positive developments that came immediately afterwards would not have been possible without the organizational and ideological support of the "Right to the City" network.

Get into Gear (Komm in die Gänge)

On Saturday, August 22, 2009, about 200 people occupied the Gängeviertel. Camouflaged as a courtyard festival, the occupation was advertised throughout the city. The initiative "Komm in die Gänge" made the invitation. Thousands of visitors attended the event and partied together in the narrow backyards between outdoor bars and open-air exhibitions. Obscured by the crowds of people in the alleys, doors to the buildings were gradually opened after having remained locked for many years. Amazed visitors entered the historic buildings and found art exhibitions and performances, which had been prepared over the course of weeks. Unlike many previous occupations in Hamburg, the houses were not barricaded, but rather opened and made accessible. A space of possibilities was created that invited everyone to participate. The art installations inside served as inspiration and as an illustrative example for the great degree and ease to which the rooms could be converted to artist studios, concert halls, or exhibition spaces. However, this approach also had a strategic aspect: the police in Hamburg had ended all occupation attempts over the past twenty years within twenty-four hours. Art and public participation offered protection from the police, because the eviction of an artists' initiative and the many visitors would have torpedoed the city marketing of Hamburg as a tolerant place for culture.

On the day of the occupation, local media reported on the action. A few days later, the international press also picked up on the subject. Even the conservative media outlets expressed their appreciation and showed understanding for the concerns of the initiative. As the official patron of the occupation, the Hamburg painter Daniel Richter took advantage of the media attention to vent his pent-up anger about his city's cultural policy. Many other cultural operators in the city also came forward with critical contributions. Shortly afterwards, an outpouring of supportive statements came from architects, urban planners, and scientists. On the evening news, Richard Florida, creator of the "Creative Class" theory, even suggested to the city government that it should develop the Gängeviertel together with the artists. Altogether, this helped the public to sympathize with the squatters. The future of the Gängeviertel was of public interest far beyond Hamburg's city limits. After the first reports began appearing in the press, politicians also began to speak up. Most expressed their understanding and appreciation for the action and signaled their readiness to engage in talks. The activists were also prepared for talks with the politicians. On the first weekend of the occupation they tried to reach decision-makers and on the first working day sent small delegations to key senators (urban development, culture, finance) to explain their reasons for the occupation.

Cultural Diversity Moves In

While the politicians asked themselves how they should react to the occupation, the occupiers provisionally organized the spaces and continued making a cultural program. They invited members of the public to weekly assemblies and formed working groups for specific tasks, such as negotiations with the city, public relations, or the design of the cultural program. Many supporters came and joined the initiative. They introduced ideas for usage, brought their labor power, helped to repair the buildings, organized events, and helped build organizational structures. Working rooms and studio spaces were set up on the upper floors of the buildings. The ground floors were used collectively and generally open to the public. Exhibitions, concerts, film screenings, and readings took place on an almost daily basis in these provisionally adapted spaces. The activists organized workshops in which future concepts were discussed and invited experts from Hamburg and other cities. They publicly debated cultural and urban development policies. Soon the squatters had become experts and were invited to podiums with politicians and scientists in other cities on topics such as art, culture, gentrification, and urban planning. Given these developments, the politicians needed to at least formalize the conditions and offered the initiative an interim usage agreement. Since private individuals could not legally sign the agreement, the non-profit Gängeviertel e.V. was founded. Since that moment, the association has been responsible for the unrenovated areas in the Gängeviertel and the management of the cultural program. This formed the basis for the establishment of various forms of usage: galleries,

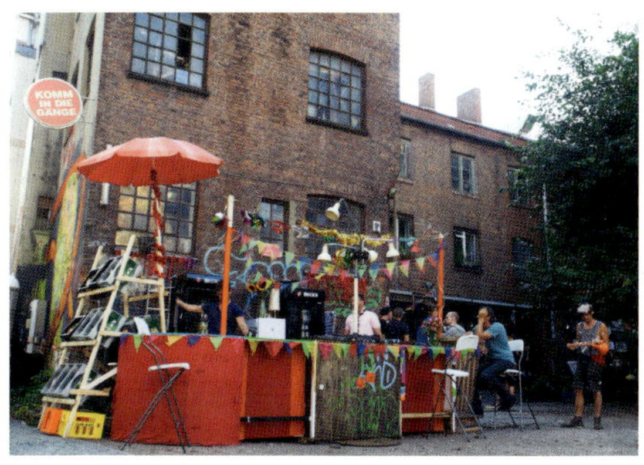

Temporary bar

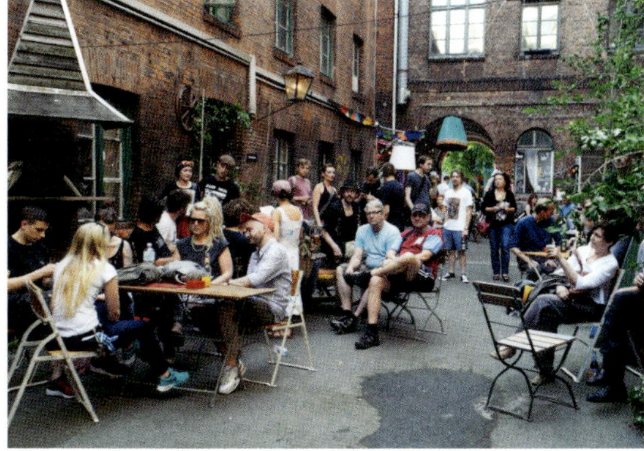

Schierspassage (Gängeviertel)

concert venues, a bicycle self-help workshop, a woodworking shop, a library, a food cooperative, a free-store, and many others.

The foundation of the association and the signing of the rental agreements were the first steps toward the institutionalization and legalization of the initiative known as "Komm in die Gänge." All the same, the open structures and informal usages were not relinquished: the weekly general assembly is still the primary body of the project; at the assembly, everyday decisions are made on a democratic basis. Furthermore, there is still leeway for appropriations and new usages. Many activists are involved for a time and then move on to other projects. Thus, the Gängeviertel is constantly renewed and expands its network. However, there are also many people who have been active since the first days. Since the beginning, there have been principles drawn up that must be observed: no one should be excluded by high prices and no one should make money at the expense of the Gängeviertel. Events are free of admission and open to all peaceful visitors. Drinks have only a minimal fixed price and it is up to the guests if and to what amount they would like to give as an additional donation. The proceeds go to the non-profit and, other than with very few exceptions, all work with is honorary and unpaid. Even among themselves, active participants maintain interpersonal exchange according to the solidarity principle. They have established a dense network of neighborhood assistance. Car-sharing as well as mutual material and tools are common in the Gängeviertel. Office work and other tasks are undertaken by the collective as much as possible.

The many uses, provisional extensions and components, art installations, street art, and the repairs to the buildings have created an aesthetic that bears witness to the cultural appropriation of the Gängeviertel and overlaps with the historic appearance of the buildings. The contrast could hardly be more intense in comparison with the high-priced and architecturally formalized downtown. Nevertheless, the small-scale structure has many spatial links to the surrounding urban space. In addition to the participants on-site and the guests of the cultural program, passersby and employees from the neighboring high-rises also use the many passages and backyards as a shortcut on the way to lunch or simply for relaxing. Former residents come by and tell of times when they were children and have played in the Gängeviertel. Many visitors come from other cities, because tourist guides and official city-marketing advertising brochures list the Gängeviertel as a popular destination. As a result of the occupation, the place has once again become an urban neighborhood—a place that is worked on, lived in, and celebrated, where strangers young and old meet locals. In this way the activists build upon the history of the Gängeviertel and update them in their own way. Because of its cultural, historical, and social complexity, the UNESCO distinguished the Gängeviertel as a place of cultural diversity.

The Cooperative Renovation Model

Because the Gängeviertel initiative appropriated more and more space, the city bowed to public pressure and in December 2009 bought it back from the investor. A few months later, it announced that it wanted to retain the Gängeviertel as a piece of municipal property and redevelop it according to historical conservation practice. The artists wished to be included in the planning and orient the process to stay in line with their utilization concept. The city hired a private redevelopment agency (steg) to fashion a development plan in cooperation with the initiative. In essence, it provides for the gradual renovation of the twelve buildings. This called for the creation of publicly funded social housing, studios, and culturally usable commercial space. The Fabrique, the largest building in the Gängeviertel, was to be expanded as a sociocultural center with open workshops and studios as well as seminar and event rooms. The entire cost of the renovation was earmarked at twenty million euros. Because the city was unwilling to pay this sum entirely from its own resources, a large part of the financial instruments were to be acquired from funding programs and loans. The loans were to be refinanced from the rental income of the renovated areas. In order to keep the post-renovation rent from being too expensive, it was planned that the renovated spaces should be subsidized from various public funds—at least for a certain period. The decision about the people that are allowed to move into the government-funded spaces is a decision made by an occupancy commission composed of representatives from the city and the initiative.

The collaboratively fashioned development concept basically follows the central demands of the initiative. The combination of living, working, cultural program, and low rental rates were major concerns. Thus, the initiative sought to ensure the preservation of the versatile and open nature that currently prevails in the Gängeviertel. Additionally, internal gentrification should be prevented, because due to the refinancing of the renovation costs through rental fees there was a real danger that these spaces might become too expensive for artists and for cultural usage. However, from the perspective of the initiative, there should have been binding rules for their participation in the restructuring process and for the autonomy of renovation process. The activists feared losing decision-making authority during the renovations. Therefore, in late 2010 they founded their own own cooperative and called for a firm commitment from the city that after the renovation, the buildings should be managed by the cooperative and that it should remain involved in the entire process of renovation.

After tough negotiations, the city and the initiative reached an understanding and negotiated a cooperation agreement. Accordingly, a building committee was formed, in which the cooperative, the redevelopment agency, and the architects were represented. The parties jointly chose and commissioned an independent architectural firm. After the renovation, all of the buildings should be managed by the Gängeviertel cooperative. The basis of the property management has not yet been decided: the options being considered are general rent, long-term lease, or purchase. However, precise terms have not been established for any of the three variants. Regardless of the decision that the partners ultimately agree upon, each variant requires that the cooperative acquires capital. Therefore, the users of these rehabilitated spaces must purchase a share for five-hundred euro for each ten square meters that they use. However, the usable space in the Gängeviertel only covers around 7,500 square meters. The cooperative is therefore dependent on supporters who purchase shares in order to secure the self-government of the Gängeviertel after the renovations have been completed. The cooperative is supported in its acquisition of shareholders by many well-known artists and cultural agents from Hamburg.

Problems in the Process of Cooperation and Renovation

Detailed planning for the renovation began in May 2012; September 2013 saw the beginning of the construction work on the first building. Six months later, two more

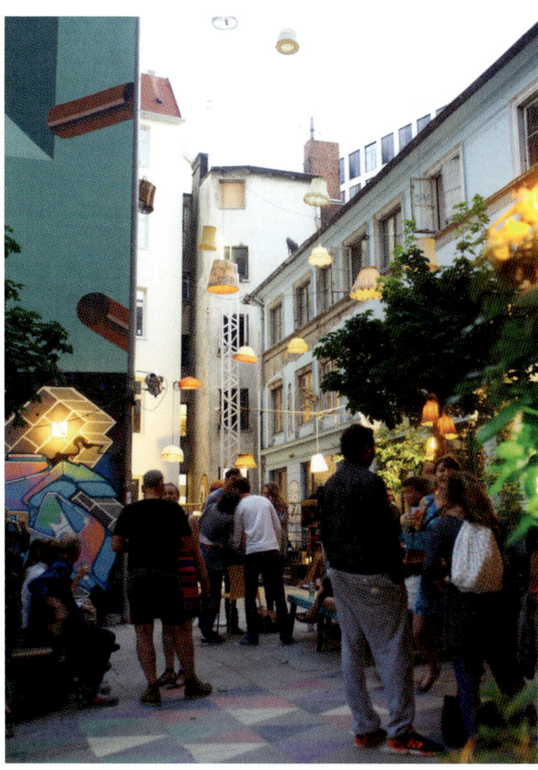

Kutscherhof (Gängeviertel)

buildings entered the renovation phase, including the sociocultural center, the Fabrique. The city council set up a renovation board, which was composed of politicians from the various parties of the city council, representatives of the cooperative, and residents of Gängeviertel. Despite this further participation in the board and the existing cooperation agreement, discontent began brewing during the planning phase of the renovation. At the commencement of the renovation, the active participants from the Gängeviertel published a statement in which they criticized the planning process and the upcoming construction. They denounced the fact that too many changes to the buildings were being undertaken and were afraid that these historic buildings might lose their unique character. Above all, they felt left out of the process and not on an equal footing in many questions.

A new round of negotiations began shortly afterwards, because the city and the cooperative had to agree on the management of the houses before they were finished. A new negotiation was launched under the leadership of the then Ministry of Urban Development and Environment (BSU). However, the discussions proceeded slowly from the outset, whereas the construction sites progressed according to schedule. The primary disagreement between the cooperation partners was mainly in the question of what powers the cooperative should have regarding the management of the properties. The initiative called for householder's rights for the cooperative. Furthermore, the cooperative should be the entity that directly signed the contracts with the residents. The BSU, on the other hand, wanted the redevelopment agency steg to be the landlord for the residents, because the steg had been commissioned directly by the city and depends on the Ministry of Urban Development and Environment. From their perspective, the cooperative should only be concerned about the financial responsibilities of gathering the rent, but not involved in decisive management tasks.

In February 2015, the first house was completed. However, up to that point there had still been no agreement. In order for the new residents to move in, provisional agreements were signed, which passed the essential tasks to the redevelopment agency. Thereafter, the cooperative was informed that the city wanted to maintain the validity of these signed contracts until the entire Gängeviertel had been redeveloped. It would not be possible for the cooperative to manage the renovated buildings. From the perspective of the initiative, the cooperation process had failed. In order to demonstrate this, the Gängeviertel representatives resigned from the board of the redevelopment advisory council. A great many regional media outlets picked up on the news of the failed cooperation. To increase public pressure, the initiative launched a solidarity campaign. Popular cultural workers signed a statement and demanded: "Save the Gängeviertel."

A few weeks after the termination of negotiations, there was a conversation at a higher political level, but in the meantime, it seemed that the Gängeviertel was preparing for protest. The confidence of the initiative in the municipal partners and the redevelopment agency had been lost. Therefore, the representatives of Gängeviertel insisted on an immediate stop to all planning as a condition for further talks. All plans for renovations according to the extant reorganization proceedings were canceled. The buildings already under construction should be finished, even though the initiative was not satisfied with the quality of the construction work. From its perspective, its fears at the beginning of the construction phase had been confirmed. In many cases historically relevant components were demolished and historic charm was lost. However, the work on the buildings had progressed very far. Stopping the renovation while it was underway would hardly have changed the results of the restoration and would have been very expensive.

The city and the initiative established working groups in order to carry out the most urgent issues in the renovation process. These included self-management by the cooperative and the methods to be undertaken in the process of further renovation. External consultants were involved in order to find solutions. In October 2015, results had finally been reached in the working group concerned with the management of the Gängeviertel. The city was now ready to meet the demands of the cooperative. One of the more important factors in this success was most likely the fact that the city of Hamburg had received a new Senator for Urban Development. Just in time for the completion of the second building, the Ministry of Urban Development and Environment, the redevelopment agency, and the cooperative signed a contract that enabled the cooperative to be the general tenant of the renovated buildings. However, this contract would remain valid only up to the point when the restoration of the entire district is complete. Therefore, the current work is focused on finding a long-term solution. It should also be a basis for a collaborative process in which the cooperative assumes more responsibility. Currently, a proposal from the city administration will determine whether a long-term solution could be that the cooperative becomes the owner of the buildings. It would then have more freedom of action and could even manage future construction. Whether property ownership is an expedient solution for the cooperative depends on the purchase price and is also a politically charged issue. Actually, the Senate no longer wants to sell the Gängeviertel. The initiative is generally critical of the privatization of public property; the same goes for a possible purchase by their own cooperative. Both politicians and the administration should remain responsible for the development of the Gängeviertel, since it represents a piece of local history and the dilapidated condition of the houses is their responsibility.

Closing Remarks

As is customary in many collaborations, the partners in the renovation of the Gängeviertel depend upon each other and still act in accordance with their own intentions.
The initiative aims to ensure the long-term self-management by the cooperative. The
city wants to keep control of the process and that their expenses do not increase. The
redevelopment agency wants to organize an efficient renovation process. However, the
cooperation is not working well. What is missing is a collaborative process whereby
city, redevelopment agency, and initiative can cooperate effectively. For a long time,
the city administration had no interest in adjusting their method and invoked existing
rules and regulations as justification, although the initiative had on several occasions
expressed that the cooperation was facing the threat of failure. It was only when the
initiative threatened the termination of the cooperation and presented this publicly,
that the town finally began to search for solutions to the problems in the cooperation
process.

The proceedings to date have burdened the cooperation and cost unnecessarily large
amounts of time and energy for everyone involved. This is especially true for the activists in the Gängeviertel. For years they have organized a multifaceted cultural program, have taken care of the buildings, and have established a cooperative. The cooperation process demands many weighty decisions from the initiative, which requires
strenuous approval processes due to its basic democratic structures. On top of those
tasks, there are also the protracted negotiations with the city. Volunteers hardly have
the time to carry out the continuous work involved in the renovation process. There
is a fundamental incongruity in the cooperation process: whereas the representatives
of the initiative are unpaid participants, the parties of the other side are paid for their
work. Nevertheless, the activists in the Gängeviertel continuously mobilize their energy
to resist. To date, it is the the only way for them to assert their interests in the cooperation process and to encourage the city to choose innovative actions in accordance with
the cooperation agreement.

Such productive resistance has been undertaken by many initiatives in Hamburg.
Often it is the cultural workers and artists who in this way successfully fight for their
self-managed spaces. Without these activists, today in Hamburg there would be neither
Gängeviertel, Westwerk, Vorwerkstift, nor Fux eG. Many places and organizations
would be missing from the cultural landscape that enrich the city and make it livable.
But resistance also causes friction. In order to manifest effective cooperation between
municipalities and city residents, it is important to find new cooperation models in
order to enable the development of the productive forces of citizens and make it possible

for activists to participate in the development process through ingenuity, self-organization, and physical work while remaining on equal footing with the politicians and the administration of their town. The Gängeviertel is a valuable place of learning for that. City administration, politicians, the activists, and the redevelopment agency can learn much from each other for the future. In this respect, the debate about the Gängeviertel is not only about the preservation and self-government of twelve historic buildings, but also about the negotiation of sustainable urban development policy, which focuses less on the interests and capital from investors, and more on the needs and skills of urban residents.

das-gaengeviertel.info
gaengeviertel-eg.de

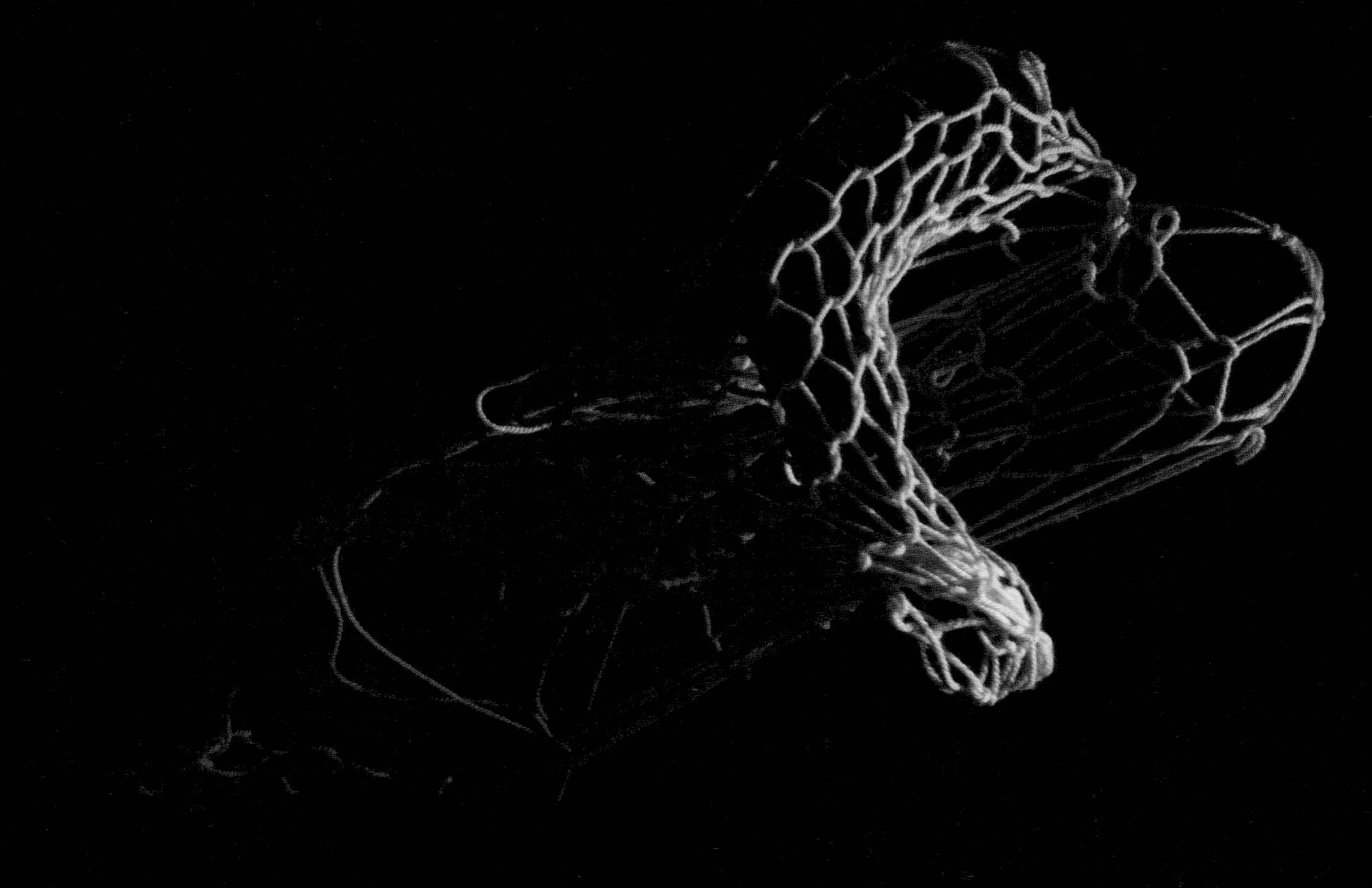

Video still *Continiuos Constellations* by Julie Sparsø Damkjær at Westwerk

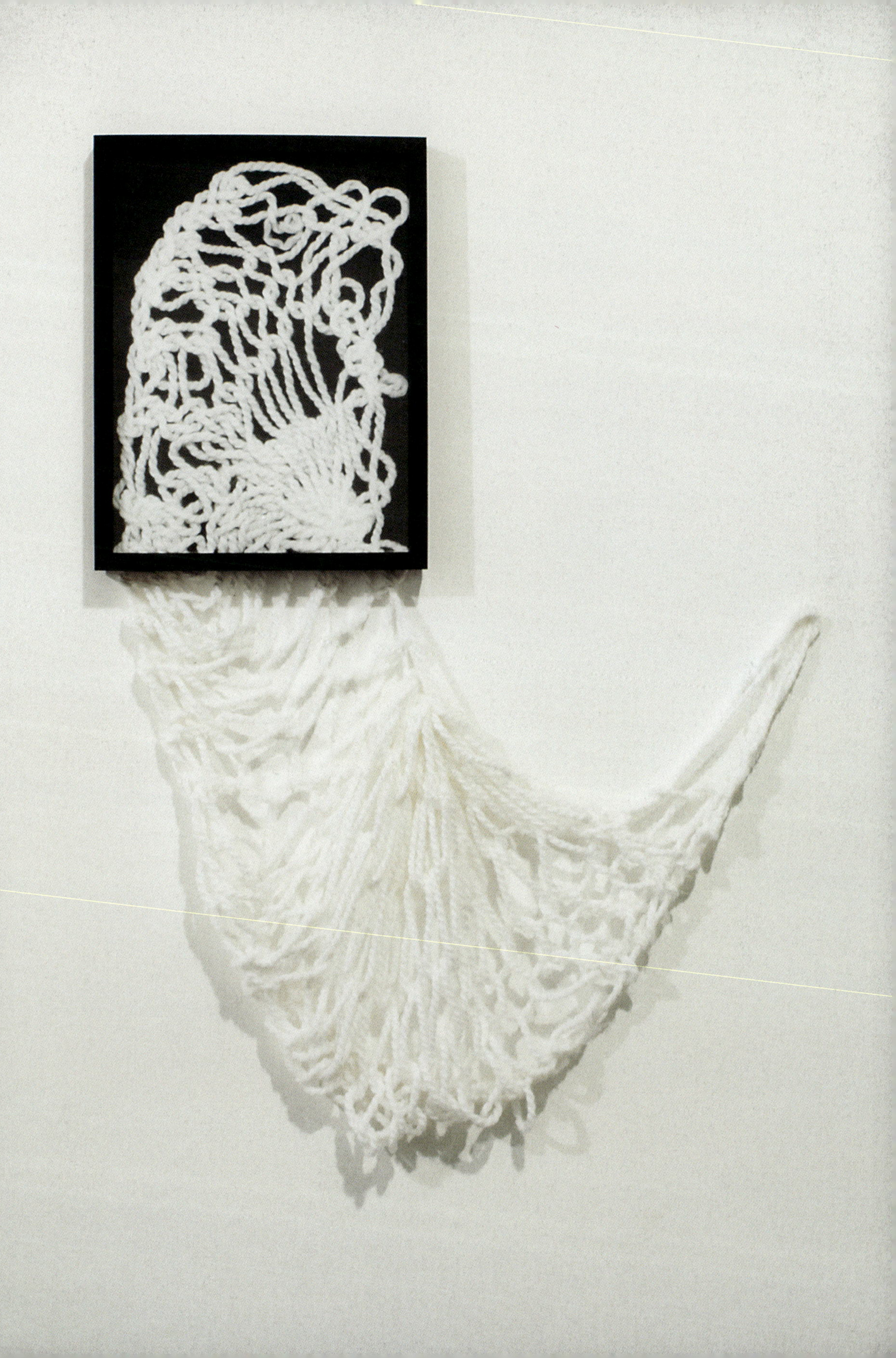

Framed Constellations by Julie Sparsø Damkjær at Westwerk

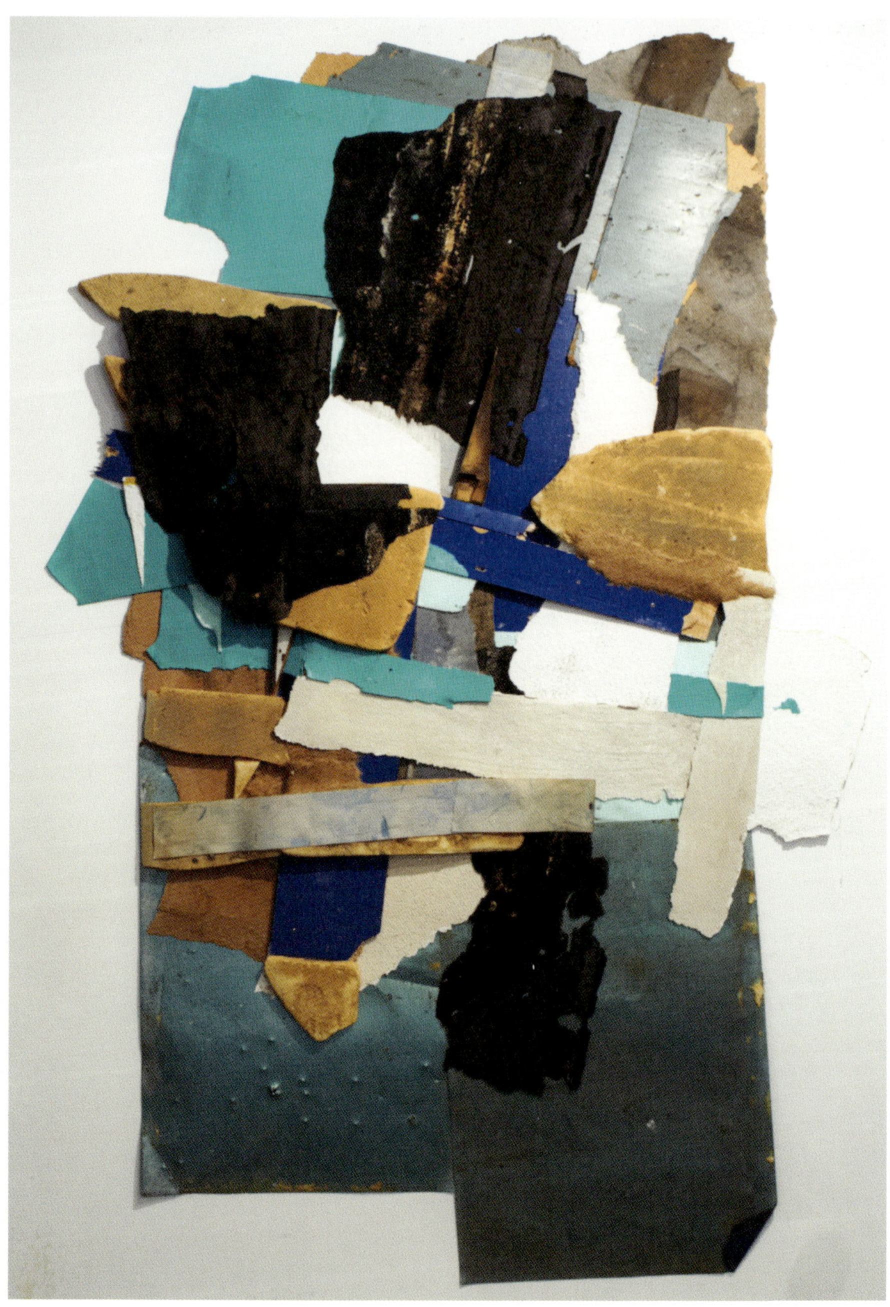

Rokildevej, Otto Busses Vej, Krimsvej, Ved Amagerbanen, Voldgaden, Billhafen Löschplatz, Peute-straße, Brandshofer Deich, Lippmannstraße by Christian Elovara Dinesen at Westwerk

Small Scale with Big Potential: The Story of PB43

Steen Andersen

At PB43's original location on Prags Boulevard 43 in the southern part of Copenhagen, more than 150 self-organized users in a number of member groups, associations, and creative businesses succeeded in transforming a former paint factory into a platform for creative and cultural entrepreneurship. After a period of much uncertainty and an exhausting struggle for survival as a consequence of the sale of the real estate, PB43 has found another location. The vision is to continue developing the potentials for small creative businesses as well as alternative cultural and social projects. In short, it is about creating a sustainable environment for creative growth, culture, and social innovation. In this essay I will have a closer look at the development of PB43 from its beginning in 2010 to its relocation in 2015.

The Beginning—2010

PB43 was situated in one of the last industrial areas in Copenhagen that in recent years had begun the de-industrialization process in which production closed down and moved out of the city. Such areas often lack official planning and distinctive functions, which altogether creates a spatial vacuum—a form of empty space—away from the real estate market and the public's interest until it is absorbed by the normalization process of city development, typically with new office buildings, upper-scale apartments, shops and cafés. The non-profit organization GivRum negotiated a two year contract with an option for extension with the real estate owner, the international chemical company Akzo Nobel. This temporarily opened up the former factory and its grounds for new uses, a re-definition of its function that was suitable for people who had a project or idea they wanted to try out. The keywords were: low rent, flexible space, high degree of freedom, self-organization, interdisciplinary cooperation, local interaction, and sustainable bottom-up city development. This seemed like a space of possibilities. A space of unlimited use. A space of re-creation. A space of action. A space to be. So when GivRum invited the public to come to the first meeting, I went there hoping to learn more about the project.

In the main building there was a sharp smell of chemicals and the panes in several of the windows were missing or broken. There was neither heating nor lighting in the hallways and in the rooms, since the electrical installations and the wiring had long since been stolen for the resale value of the copper. It was truly hard to imagine anyone

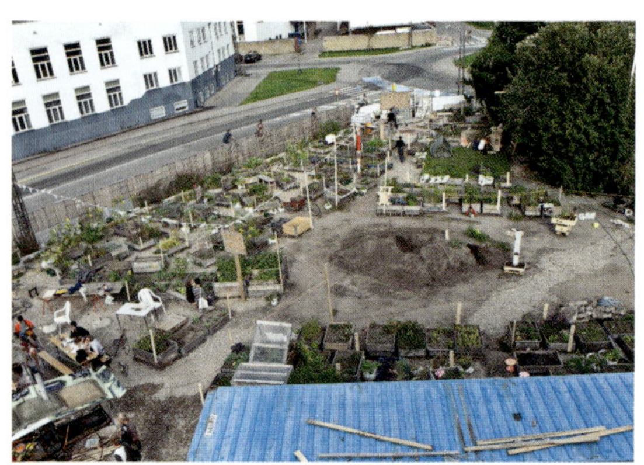
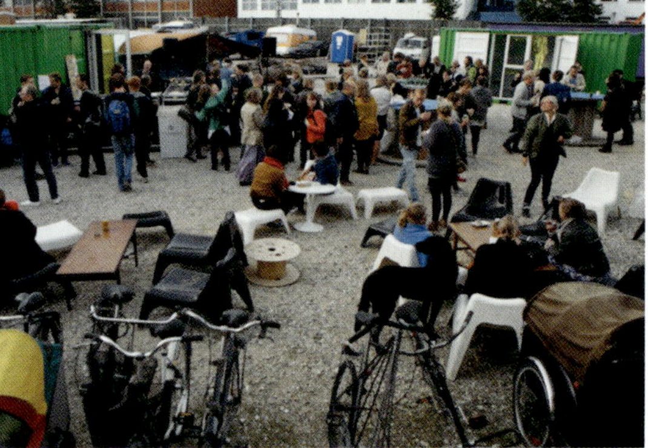

PB43 urban garden project   Public activities on the site

wanting to use the buildings of the former paint factory. Still, between thirty and thirty-five hopeful project makers, entrepreneurs, and artists gathered on this chilly November afternoon in 2010 to hear about the plans and discuss the reanimation of the 6,400 square meter plot, including four empty buildings, into a self-organized working community.

The Property Owner

Akzo Nobel wanted to hold off selling the property until the Copenhagen Municipality had decided on a new development plan for the local area in 2012. Meanwhile the renters would be house-sitting, taking care of the property and preventing vandalism, while their cultural and social activities would help Akzo Nobel in giving something back to the neighborhood as a kind of compensation for the loss of jobs that occured when Akzo Nobel closed down the production facility. This was the explanation that the director of Akzo Nobel had given when asked why they agreed to rent out the place more or less for free—the users only had to pay the property taxes, maintenance expenses, and the usage of water and electricity.

Organization

The users were to be organized as a volunteer member association called the Working Community Prags Boulevard 43 (PB43), which was responsible for the day-to-day operations of the facility, renovation of the property, various administrative tasks, coordination between internal and external projects, arrangement of various social activities, and maintaining contact with the authorities, the press, and the neighborhood. On a longer term, the plan was to transform the association into a cooperative, which would have brought certain tax and legal advantages. The users would then also be given the legal and economic responsibility for the area. Those who rented a space had to be registered members of the PB43 association.

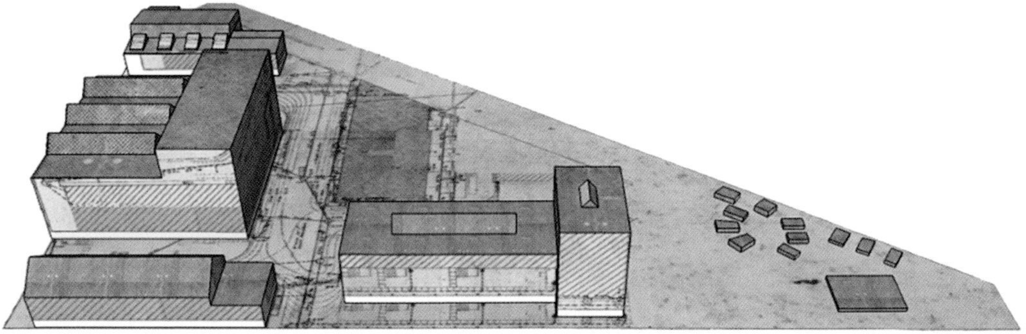

Rendering of the area

Contracts

The legal contract between PB43 and the renters would be business rental, but with status of borrower. The renters would, by this arrangement, give up many of the normal rights of a rental contract. In return they had the possibility of using the place at a very low rent for an undefined number of years. A law firm was engaged to ensure that the contracts were legally binding. The users' rental contracts were subsumed under all the limitations included in the contract with the property owner, Akzo Nobel, the expenses for which had been covered by Akzo Nobel. The contract with Akzo Nobel was based upon an arrangement to borrow the property instead of a normal rental agreement, since the rights of a normal tenant would make it more difficult for Akzo Nobel to terminate the contract and get the users off of the property.

Rooms

In the four buildings there were thirty-nine rooms, some of which were halls so large that they could either be split up and rented out individually or used for cultural and social activities. Some of the rooms were almost ready to use, while others needed more work and investment to be used. It was primarily groups and associations that rented the spaces. The tenants were individually responsible that their own users stayed within the regulations in the contracts, especially with regard to the communal areas. Most renters had their own internal rules for the use of their individual rental space. One communal rule was that the space should be used for working, so living in a space was not allowed. Furthermore, the individual tenant could have their contract terminated if there was no activity in a rented space over a certain period of time or if the type of activity taking place was not that which was agreed upon in the contract.

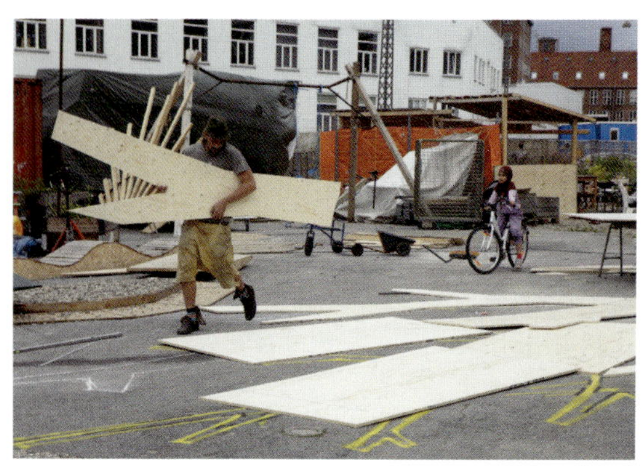

Workshop in the outside area

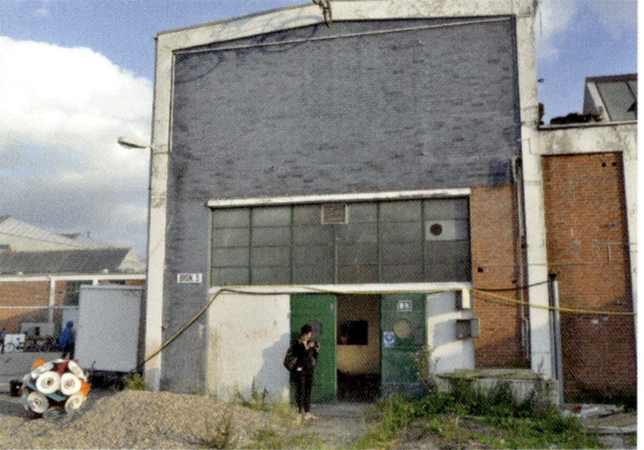

The cultural hall Building 5

Costs

Each member had to cover the costs for their own construction and the installation of electricity, water, and locks for their rented space. The overall installation of water, electricity, gates, main doors, et cetera would be undertaken by the communal budget. There would be free rental until March 2011. Thereafter, rent would be at a reduced rate for several months, depending on the state of the rented space. After this period, the rent for all spaces would be forty euro per square meter per year, which was less than one third of the market price in Copenhagen. The rent would primarily go to cover communal maintenance of the property, administration, taxes, waste disposal, and some degree of daily coordination. Since neither GivRum, the PB43 association, nor its members had the economic standing to pay the deposit for a property of this size, the association came to an agreement with Akzo Nobel that the renters should collectively save up a deposit of 1,000 euro per month, which would be returned if they left the property and cleaned up after themselves when the contract ended. There was a chance to lower the rent for all spaces if some income was generated through communal events and a higher degree of the practical and administrative work was carried out by the users. Individually, there were also ways to decrease the rent if a project had a focus on involving the local neighborhood or arranged free cultural and social events.

Outdoor Area

The rent for the usage of the outdoor area would be 25 euro per square meter per year if the purpose were non-profit or the renter already was a member of the working community. When renting for commercial purposes or short-term rental, an individual deal would be negotiated. Member projects did not have to pay rent if they needed to use outdoor space for no longer than two to three weeks and if they had no need for setting up a roof or some walls.

After some discussion about the basic structure and the organizing of the Working Community PB43, it was decided to meet some weeks later to approve the association charter, elect the board, and the meeting was adjourned. Beers were opened and cigarettes lit. The mood was cheerful. But people were also tense. No one had a clear sense of where they were going to be in a couple of years.

Establishment, Conflicts, and Inclusion—2010–2012

In December 2010 the users finally approved the association charter and on the same evening the board had its first meeting. It was important for the users to get started as quickly as possible, since they could only use the place for two years. The owner had no objections to the plans, as they conflicted neither with the usage contract nor the local municipality's zoning of the plot. So the implementation of the concept described above could be undertaken as agreed by the users and GivRum.

From the start of the project in 2010–12, the focus was primarily on the establishment of the communal infrastructure, reconstruction of the users' individual spaces, and planning of the use of the communal outdoor area; and only secondarily on developing the organization itself, the association known as The Working Community PB43. The installation of water, electricity, a lock system et cetera was coordinated by the Go To Guy—one of the users who for a monthly fee ensured that the basic infrastructure was established, either by authorized craftsmen or by the users themselves. The Go To Guy also took care of practical tasks, such as ordering waste disposal, advising users about their individual construction plans, the signing of contracts and giving new users general information about the place. He also functioned as the communication link between the users and GivRum, which was not present at the place on a daily basis. Most of the formal decisions over the first six months, such as who could rent a space and for which amount of money, was made by GivRum, while the PB43 association was mainly concerned with the maintenance of the property, social events, and cultural aspects. The real estate owner on the other hand, did not have any objections regarding the use and the activities as long they were not illegal, in direct conflict with building regulations, or could do harm to people.

After a short amount of time it became clear that there was a lot more to do than just practical daily work and having a monthly board meeting in the association. The maintenance of the property was a shared responsibility, so work-weekends needed to be organized where the communal areas were maintained: walls repainted, toilets, rainwater pipes, and fences repaired. Furthermore, various outdoor project began to pop-up: people wanted to park containers, trailers, boats, buses, and even a huge circus tent. Two different groups even planned to use the same large part of the outdoor area: one for an open urban communal garden for the local neighborhood and the other for a showcase forest for alternative park development. In addition, there arose a growing number of cultural and social activities such as parties, concerts, festivals, and exhibitions. The authorities began to take a closer look at some of the projects: did they have a permit, was the area legally approved for urban gardening, was the swing for the kids built within the regulations, were the public spaces approved by the fire authorities, was there a liquor license, who was in charge of this and that project, who was the official contact for the whole PB43? The press took notice that something interesting was happening and wanted interviews, photos, and background information. Students from universities wanted to do project reports and internships; others inquired about renting a space temporarily for events, projects, photo shoots, and music videos; and other self-organized projects, urban networks, the local council, various municipalities and companies wanted to cooperate and learn more about the experiences of the project.

One partnership, however, arose from simple basic human needs: access to toilet, water, hot food, and a warm place. In the beginning there was no running water at PB43 and therefore no toilet facilities, the heating was not strong enough in the winter for office work and meetings, and there was not a place to buy warm meals. Prismen, a local sport-center across the street, could fulfill all of these needs. To this end, a deal was struck to use their facilities temporarily by which PB43 members would receive a discount when buying soup and coffee in their café. This mutual understanding developed over the years, culminating in a collaboration between PB43, Prismen, the Copenhagen Municipality and Copenhagen Cooking: in 2013–2014 they arranged the "Taste The World" ("Smag Verden") festival, where eighty local associations and a number of restaurants showed around 25,000 people from all over Copenhagen a range of what today's urban ethnicity and cultural variety tastes like.

It was, however, only a few projects and activities that were open to the general public, since most spaces served as the daily workplace of the tenants. In the first couple of years there were mainly three open projects: the urban garden Prags Have, the exhibition space 68 m2 Art Space, and The Urban Laboratory that arranged lectures and courses in urbanism, architecture, and culture. These three projects functioned as a bridge to the city, which helped to create the first official collaboration between PB43 and various partners. It was essential for the place that it did not remain a closed "shop," but rather invite people to come inside. In this way it functioned as a showcase for open and sustainable city development. This was also important because the deal made with the real estate owner to use the property rent-free required that there should be cultural and social activities for the local neighborhood.

Later, the association managed to renovate the two large halls in Building 5 in order to create a cultural venue with enough room for up to 500 people. It also took on a large part of the coordination and communication with internal and external users that wanted to make events, while Prags Have, 68m2 Art Space and the Music Association PB43 began to make activities together with and for the local kids and their families, others organized the people's kitchen, urban gardening, and photo workshops. They even began to invite older kids to help at concerts and festivals.

Have Gold, But More Gold Is Needed—2012–2015

After the first couple of years, PB43 had grown into a larger and more professional organization. It was transformed from a volunteer association into a cooperative, which took over the economic and legal responsibility from GivRum in order to negotiate a new four-year contract with the real estate owner. It had two daily coordinators, more tenants and users, and managed to rent out all available indoor space. This is why a vacant part of the outdoor area was reclaimed for parking more containers and trailers in order to meet the increasing demand for workshops, studios, and offices. A number of communal projects and associations had also been established that continually arranged festivals, concerts, performances, talks, parties, movie-nights, and project consultancy. There was a growing demand for renting out space for temporary use such as events, concerts, and seminars. The cooperative was contacted by local, national, and international people who wanted to hear more about the project, have lectures, receive consulting, hold interviews, cooperate on urban projects, and become active parts of the network. The communal PB43 Publishing released its first book, *The City Becomes (Byen Bliver Til)*, about the development of PB43 and twenty other urban projects in Copenhagen. The urban garden won four prizes, which resulted in a huge public interest in the entire project. Locally the second phase also enjoyed the fruits of major developments: PB43 was given two seats in the local council, it appointed a member of the editorial team for the local newspaper, and coordinated a number of art, culture, and music festivals that involved the local neighborhood in various ways. Around the same time, PB43 was granted a property-tax reprieve by the authorities, which halved the annual amount the organization was committed to pay.

One of the most significance steps in the second phase was the development of a sustainable economical model. After a financial deficit in the 2010 and 2011 due to higher establishment costs and a lower rental income than planned, 2012 was a turning point with a more than one-third rise in income. This was due to an increase in the number of activities, as well as a considerable profit after basic expenses, which also continued over the following years and made the organization economically viable on the longer term. Beginning in 2012, the sources of annual income could be divided into five categories: permanent rental of space (internal), temporary rental of space (internal/external), co-coordination of events (internal/external), consultancy (external), and projects and partnerships (external). This proof of economical viability was especially important for the PB43 organization, showing that it could not only survive, but also develop without the need for acquiring external public funding; hereby retaining a high degree of independence while continuing its work without making too many compromises concerning the ideals of the organization and its users.

The model was based on the idea of "how low can we go to survive?" meaning: what are the most basic needs of the users and what resources are needed to fulfill these requirements? Everything else was merely icing on the PB43 cake: nice to have, but not necessary. The primary need of the users was a space to work, which should be secured by the income from internal sources, i.e., the permanent rental of space to the users, which covered the expenses for running the property: property taxes, monthly deposit saving, communal electricity, water, internet, waste disposal, and the basic administration and maintenance of the property. The rest of the income could then be channeled into a swath of secondary activities such as project coordination, development of the property, organization, and networking as well as social, cultural, local, and international activities.

The development and success of PB43 seemed to have no end. The finances were healthy, the political influence was increasing, PB43 had become an important local factor, the waiting list for renting a space was growing every week, more potential partners wanted to cooperate, and the international dimension of the project made important steps. Everyone was convinced that 2014 would be the year where the project entered a new phase of development, showing its real potential and proving that self-organized projects had to be taken seriously. Then one day in the beginning for 2014, PB43 received a letter from Akzo Nobel, saying that the property had been put on the market for sale and that the contract with PB43 was therefore terminated. PB43 received one year notice, which meant that everyone had to leave the property at the end of February 2015. This message put an abrupt hold on all further development, but only temporarily: PB43 hired a law-firm and a real estate agent. Over the next six months they gave Akzo Nobel two offers to buy the property. The users wanted to turn the imminent threat into a strategic opportunity: the plan was to become the owner of the property and evolve from a temporary project into a permanent project, thereby securing the users and the organization on a long-term basis.

The question, however, was first and foremost whether or not a large group of self-organized creative entrepreneurs could raise enough capital to buy the decommissioned paint factory. After the first meetings with real estate institutes, banks, and potential investors it turned out that PB43 was regarded as a creative business organization with a healthy economic standing, an interesting vision, and possibilities for development—all of which meant that the financiers were interested in helping to buy the property. The organization could get 50–60% of the money needed at a low interest rate as a mortgage, and a bank loan for remaining amount. The challenge was that the bank loan had a high interest rate, which meant compounded interest while repaying the loan and therefore a higher amount of rent for the users. A more acceptable solution for the users was a mix of the real estate loan and an installment agreement, whereby Akzo Nobel received a large part of the payment upfront, and the rest over several years. Another possibility would be that Akzo Nobel used PB43 as an example of Corporate Social Responsibility and sold the property at a lower price. PB43 ultimately created a proposal that showed Akzo Nobel the activities and development that had taken place on the property, and in the local area, and what would be undertaken if PB43 became the new owner.

The news about the forthcoming sale of Prags Boulevard and the possible end of PB43 also reached the city council and two of the political parties asked if they should raise the issue and try to convince the municipality to buy the property and rent it out to PB43. One of the largest private funds in Denmark also showed interest in buying the property and letting PB43 rent it afterwards. Unfortunately, both the municipality and the private funds would necessitate broad and expensive renovation; after which the property would be rented at market price and most likely place various demands that would limit the use and the organization of the place—a solution that would mean low independence and high rent. In fact, the fund suggested unofficially that PB43 should try to find another solution because their involvement had a chance of "suffocating" the very idea of the PB43 project. In the end both offers were turned down.

In spite of the fact that PB43 had different financing options and that the organization made two offers to buy the property, Akzo Nobel decided to sell to an international investment fund that had plans to build a self-storage building on the plot. PB43 could not match the investor's much higher offer.

A New Place With A New View—2015 Until Now

The alternatives were either to dissolve PB43 or to find a new place to continue the activities. The users of PB43 chose the latter by unanimous decision. However, the search for a new place turned out to be a difficult task, since the real estate market and the city development in Copenhagen was shifting into a higher gear after a long

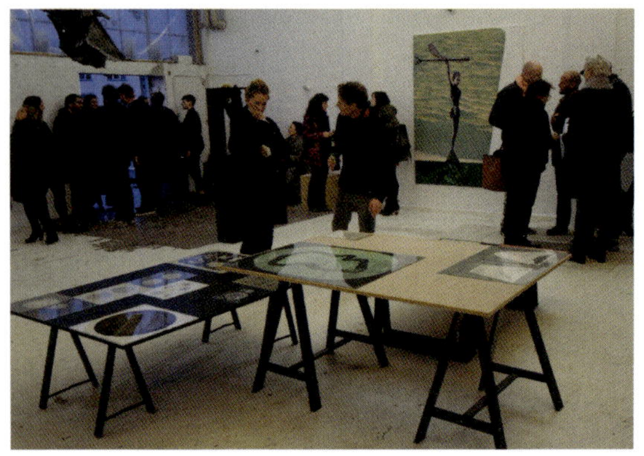

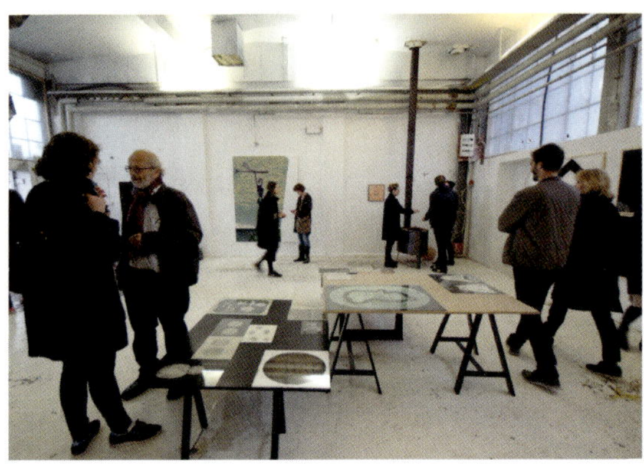

Archaea curated by Carsten Rabe at PB43
(Beton Art Space)

Archaea curated by Carsten Rabe at PB43
(Beton Art Space)

period of recession. So vacant places with low rent and a high degree of flexibility that suited a large differentiated group of self-organized people were now less available and much more expensive to rent than just a few years earlier. Many real estate owners and developers seemed at the same time to have learned that disused worn out industrial properties also contained some value—especially for creative users and leisure projects—while waiting for a change in the local municipality zoning plans that would open up for the establishment of new expensive flats and office buildings. Amazingly, just two weeks before PB43 was to vacate Prags Boulevard, they succeeded in finding a new location at the Copenhagen's North Harbor for some of the existing users as well as for a number of new ones. So, in March 2015, PB43 moved to its new location in Copenhagen's North Harbor and is now reestablishing itself.

Here PB43 wishes to secure and develop its vision further, to benefit the users, the local area, Copenhagen, and its many national and international partners. Unfortunately, it is doubtful that PB43's vision will have the same opportunities of development at the new site. The agreement with the real estate owner in the North Harbor does not contain the same favorable conditions as on Prags Boulevard, so the project is now facing a range of new challenges. If the establishment and further development of PB43 in the North Harbor is undertaken at a rent level and under inflexible user conditions based on market terms, it will be the up-and-coming creative businesses, social, and cultural non-profit projects especially that will face the risk of either giving up their activities or radically pivoting their focus. This is because of the simultaneous economic challenges involved in reestablishing working spaces and an amount of rent that has more than tripled when compared with Prags Boulevard. If PB43 is to continue to seriously participate in the development of a sustainable environment for creativity in Copenhagen, it will require active investments and alternative decisions.

For the first time, PB43 has applied to the City of Copenhagen for funding for the establishment and development of various projects. The organization is also considering whether or not it should apply for the funding of daily operating costs, which runs the risk of enabling the municipality to potentially dictate certain conditions that are in line with its vision and guidelines for ways that creative environments should be developed in Copenhagen. This is problematic when the core ideals of PB43 require it to remain entirely self-organized and independent. Furthermore, it is also unlikely that PB43's economic model, which is a major pillar of the organization's vision, can simply be transferred to the new conditions.

Conclusion

When reflecting upon the process of trying to buy the property, it seems that PB43 unwittingly participated in "business as usual" city development, where investors and real estate developers benefit from properties that, for a relatively short period of time, are placed in a vacuum outside of the real estate market. PB43 had the vision and the possibility to create cultural, social and economic value for as many people as possible, whereas the investors wanted to create economic returns for as few people as possible (themselves). Akzo Nobel explained that they were in a period of financial difficulty, which is why they needed to sell their non-productive properties. This approach made it clear that they were not really interested in helping to ensure sustainable city development: they chose to sell to the highest bidder and not to the one that had the best plan for how the city and its citizens could get the most out of the situation in the long term. On the other hand, Akzo Nobel basically donated a space in Copenhagen for five years; a space where it was possible to experiment with ways of using and organizing the city.

For five years PB43 had a unique loan agreement with Akzo Nobel, which in addition to the obvious advantages for the users and the local neighborhood also manifested a mutually advantageous economical agreement for both Akzo Nobel and PB43. It was an agreement that made it possible to establish PB43 as an alternative space within the context of official city development in Copenhagen; meaning low rent, flexible use, a high degree of self-organization, and interdisciplinary exchange. These factors are necessary conditions for developing a favorable environment for fostering creative growth and effecting social change. Had PB43 succeeded in purchasing the areal at Prague Boulevard 43, it would of course also have resulted in very different economic and organizational conditions than was the case over the first five years of the project. The organization would have had to have borrowed a significant amount of capital and paid off the loan plus interest over many years. This would have manifested a huge challenge and at least doubled the rent for the users, but they would nevertheless have been "masters of their own destiny" and enjoyed a high degree of independence with a unique opportunity for organizing their own environment. Unfortunately, this ideal degree of independence does not seem possible at the new site, since there is not only a tripling of the rent when compared to that of the Prague Boulevard 43 property, but also because the owner in the North Harbor has certain demands and procedures for the use and maintenance of the property.

Perhaps there are both advantages and disadvantages to this new situation. PB43 is now forced to function according to market conditions, which will require adjustments and hard work, but it will also be a test of whether the users, their organization, and the shared vision is capable of standing on their own feet. The most important thing is that the guiding idea behind PB43 has thus far survived the move from one place to another, and that a large part of the overall experience, network, and goodwill has moved with PB43 to its new site. In this way it is possible for PB43 to continue to work for a more open and sustainable urban development for creative growth, cultural innovation, and social evolution. It is not just about securing a dynamic and self-organized environment; as with all sustainable development it is also about manifesting a solid backbone with conditions necessary for survival—a reasonable foundation for change and growth. We must secure the conditions needed by creative entrepreneurs for their work: flexible space, reasonable and affordable rent, possibilities for open sharing of interdisciplinary knowledge and experiences, and a strong ongoing network where projects, products, and ideas can develop through both local and international partnerships. It is this task that PB43 wishes to uphold and support and is what PB43 has come to be: an environment that has set a new standard for creative entrepreneurship, cultural innovation, and social evolution. It will be interesting to follow PB43 as it faces new challenges and develops further.

pb43.dk
forlagetpb43.dk

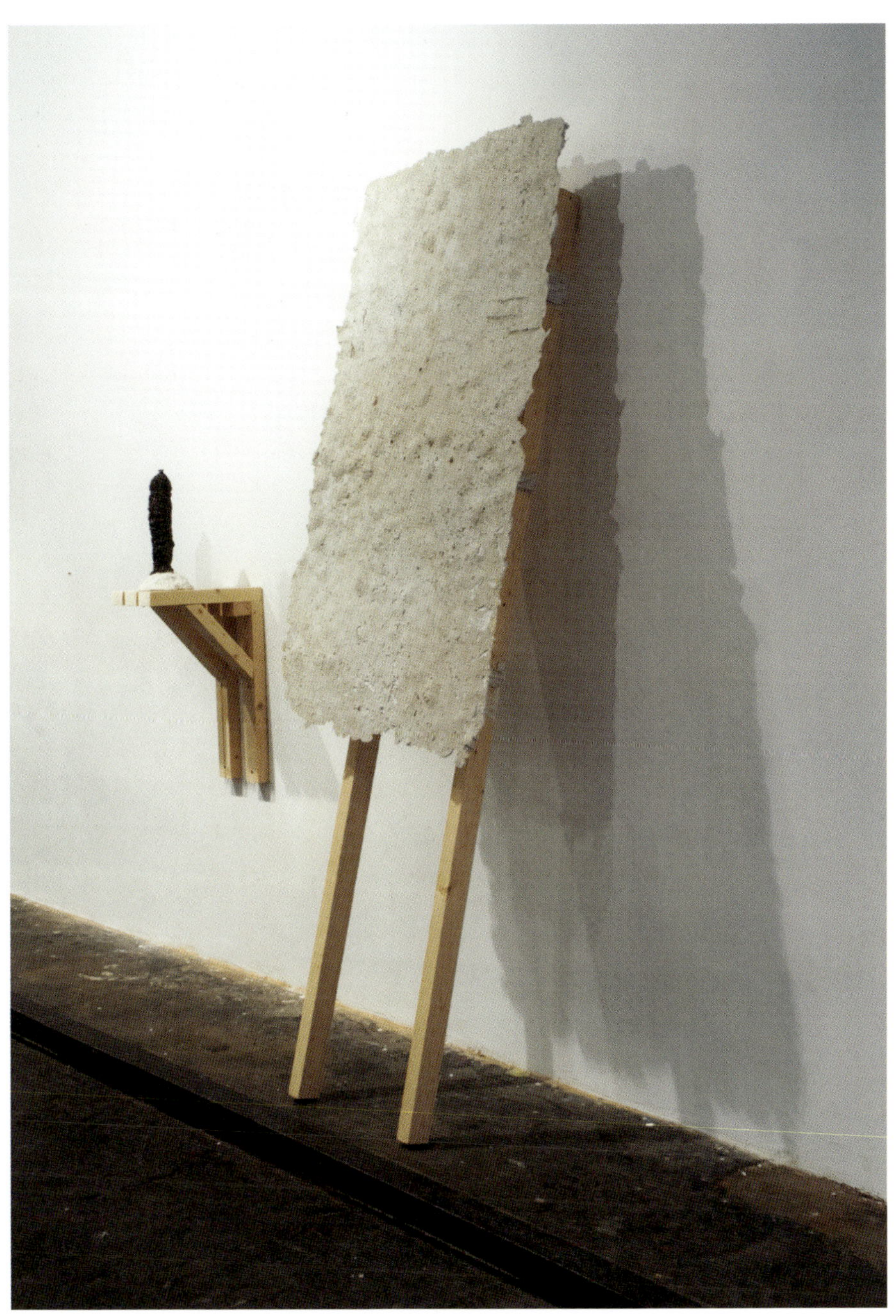

Material Retention by Julie Bitsch at Westwerk

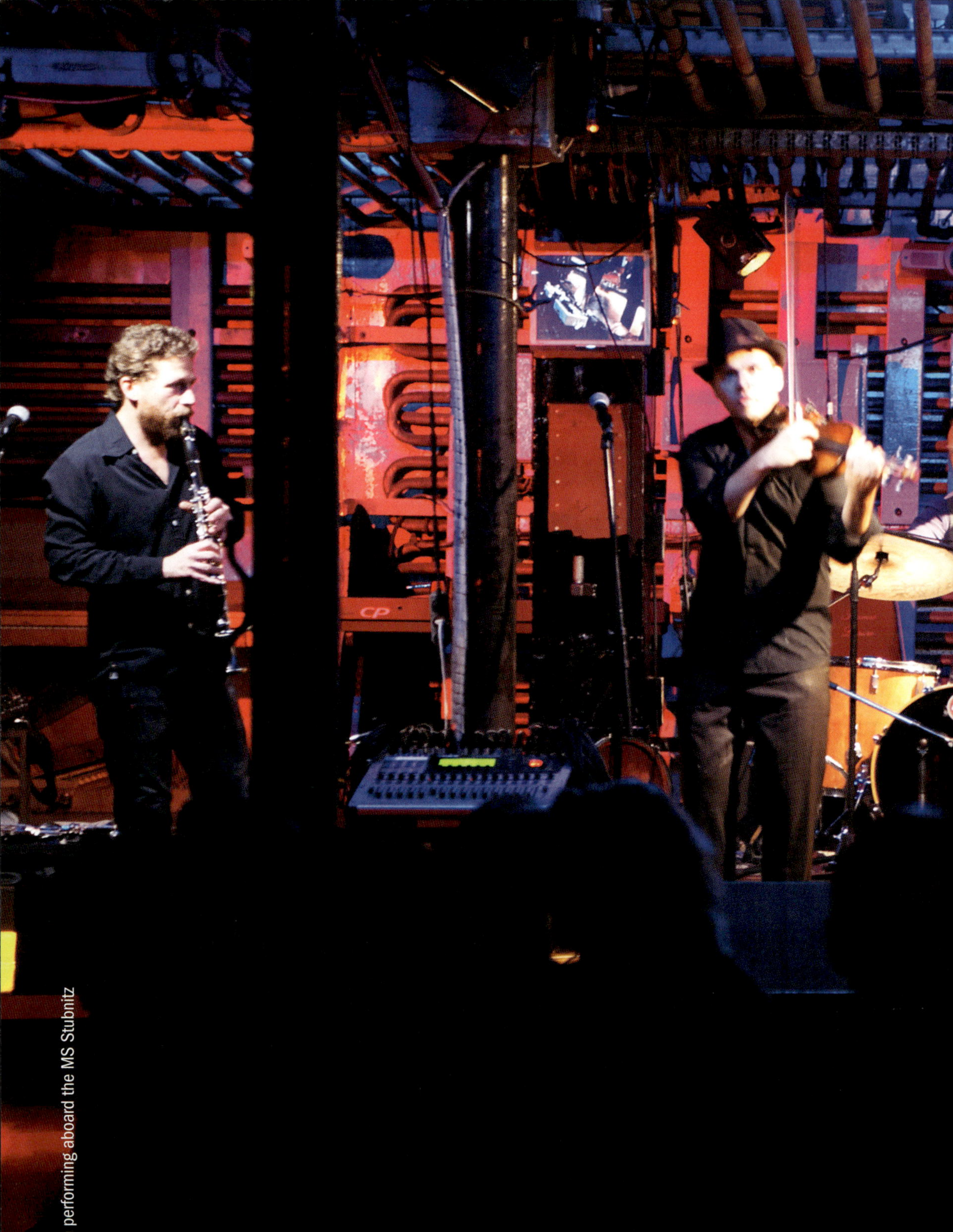

Afenginn performing aboard the MS Stubnitz

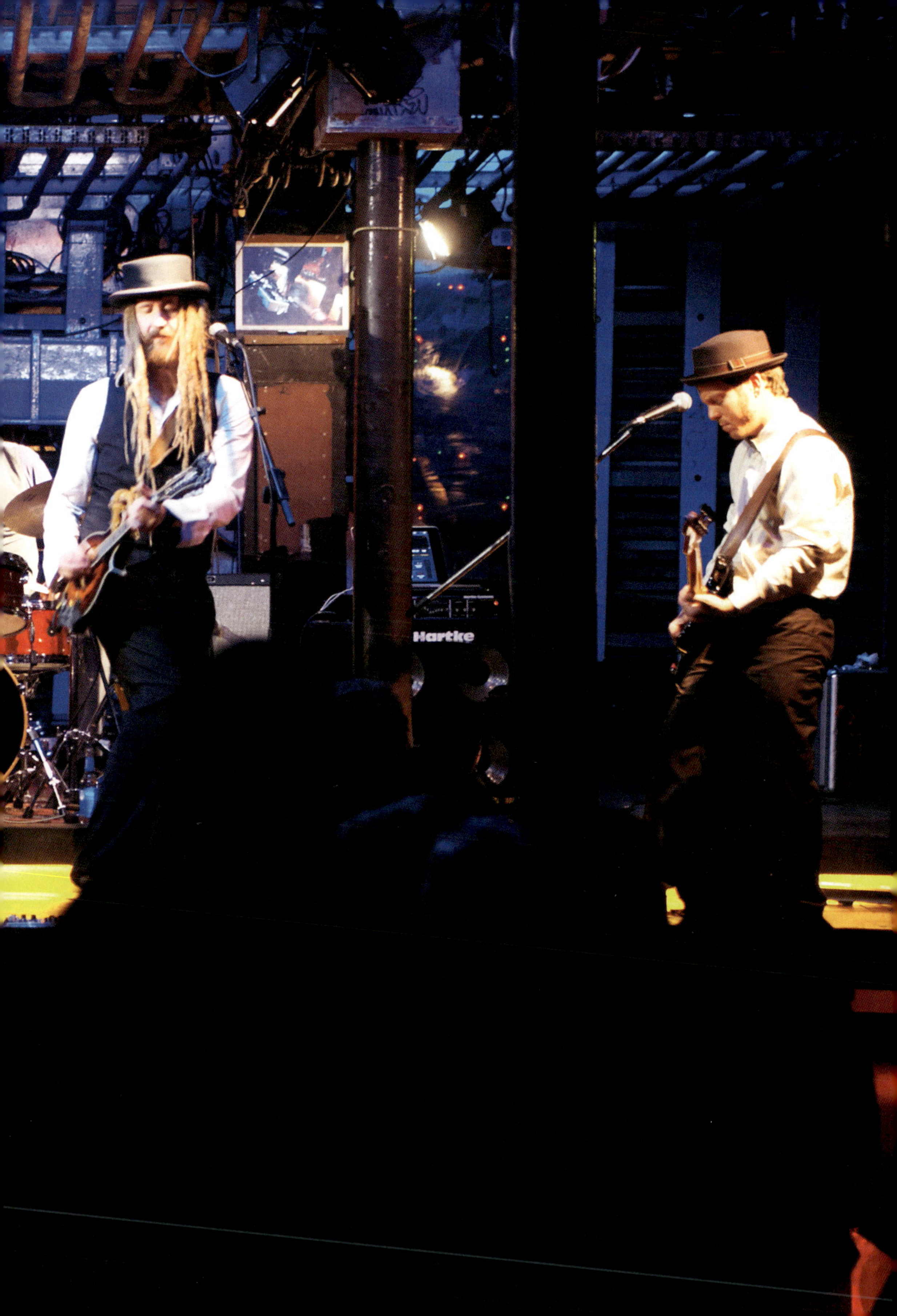
Hartke

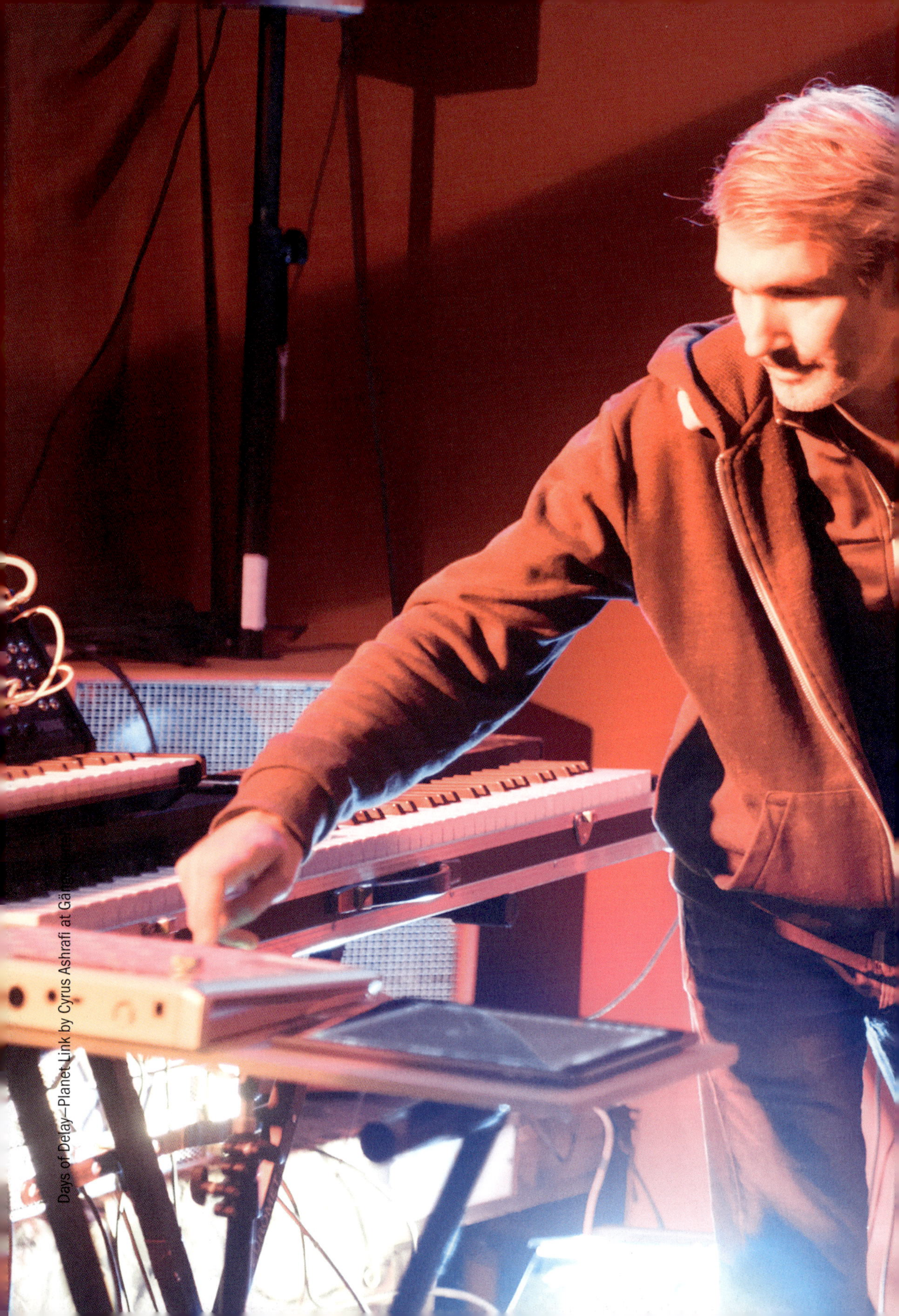

Days of Delay–Planet Link by Cyrus Ashrafi at Gäl...

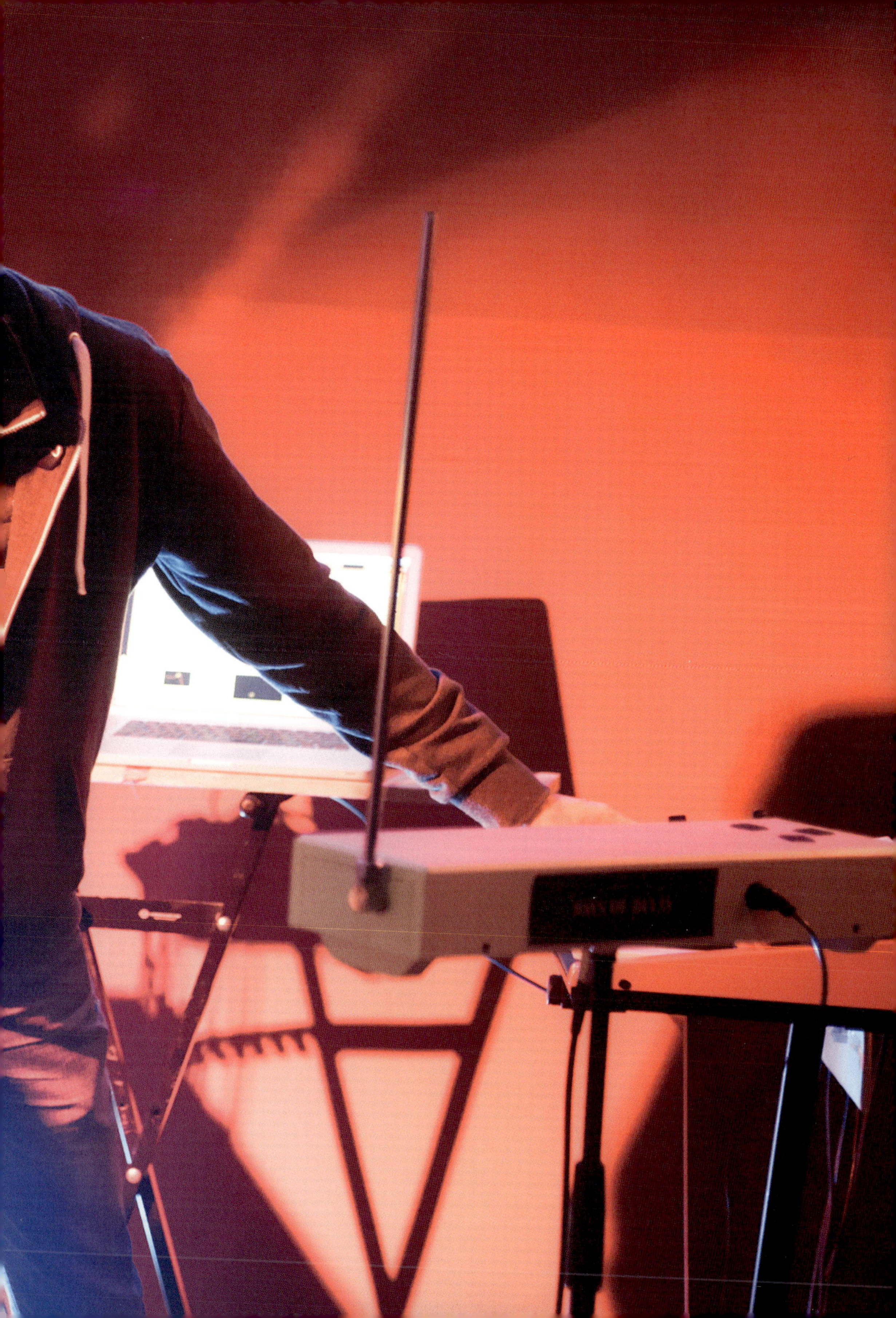

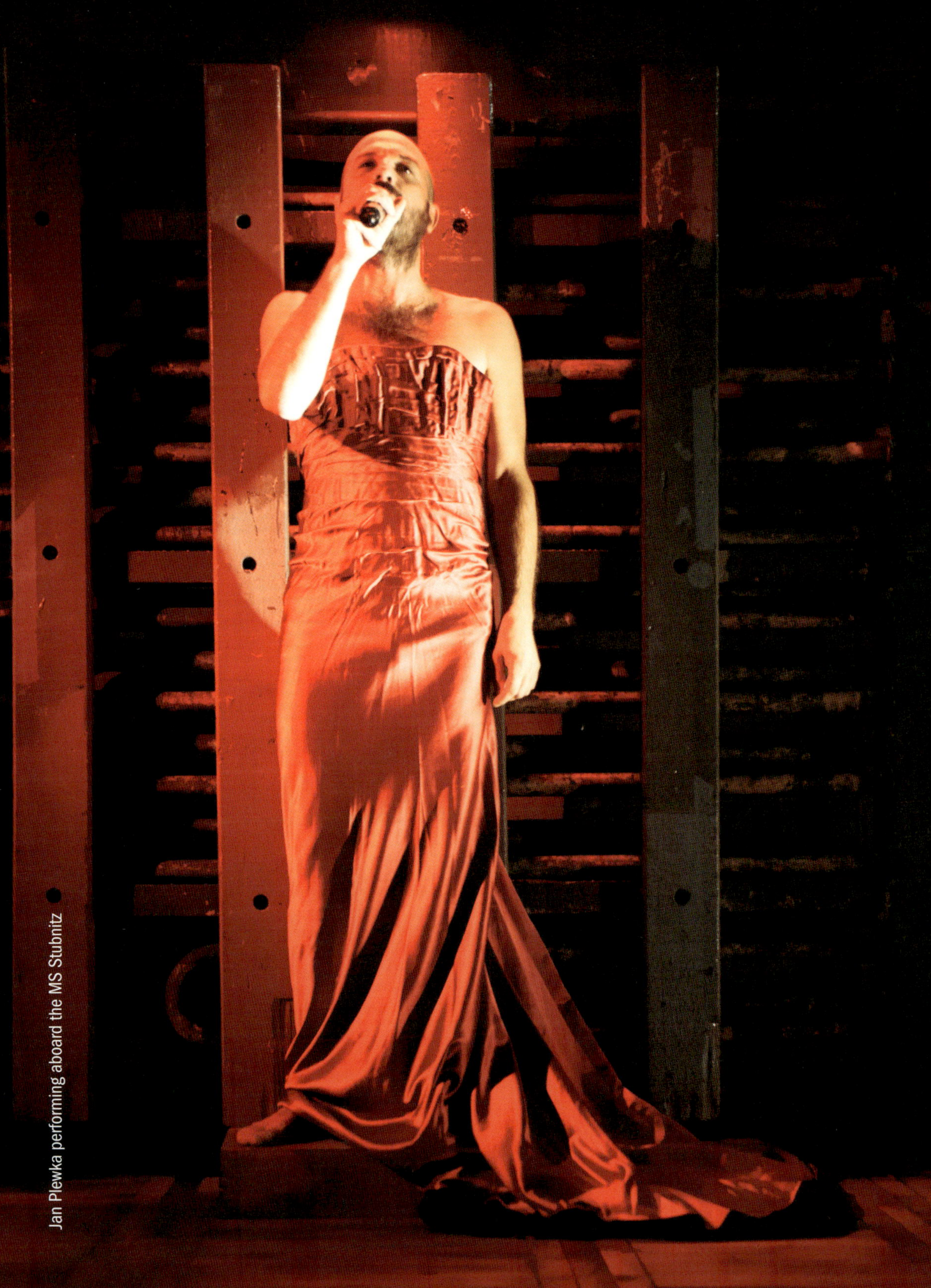

Jan Plewka performing aboard the MS Stubnitz

Artist-Run Spaces and Projects

In the following section, twelve artist-run spaces and projects from Hamburg and Copenhagen will be presented with short profiles. The range does not encompass the entire spectrum of self-organized art spaces and projects in the two cities, but gives insight into the variety of places, the range of practices, and the different aims of the operators. These artist-run spaces and projects all took part in the City Link Festival in Hamburg. They made their spaces available for events, and their operators participated both as curators and artists. This is a reference to the organizational structure of the festival: art exhibitions were organized in two different manners, some were curated group shows of invited artists from Copenhagen and others were self-organized artist-run spaces with different exhibitions complemented the program. Many of these projects have a broad variety of cultural entrepreneurs in their midst, such as musicians, DJ's, theater producers, actors, and dancers. This made it an obvious choice to include these artists within the festival program. In addition to the curated exhibitions, a small number of art spaces in Hamburg also participated. To be part of the festival they either invited artists from Copenhagen or organized shows independently.

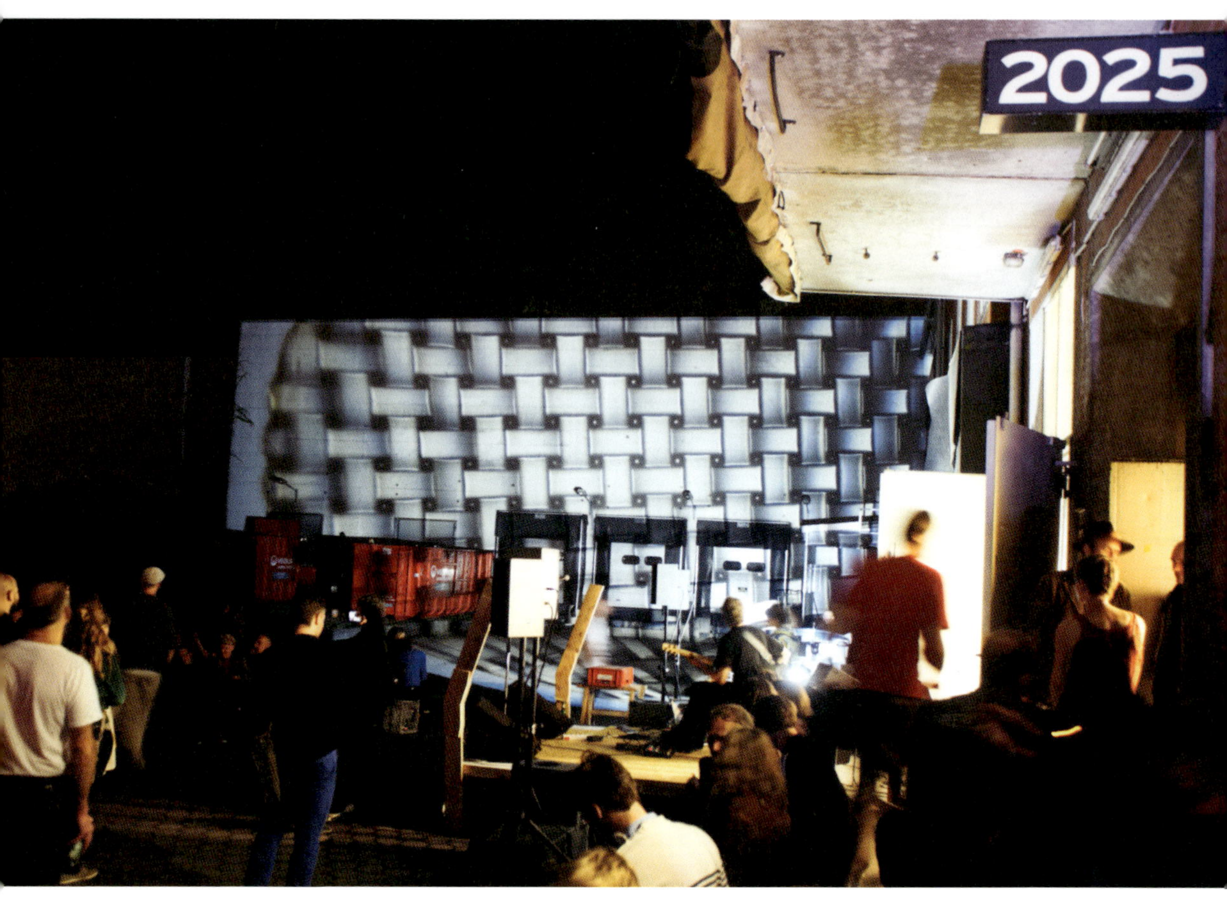

Visual projection by Katrin Bethge and John Eckhard at 2025 and Achterhaus

2025

2025 e.V. is a studio and exhibition space in Hamburg-Bahrenfeld. It opened after extensive construction work in October 2009. The reason for its establishment was that most members were forced to leave other locations in the city. They came together to jointly open affordable working spaces, since a group of like-minded individuals has a greater chance of renting a suitable property. The project is operated by a non-profit association founded by the artists. The eighteen members pay rent to the association for their studios and jointly operate the exhibition space. They share tasks such as press relations, external communications, fundraising, and curating the program. Furthermore, there have been a number of artistic collaborations and joint exhibitions among the members, but they do not consider themselves to be an artists' collective.

The association has obtained annual program funding from the Ministry of Culture in Hamburg since 2012. Therefore exhibitions need not be filled to overflowing and artistic experimentation is welcome. The exhibition room provides space for diverse forms of artistic expression and technical facilities for various exhibition formats. For example, every Friday at 2025 the event series ACTION takes place. ACTION focuses on ephemeral moments in art in these times of oversupply and twenty-four-hour availability. The format provides the opportunity to respond quickly to current events and allows artists from all sectors "to enjoy failing" without any market pressure.

2025ev.de

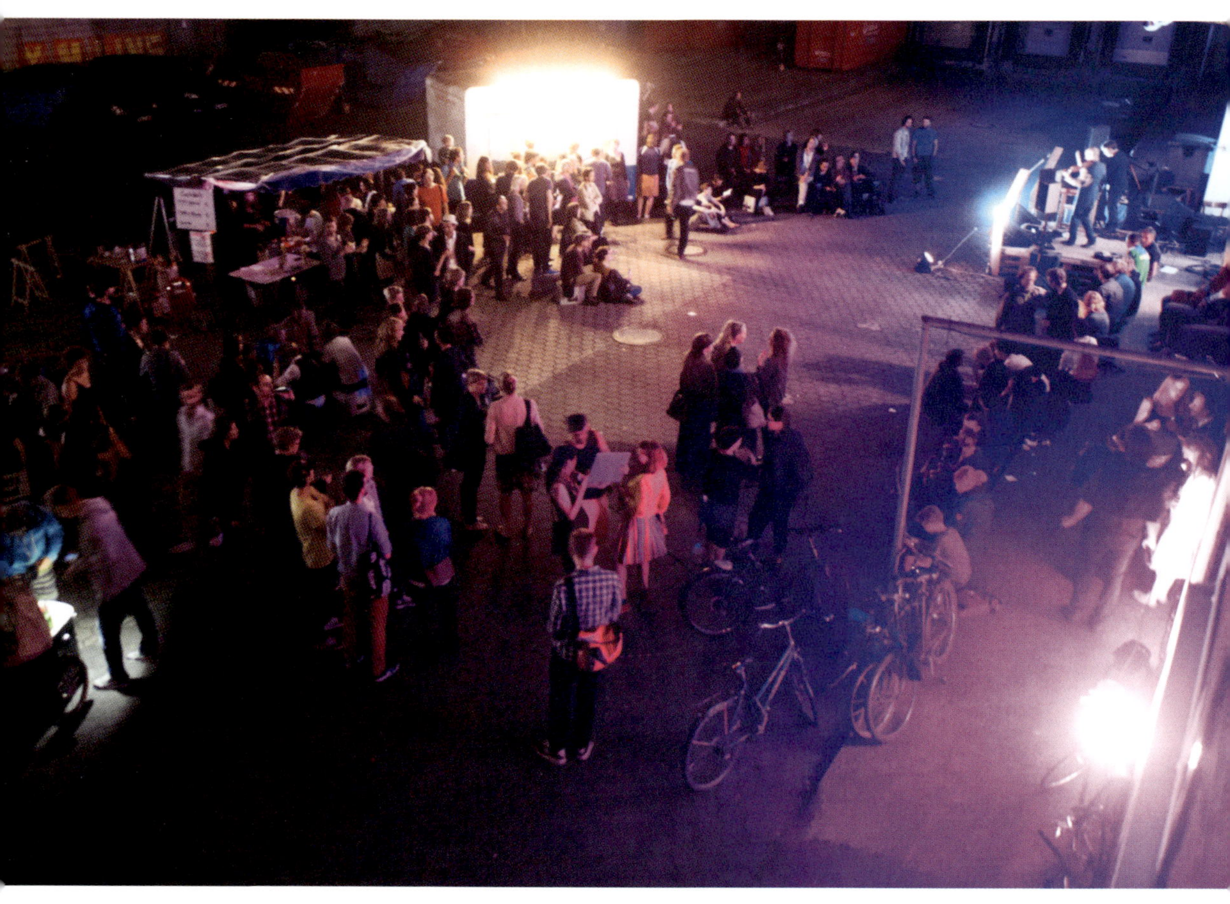

Open studios and Summerparty at 2025 and Achterhaus

Achterhaus

The Achterhaus | Ateliergemeinschaft e.V. is an artists' house located in a backyard of the highly industrialized west-district of Hamburg-Bahrenfeld (next door to the 2025 e.V.). Originally, the three-story building housed the administration of a wallpaper factory and later the office of a department store. Today it provides twenty-two working spaces that are currently used by thirty-one artists of different professions. Each of the artists is a member of the Achterhaus Ateliergemeinschaft e.V. association and undertakes a role within the project's management, ranging from communication, press relations, and building maintenance to financial and legal matters.

The association was founded in 2012 with the goal of providing long-term working space for independent artists in Hamburg and supporting a versatile and sustainable network between them. An important objective of the association was to promote and protect the heterogeneous composition of its members. In the Achterhaus, many different trades work alongside each other: sculptors, stage designers, painters, drafts-people, illustrators, product designers, and photographers. After initial financial support from Hamburg's Ministry of Culture for the purpose of important and necessary reno-vation, today the members bear the costs for upkeep. The Achterhaus Residency is a studio for international artists in ongoing cooperation with the Ministry of Culture, where the residents receive a stipend and can stay for a duration of between one and three months.

atelierhaus-ruhrstrasse.de

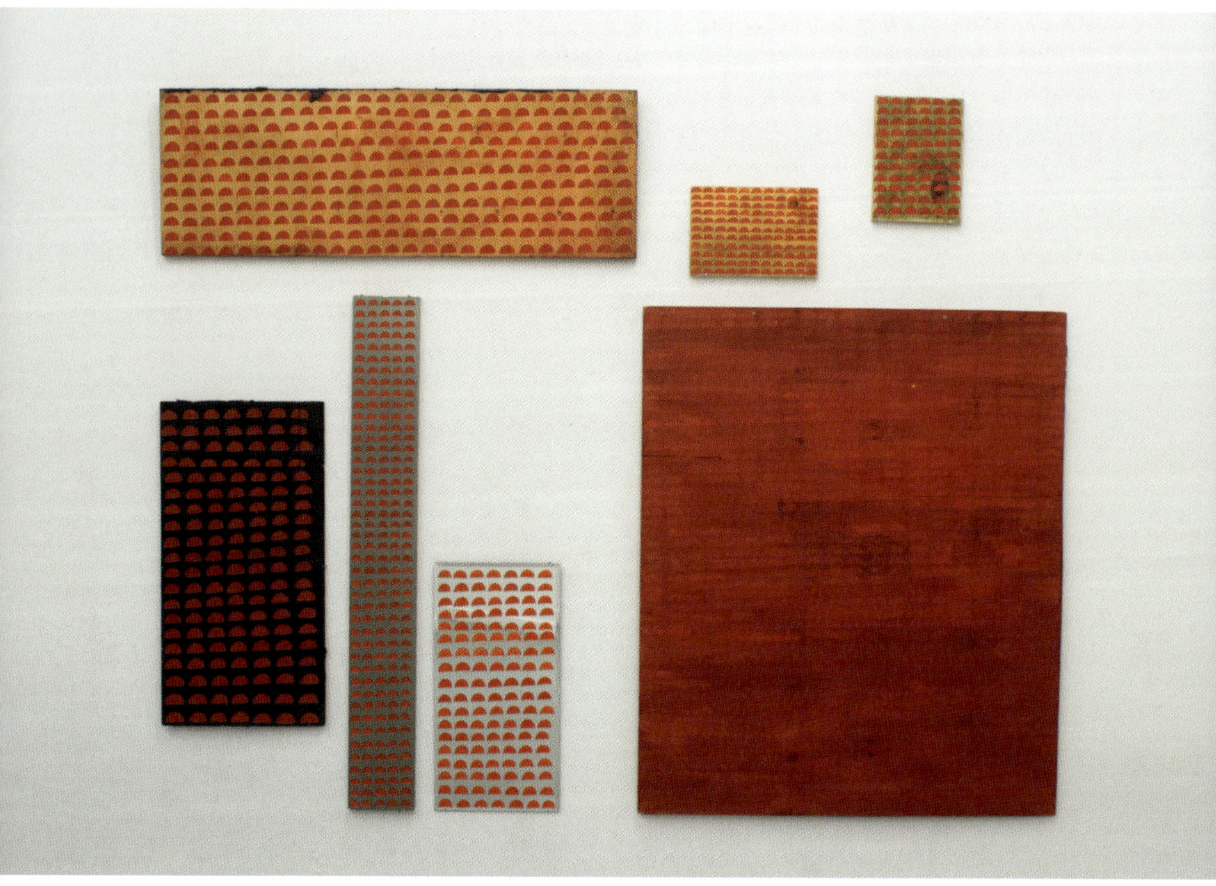

Sunsets by Nina Wengel at Viktoria Kaserne (fux eG)

Fux eG

Fux eG is a cooperation with the goal of turning an old Wilhemine military complex (known as the Viktoria Kaserne) into a self-managed production and cultural center. Its history is closely connected to protests of local residents in the Winter of 2009–10 against the establishment of an Ikea store in Hamburg-Altona. The protests were supported by the tenants of the Frappant building, which Ikea wanted to demolish (and has since been torn down for the construction of the store). After a large occupation party with weeks of activities and events at Frappant, local politicians were forced to offer an alternative venue to the former tenants. In February 2010, the Viktoria Kaserne was rented to the Frappant association (Frappant e.V.) and became the new home for around 140 artists and tradespeople. Since that time, the place has established itself as a venue for art, labor, and events in Altona. Simultaneously, Lux & Konsorten was founded as a political association of small businesses in Altona that sought affordable working spaces at various locations that could be collectively managed. When it became apparent in the fall of 2011 that there was an opportunity to purchase the former barracks from the city, Lux and the Frappant association began to discuss the possibilities of a cooperative organization. In October 2013, the fux Cooperative was jointly founded. After one and a half years of negotiations with the City of Hamburg, fux eventually bought the enormous complex.

Fux Cooperative is a union of cultural workers, small businesses, educational institutions, and social organizations: there are artists, a bicycle repair shop, graphic and fashion designers, a free shop, a food cooperative, illustrators, architects, urban planners, a cabinet maker, project spaces for youth workshops, a tree care company, a canteen, photographers, film-makers, musicians, theater people, programmers, book and film publishers, an accounting office, a training provider, a journalism office, an upholstery, an instrument workshop, a tailor, and a sound and lighting system rental. In addition to individual and group workshops or studios, Viktoria Kaserne hosts guest facilities, seminar, project and workshop rooms, banquet facilities, exhibition spaces, training and rehearsal rooms for dance, theater and music, as well as a self-organized youth club and much more.

Fux Cooperative was founded as a cooperative in order to use this form of organization to express the idea that collective nature plays a key role in the project. The founders' aim was to put responsibility into the hands of all those involved. In addition to general meetings of the cooperative, there are monthly informal meetings and various working groups devoted to many aspects such as renovation and construction, publicity, and self-governance. The building is divided into sectors that are self-organized by the members of the cooperative, upon whose shoulders the financing of the project depends. Each member is required to invest three thousand euros. This amount does not exclude anyone from membership in the cooperative: even recipients of unemployment benefits can receive a credit guarantee for this sum of money. In addition to the financial resources brought by the members, the cooperative also counts on so-called solidarity loans from investing members that simply want to support the project.

The history and idea of running the former Kaserne as a self-managed space of production are both closely linked to the "Right to the City" movement in Hamburg: gentrification is not just a problem for living spaces, but also means that affordable rooms for small commercial, social, and artistic projects become more and more scarce. Backyard workshops, artists' studios, and non-commercial premises have no chance against big stores, the franchise economy, and chain gastronomy. Ultimately, it is about centrality, and therefore, that the much-vaunted "city of short distances" should not be one of the benefits only for those who can afford to pay the most money. So, out of the resistance against an Ikea store in Altona, there arose a cooperative as an alternative to an urban-environment defined purely from the perspective of profit and sales.

fux-eg.org

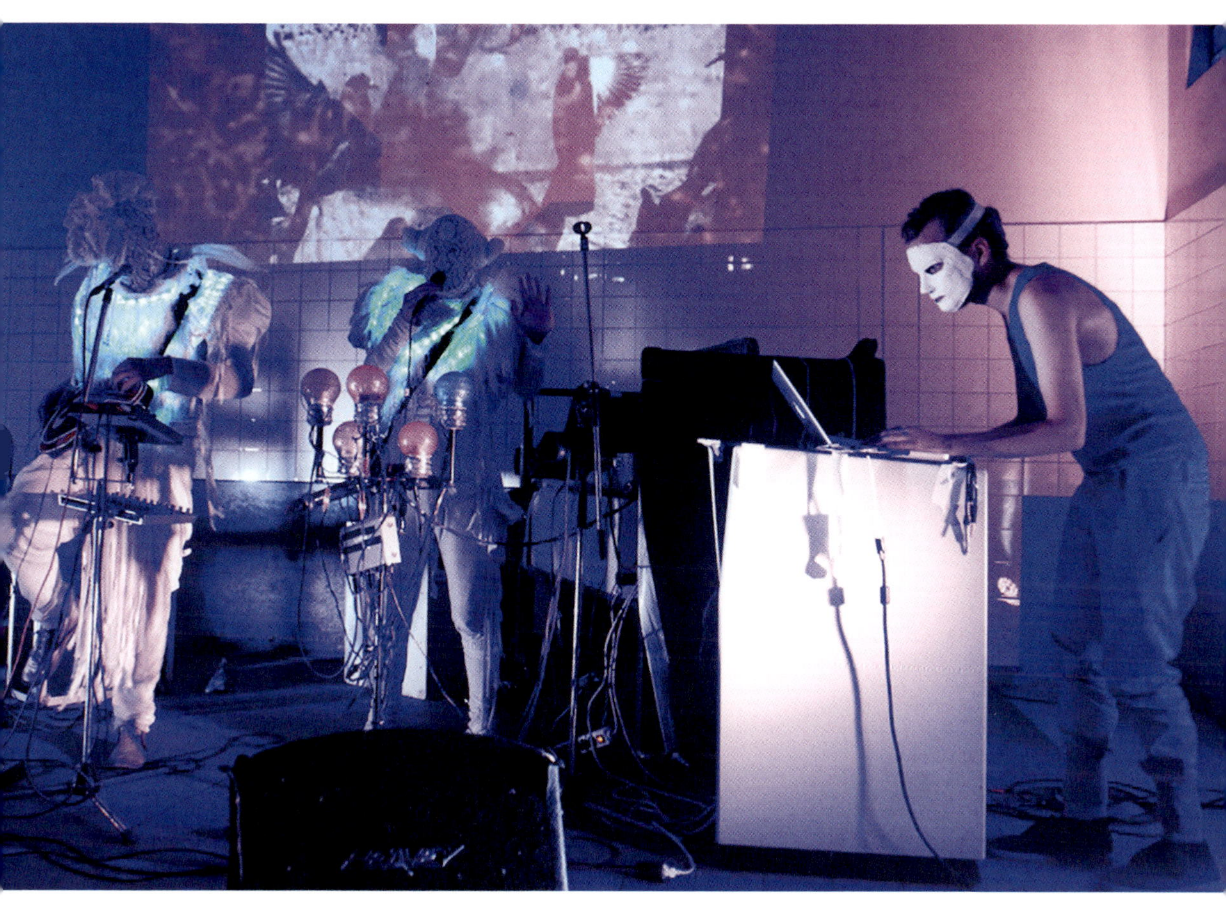

LUR performing at Viktoria Kaserne (fux eG)

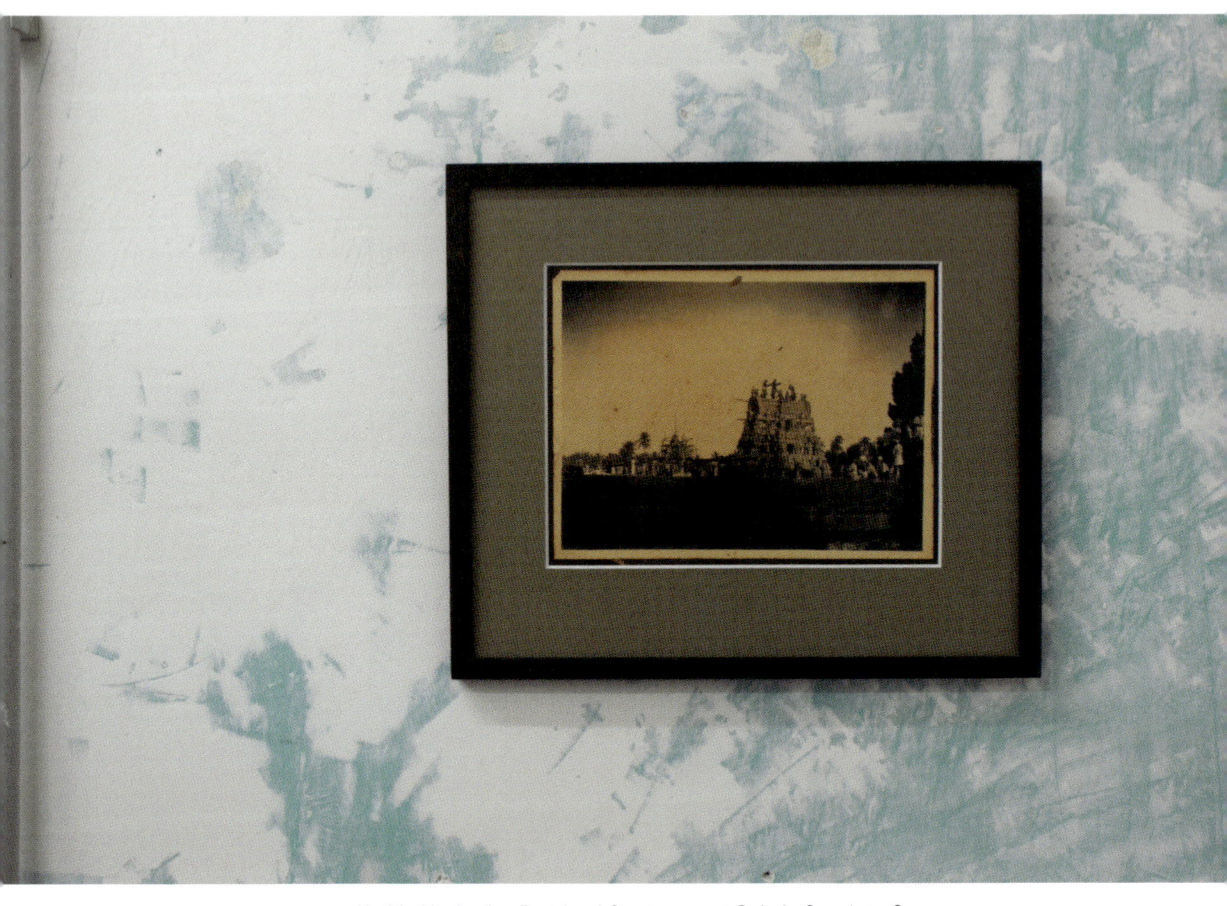

Untitled by Louise Bøgelund Saugmann at Galerie Speckstraße

Galerie Speckstraße

The Galerie Speckstraße is one of many exhibition spaces in the Gängeviertel, a small central part of Hamburg that was occupied in 2009 (Ziehl, this volume). The non-profit Gängeviertel association (Gängeviertel e.V.) provides the organizational structure of the exhibition space. Additionally, the exhibition activity has been financially supported over the years by Hamburg's Ministry of Culture. Since the first day of its cultural re-appropriation, the gallery at Speckstrasse has developed into a lively and versatile place. Exhibitions, lectures, performances, and concerts have taken place in two apartments on the raised ground floor of the building. The place remains a magnet for artists and art lovers from Hamburg and all around the world, for people of all generations and backgrounds.

Since its opening, it has become clear that the gallery is especially suitable for group exhibitions. Due to the variety of rooms and their respective qualities of shape, size and surface, individual positions can be treated accordingly. Furthermore the concept of exhibitions often pays respect to the history and memory of the place visible in the curling wallpaper, wooden floors, and other details. Here, the curators focus on inviting groups of artists whose work can coexist in dialogue. Although the staffing has changed repeatedly over the years, the curators of the gallery are generally artists working in the same house or are otherwise active in the Gängeviertel. In addition, the gallery occasionally invites external curators. Over the years, a special focus on international cooperation has developed, which among others welcomed guest artists from Latvia, South Korea, Denmark, and China.

das-gaengeviertel.info

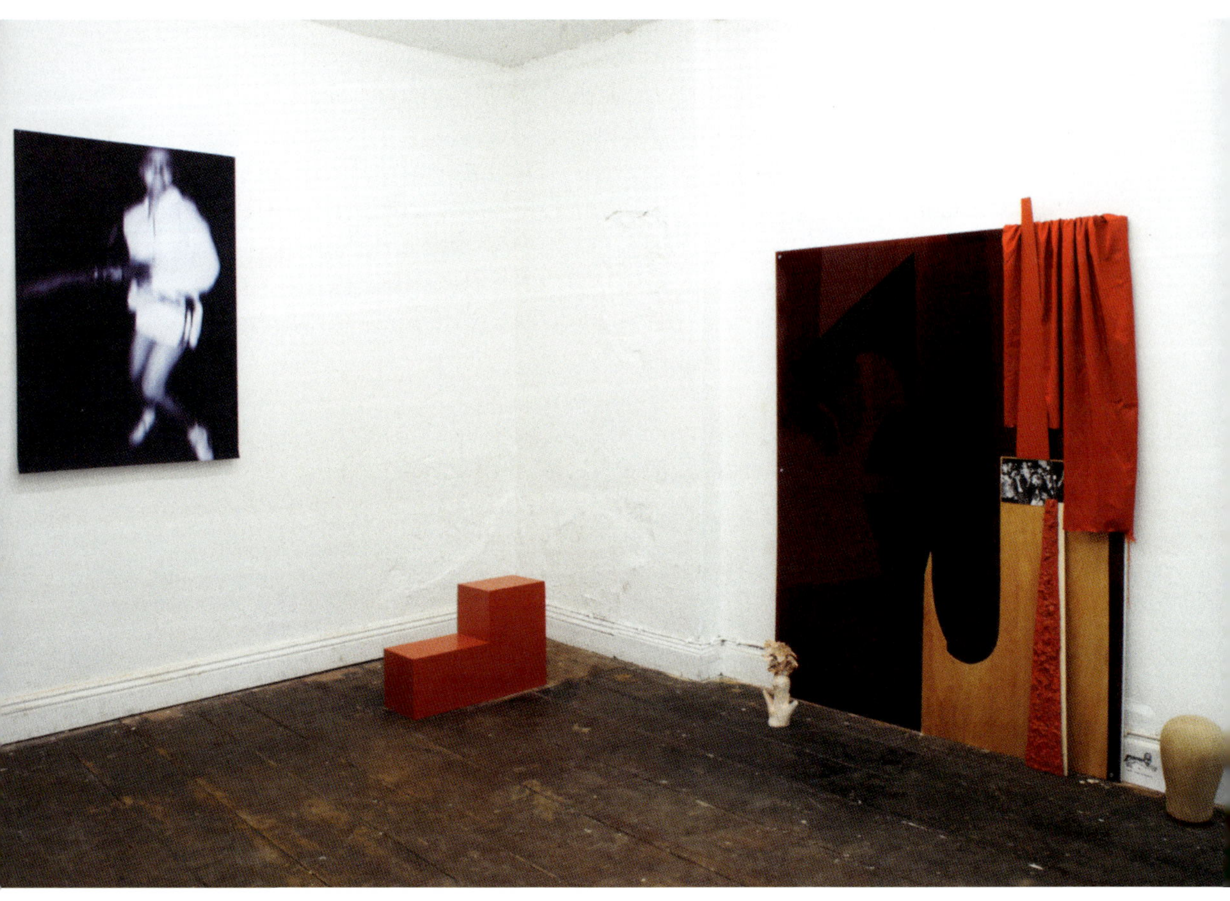

Installation Based on the Color Red by Sian Kristoffersen at Galerie Speckstraße

GREEN IS GOLD

GREEN IS GOLD is a Copenhagen based, non-profit, arts organization run by Danish artists Amalie Bønnelycke Lunøe and Ditte Knus Tønnesen. The pair met while studying at The Glasgow School of Art, Scotland in 2006. Upon returning to Denmark in 2010, they set up a studio in an old apartment space on Hyskenstræde in the city center of Copenhagen. This in turn led them to open the exhibition space, GREEN IS GOLD, as both a natural extension of their own art practices and a basis upon which to create opportunities for exhibiting pioneering contemporary visual art. Nearly four years and 35 projects later, GREEN IS GOLD is now a nomadic organization that focuses on curating and developing projects and exhibitions in a selection of venues both local and international.

The concept of GREEN IS GOLD is to create opportunities and to be involved in opportunities created by others. As a non-profit organization, it operates on private investment, goodwill, and a joint funding application system undertaken with the respective exhibiting or involving artists. Each party is involved in the acquisition of financial support, since each project is funded individually. The exhibitions and projects are composed of both proposals submitted and works by invited guests. Although Knus Tønnesen and Lunøe look first and foremost for quality, they also believe in taking risks. Their wish is to provide artists with the opportunity to present a variety of multimedia work and focus on the process behind the work instead of only taking on "finished" and therefore "safe" projects. The founders strive to re-engage the artists that have exhibited in GREEN IS GOLD in other projects with which the organization is involved; thus these artists are continually promoted in the art world. The same goes for Knus Tønnesen and Lunøe themselves: rather than being mere organizers and curators, they are also artists involved with projects and exhibitions that are suited to their respective practices. Both have been involved as exhibitors and curators in projects in Iceland, Germany, Sweden, Denmark, the UK, and Mexico.

gigstudio.dk

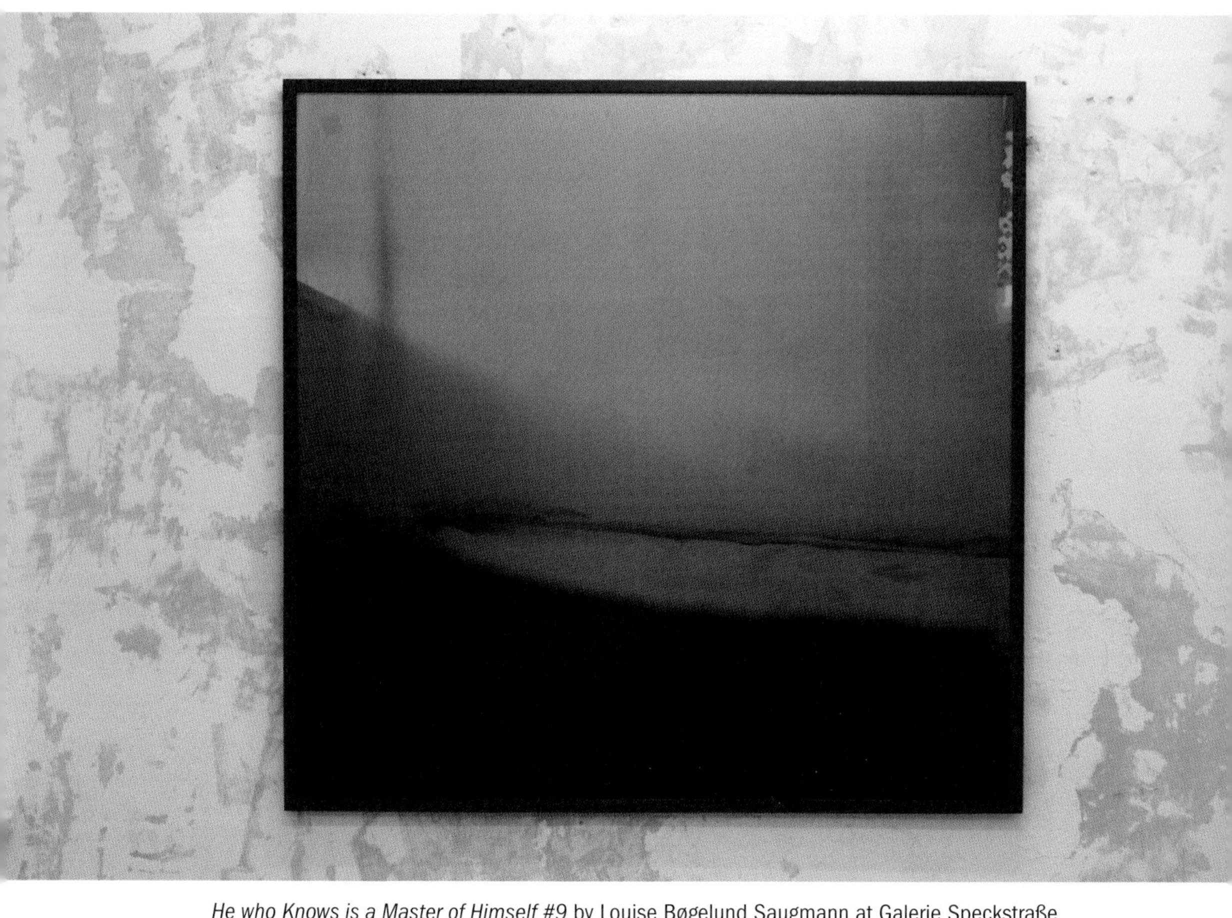

He who Knows is a Master of Himself #9 by Louise Bøgelund Saugmann at Galerie Speckstraße

KONTORprojects

KONTORprojects is an artist-run art curatorial project in Copenhagen. It opened in 2011 as a platform for the work of the founders as well as contemporary photography in Copenhagen. Jenny Nordquist and Louise Bøgelund Saugmann worked together to develop a unique space that could support their own careers as well as help other artists. They felt that the art photography scene in Copenhagen needed a small exhibition space managed by artists for artists—a space that allowed them to create innovative work without commercial or institutional limitations. The central purpose of the space is to present work that pushes the medium of photography by exploring unconventional subject matter and presentation in order to examine what photography can achieve as an art form. It should also foster dialogues and networks that transgress genders, cultures, and geographical borders in order to expand the knowledge of art photography and strengthen cultural diversity. The program ranges from solo shows, group exhibitions, and performances. Another major purpose is to create connections with similar initiatives in Copenhagen and abroad. Artists from Scandinavia are regularly invited to exhibit in collaboration with artists from other countries.

KONTORprojects is a non-profit organization that is funded and kept operational by cultural support, fund-raising, volunteer work and personal investment. One of the main challenges is finding ways to create revenue, organizing and carrying out fund-raising, and managing the exhibitions while still finding time for individual art practice. Another challenge is the management and organization of the exhibition space. From 2011–15 KONTORprojects shared their space with a larger group of people with various interests. The space had housed photographers for nearly two decades; a photographic collective with darkroom facilities developing into a working space for individual artists and photographers. Within this structure, KONTORprojects was just one of many activities taking place. The space managed to retain a relatively low rent in an area that had become highly commercialized and expensive over the years, and KONTORprojects was very much an alternative to the surrounding boutiques and restaurants. It contributed not only to the art scene but also to the local community.

In 2015 KONTORprojects decided it was time to move on by leaving the specific space connected to the practice. Today KONTORprojects is a curatorial project, collaborating with various artists, artist-run spaces, and institutions around the world.

kontorprojects.dk

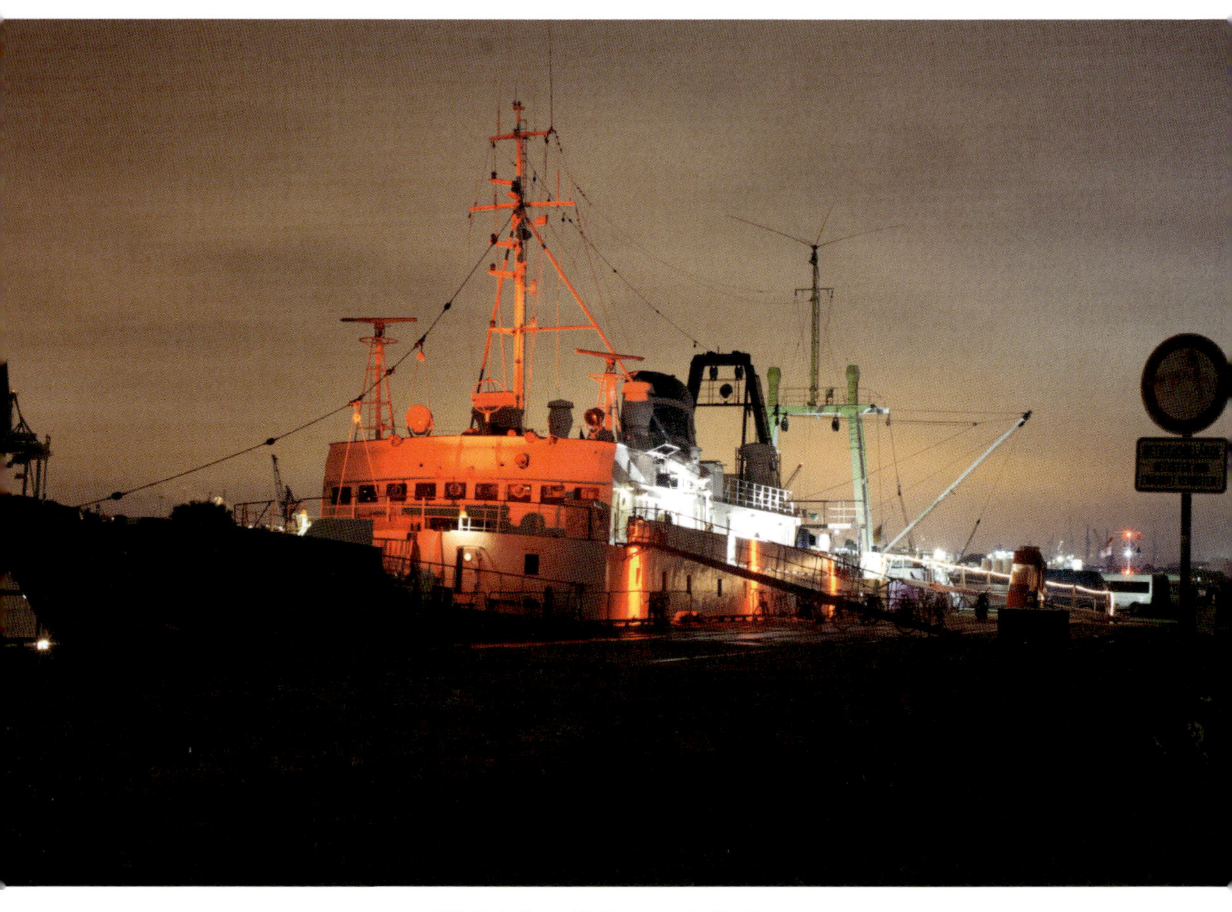

MS Stubnitz at Kirchenpauerkai in Hamburg

MS Stubnitz

The Motorschiff Stubnitz e.V. has two histories. The ship was commissioned by the German Democratic Republic in 1964 and launched from Stralsund. She and her sister ships marked the start of flotilla fishing in the Baltic: large catches of herring were shock-frozen and transported aboard these vessels. As a result of German reunification, most of the shipping industries were abandoned and the MS Stubnitz was decommissioned in 1992. In the same year, a collective of artists overtook the responsibility for her further existence. Their intention was to create a mobile center for music and the performing arts while facilitating cultural cooperation in northern Europe. With their ambitious aims they have enjoyed great success: the MS Stubnitz was listed as a historic monument in 2003. As a venue, it has a positive reputation in the music world and won its first prize for its rock/pop/jazz program with the title "Venue of the Year 2013." Meanwhile the ship has undertaken 140 projects in 22 ports and 11 countries.

The project is independently operated by the non-profit association Motorschiff Stubnitz e.V., which consists of an international collective of individuals. Although the organizational structure aboard is very horizontal, the elaborate know-how that is required of certain tasks is not a matter for collective decision-making. To this end many decisions are made by those few members in charge. The financing of the project is dependent on earnings of the cultural program and is supported by corporate events, public patronage for specific projects and the goodwill of its donors, but the only way for the laborious project to survive is through the engagement and steady influx of unpaid volunteers.

The aesthetic and acoustic qualities of the large spaces inside the ship provide many opportunities to further develop it as a location for all kinds of meetings, presentations, and exhibitions involving state-of-the-art audiovisual presentations. Unfortunately, the continuation of the project faces growing challenges. The operation and maintenance of a historic seagoing vessel of such size has become more complex and costly. Waterfront development projects are decreasing the number of suitable mooring spaces in Europe and the complexity of regulations for public events in harbors is growing inexorably. For these reasons, the MS Stubnitz has put a great deal of energy into settling in Hamburg HafenCity where goodwill to retain the ship as a cultural complement to the neighborhood has been shown not only from audiences but also from the local development society (HafenCity Hamburg GmbH), the municipality, and the Cultural Office of Hamburg.

ms.stubnitz.com

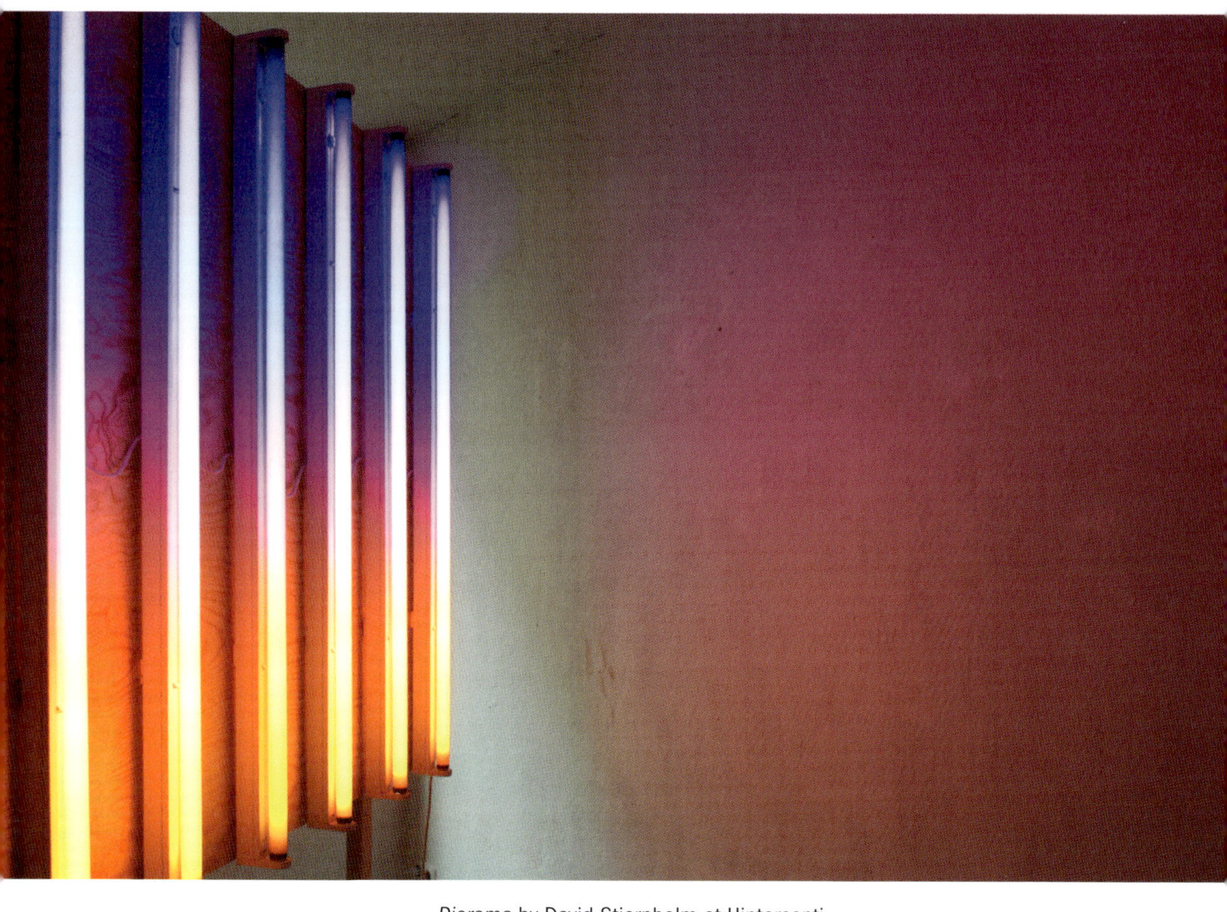

Diorama by David Stjernholm at Hinterconti

SixtyEight

SixtyEight opened as 68 Square Meters Art Space in May 2011. Originally 68 Square Meters was located in the East Amager quarter of Copenhagen as part of the creative platform PB43 (Andersen, this volume) but was relocated to the city center of Copenhagen. When it was opened, exhibitions of foreign artists in Copenhagen tended to be more commercial in nature. The goal of the founders was to bring Danish and international artists together in an experimental curatorial context and to expand the context of exhibitions by also hosting events around the questions and themes of the respective exhibitions. The aim is to allow the process leading up to the exhibition to translate into the exhibition itself, while also taking the opportunity to dwell on debates opened up by artistic and curatorial practices.

The profile of Sixty Eight has not been narrowed down to one that only presents a specific medium or group of artists because its founders are not interested in maintaining the separation between genres, trends, or concepts. The space is an open laboratory for artists and curators, which has resulted in numerous collaborations across generations, national identities, and methods of artistic research. Curatorial research in SixtyEight is based on analyzing artists' practices in relation to each other and how they correlate with or contradict philosophical and political questions. This framework facilitates the examination of the ways in which the politics of representation alter with time and how artists and curators relate to these changes and challenges.

SixtyEight has mainly been financed through funding provided by the Danish Art Foundation and the Municipality of Copenhagen along with private investment by the organizers. So far it has not been possible for the two operators to make a living from the work with the exhibition space, although it is hoped that this will be different in the future as a result of the adoption of a new approach to funding acquisition. In order to change the precarious conditions for younger artists and curators, SixtyEight is going to initiate new approaches to the structures within which the work takes place by continuing to insist on the importance of alternatives to institutional and commercial endeavors. This entails taking risks, expanding funding networks beyond state support, and trying out new platforms that focus on the quality of spaces run by curators and artists.

sixtyeight.dk

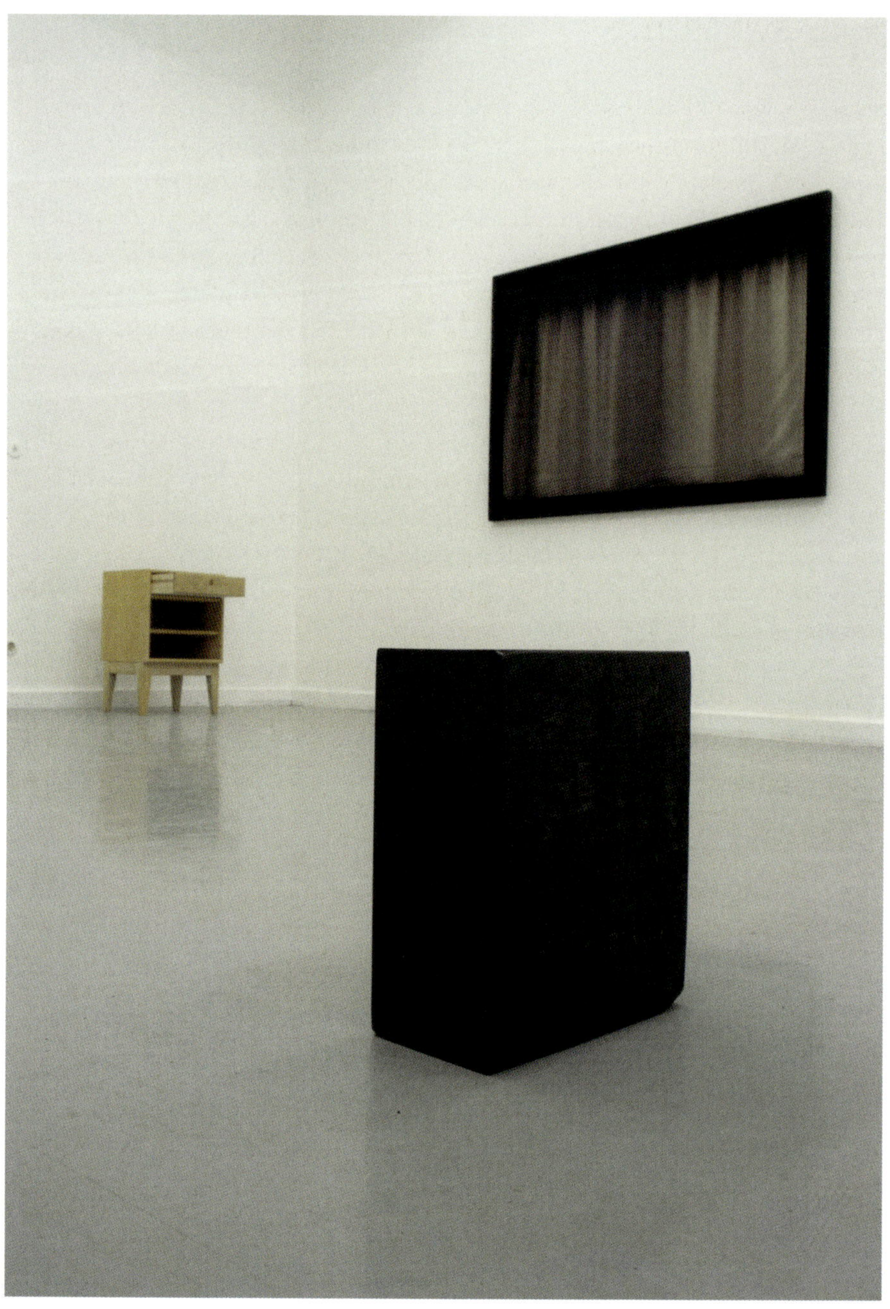

Black-out curtain 3 by Camilla Rasborg and *Rebus* by Heidi Hove at Viktoria Kaserne (fux eG)

Sydhavn Station

Sydhavn Station was established in 2012 in the former ticket office at the city train station of Sydhavn—a mixed residential area of the south harbor in Copenhagen. Although it is a mere five minute ride from the central train station, the surroundings make one feel like being in the suburbs. The setting is mostly dominated by red brick apartment buildings, take-away food stands and supermarkets. Sydhavn Station consists of two office-like rooms from the 1980s and five studios in use by some of the artists involved in the space. The space was founded under the tenet of an artist-run, DIY, and build-your-own experimental platform.

Sydhavn Station and its unpretentious office premises stand out as a statement in and of itself. It bears an aesthetic and physical distance to the professionalism that has become a commonplace style in Copenhagen over the past few years. The premises of the station beg for experiments and offer opportunities for experimentation with art in the public sphere: here works are able to descend into the context and vantage point of the everyday by absconding from the artistic context of the traditional white cube.

Ten artists are currently running the space. Each of the artists has their own artistic approach, which is mirrored in the varied exhibition program and the fluid profile of the space. The exhibition program focuses on contemporary art of experimental and conceptual character, such as solo and group exhibitions, poetry readings, concerts, performances, talks, and events by artists from Denmark and abroad. The aim is to create a framework in which even incomprehensible artistic experiments can meet another audience without necessarily entertaining, banalizing, or regurgitating. The exhibition program received a grant from the Danish Arts Foundation for the first two years, but is now exclusively financially supported by the artists running it and a small grant from the local neighborhood for promotion of its activities in the community.

sydhavnstation.info

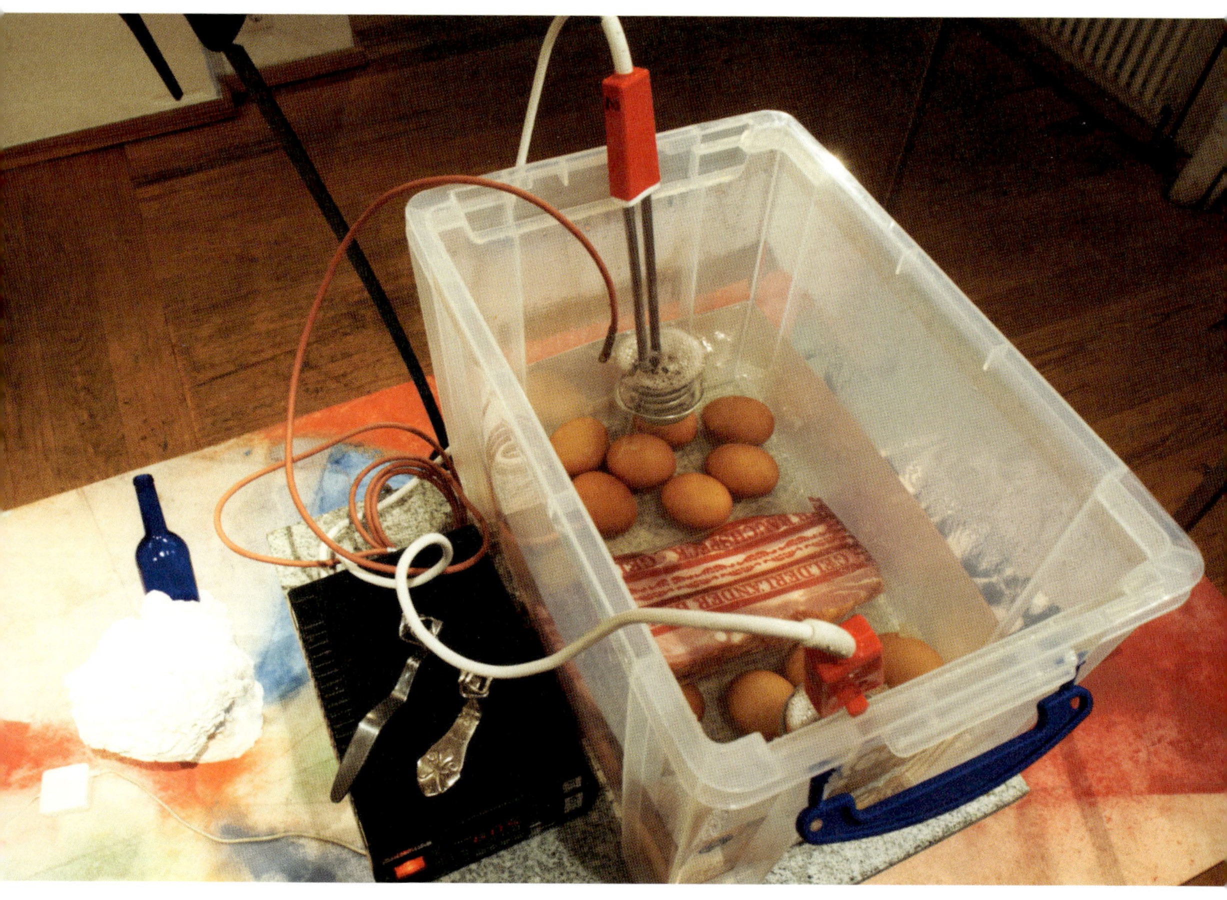

Financial Time by Years (Steffen Jorgensen, Anna Margrethe Pedersen, Merete Vyff Slyngborg, Ditte Soria and Søren Aagaard) at Vorwerkstift

Vorwerkstift

The Vorwerkstift building is located in Hamburg's St. Pauli district known as Karolinen-viertel. In 1866 it was donated by the Hamburg merchant Georg Friedrich Vorwerk as a refuge for those who, through no fault of their own, found themselves destitute. Although it was scheduled for demolition, the building was conserved and listed as a historic monument in the 1980's. Since then, the Vorwerkstift (Vorwerk e.V.) has been a work-place and residence for artists, cultural workers, and scientists. The history of today's usage began with the squatting of a former fire station, where artists wanted to estab-lish a studio and residence. Politicians proposed the Vorwerkstift as an alternative. The municipality agreed to rent out the building and its garden to the Stiftung Freiraum e.V. that for thirty years since has managed and maintained the Vorwerkstift as a studio house.

Besides the studios, the building has an exhibition space, work spaces for photography, woodworking, printing, music, and offers accommodation for nineteen permanent resi-dents and three short-term guests. Those who live in Vorwerkstift should be able to further develop themselves artistically and only have to pay the costs of operations and utilities. This particular form of artistic support should be open to as many young people as possible. Therefore, the length of residence in the house is limited to three years. Every year, vacancies are awarded via a residential scholarship granted to applicants by a jury composed of current residents and members of the Stiftung Freiraum e.V. On the ground floor, the artists of the Vorwerkstift run an exhibition space just recently named Galerie 21. Since the beginning, the project hosted exhibitions and concerts here. With its narrow rooms, the space offers various possibilities for presentations. An in-house gallery group coordinates the assignment, schedule, and execution of the exhibitions. Over the last few years, the initiative of the residents has repeatedly led to the introduction of a myriad of diverse thematically connected events.

Recently the relationship between the artists and the Stiftung Freiraum e.V. has been darkened over the course of several conflicts. In 2009, the scholarship holders declared the building as occupied in order to defend themselves against their decreasing influence on the occupancy and the artistic content. Some residents feared the commercialization of Vorwerkstift as part of the ongoing gentrification of the area. Although the relationship between the inhabitants and the Stiftung Freiraum e.V. has been restored to a certain degree, the future cooperation and the maintenance of Vorwerkstift as studio and artist house is uncertain.

vorwerkstift.de

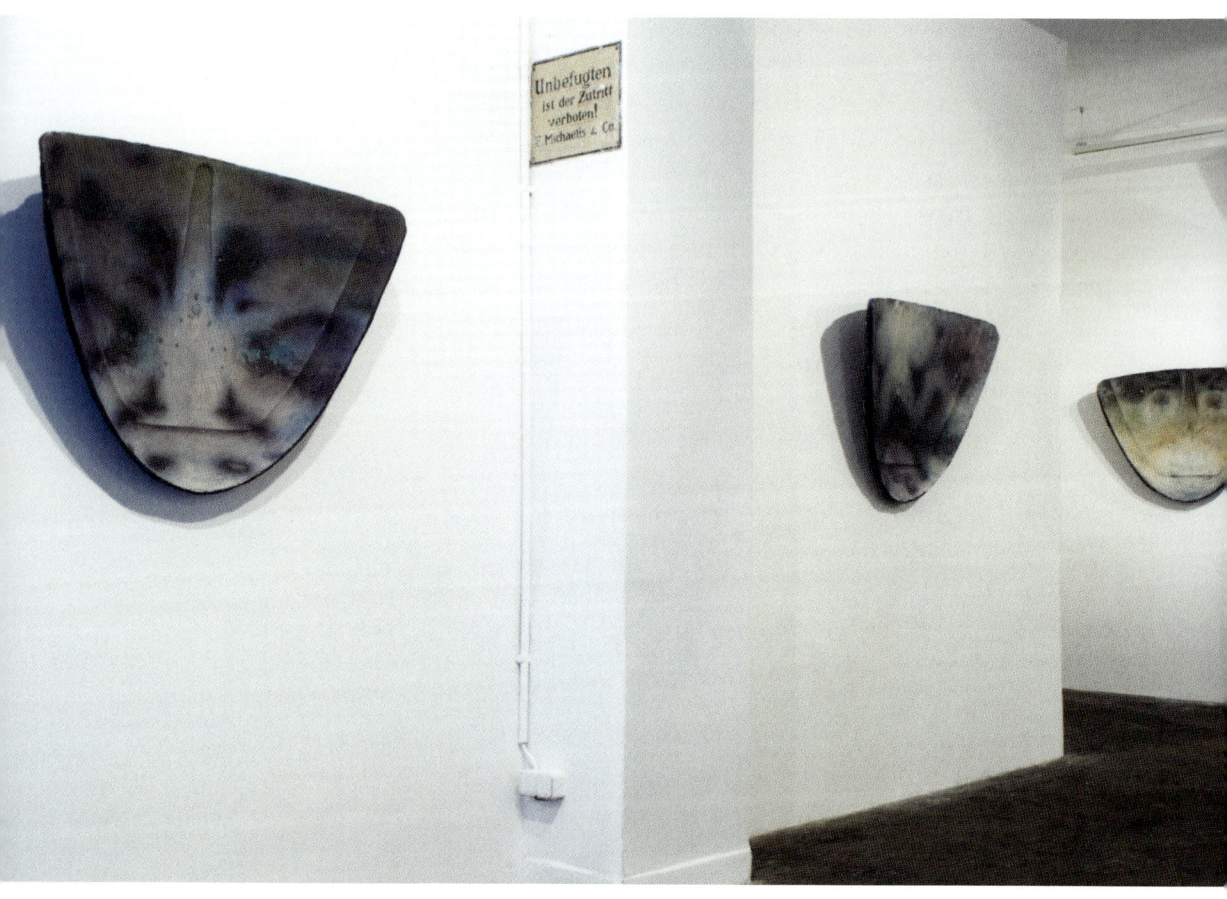

Lepidoptera Series by Silas Inoue at Westwerk

Westwerk

Westwerk e.V. is the largest non-profit, artist-run exhibition space in Hamburg. It was founded in 1985 and is located in the City Center. The building's history began as a seventeenth century harbor warehouse. Later the six-story building became the home to a paper manufacturer. Ultimately it was left vacant and scheduled for demolition, but a group of artists and musicians discovered the derelict building, founded an association (Westwerk e.V.), and rented the whole building from the city. They immediately moved in and started using its large rooms as studios and rehearsal spaces. The ground floor became a public venue presenting a wide-range of artistic events. It consists of a main hall with a floor space of around 170 square meters that is mostly used for presenting exhibitions and installations, and a large backroom, which is primarily used for staging concerts, readings, film events, and parties.

Westwerk e.V. was initially founded as a means of stopping the demolition of the historic building. The artists set it up as a non-profit association in order to apply for public grants and funding. The very mixed crowd of twenty-five young artists, musicians, writers, and others worked together spontaneously planning, organizing, and publicizing events, maintaining the space and somehow managing its limited finances. Although it has three elected chairpersons, the association works in fact entirely non-hierarchically. Rental issues, finance, and the arts program are decided jointly by all members, who also participate in running the venue. Even in Westwerk's thirtieth year, no one earns an income for working on the project. Funding for the exhibition space comes principally from two sources: a modest public grant from the Ministry of Culture in Hamburg, which Westwerk applies for once a year on the basis of the planned exhibition program. Additionally, minor financing is generated by a percentage on sales of art works shown in the exhibitions. All other spaces in the building such as studios are paid for individually by the artists and other residents in the house.

From the very beginning, the idea was to share the means of artistic production rather than producing a commercially viable gallery. Through dialogue, networking with other artist-run spaces and groups, research, and serendipity, the "Westwerkers" seek to create a lively agenda of varying formats and media that presents work and projects by experimentally inclined, young, underexposed, challenging, or awkward artists and groups from Hamburg and beyond. In practice, little attention is paid to categories that try to distinguish art from music from performance from installation from literature from video et cetera. The broad range of media, experience, preferences, and networks is reflected in how the program is shaped, artists chosen to be exhibited, and strategies developed for funding.

In terms of local impact, Westwerk has acted as a catalyst for the local arts scene. By resisting the demolition of the historic building in the 1980s boom for urban redevelopment, while persistently publicizing its work as an artists' community, Westwerk led the way to transforming the neighborhood into an ensemble of galleries, bookshops, venues, and meeting places for people interested in contemporary culture.

westwerk.org

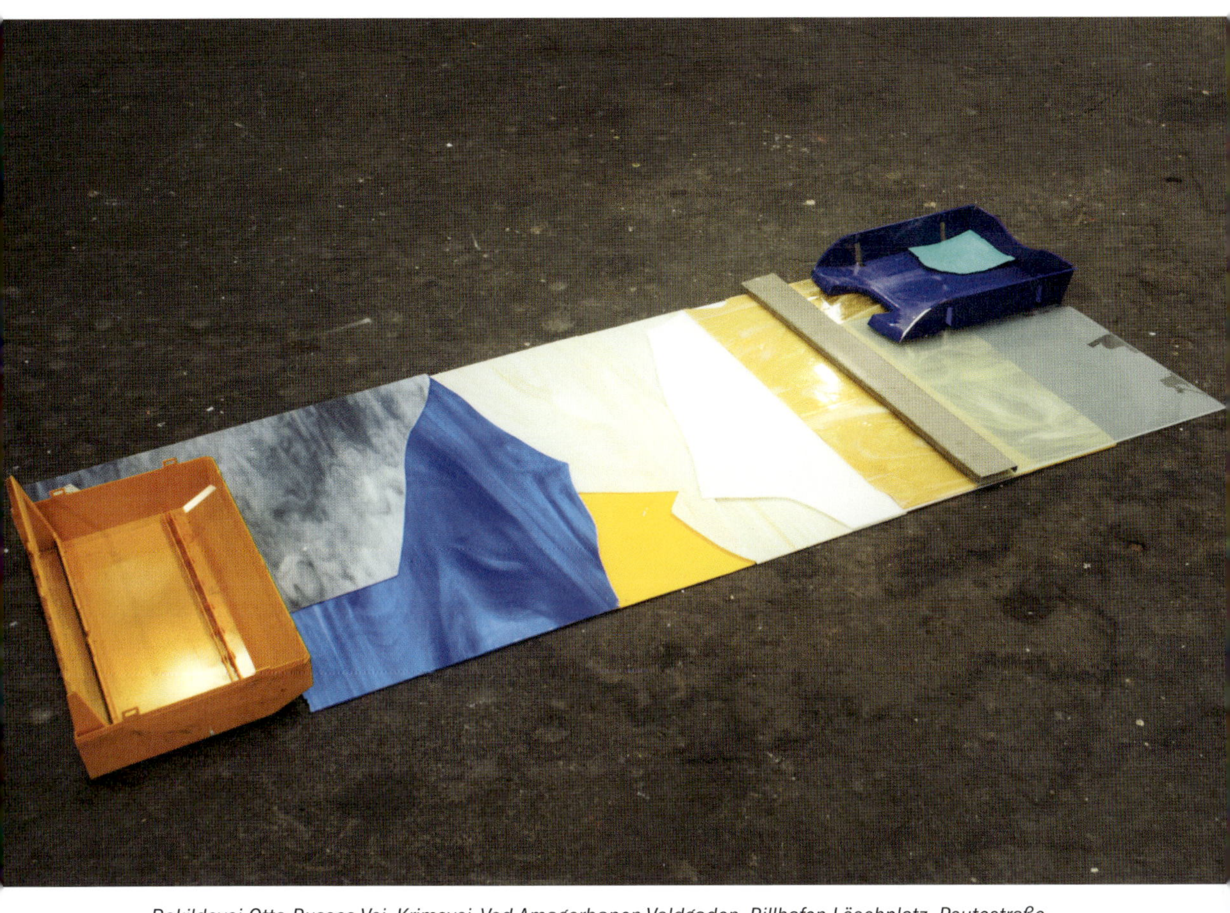

Rokildevej Otto Busses Vej, Krimsvej, Ved Amagerbanen Voldgaden, Billhafen Löschplatz, Peutestraße, Brandshofer Deich, Lippmannstraße by Christian Elovara Dinesen at Westwerk

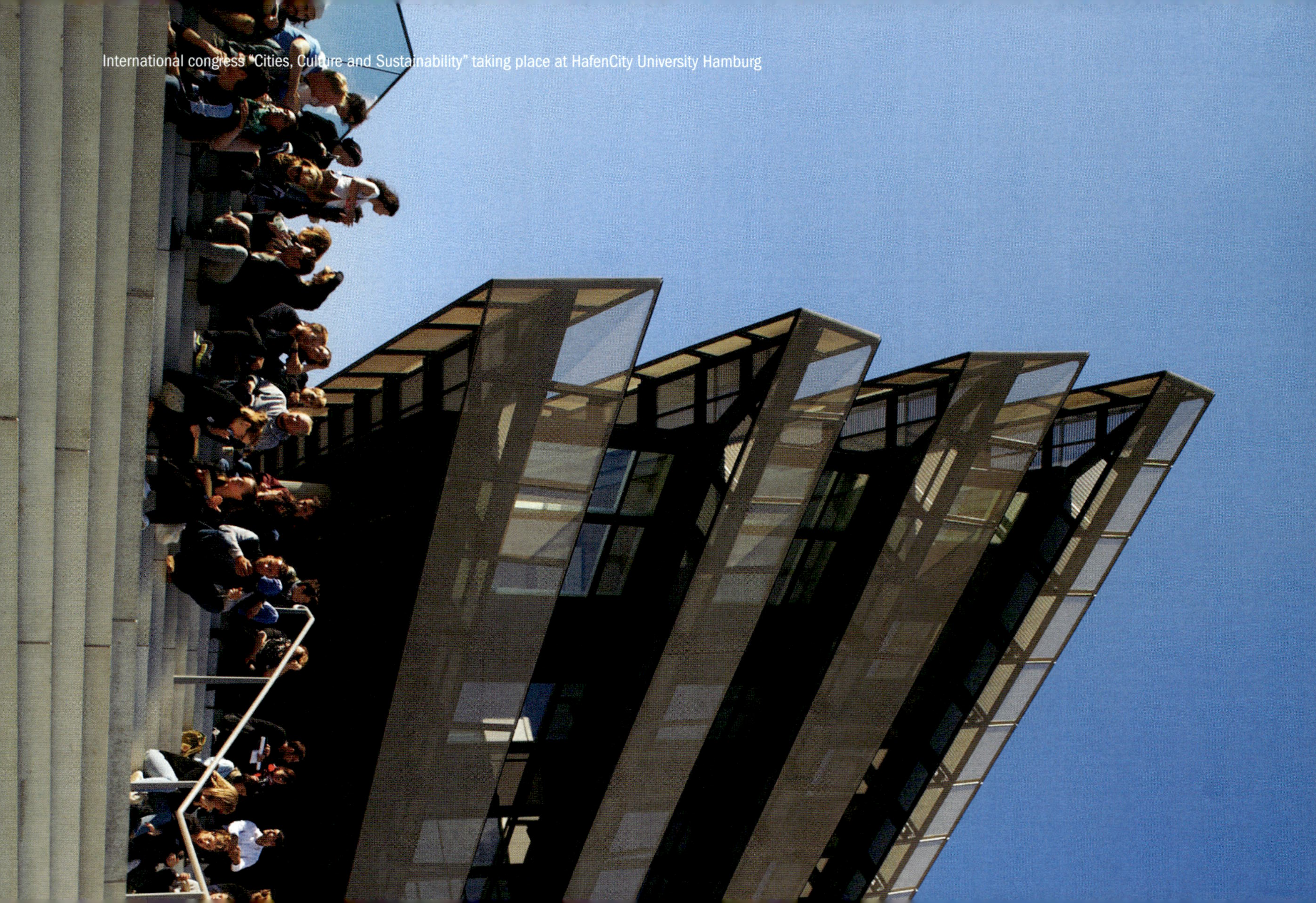

International congress "Cities, Culture and Sustainability" taking place at HafenCity University Hamburg

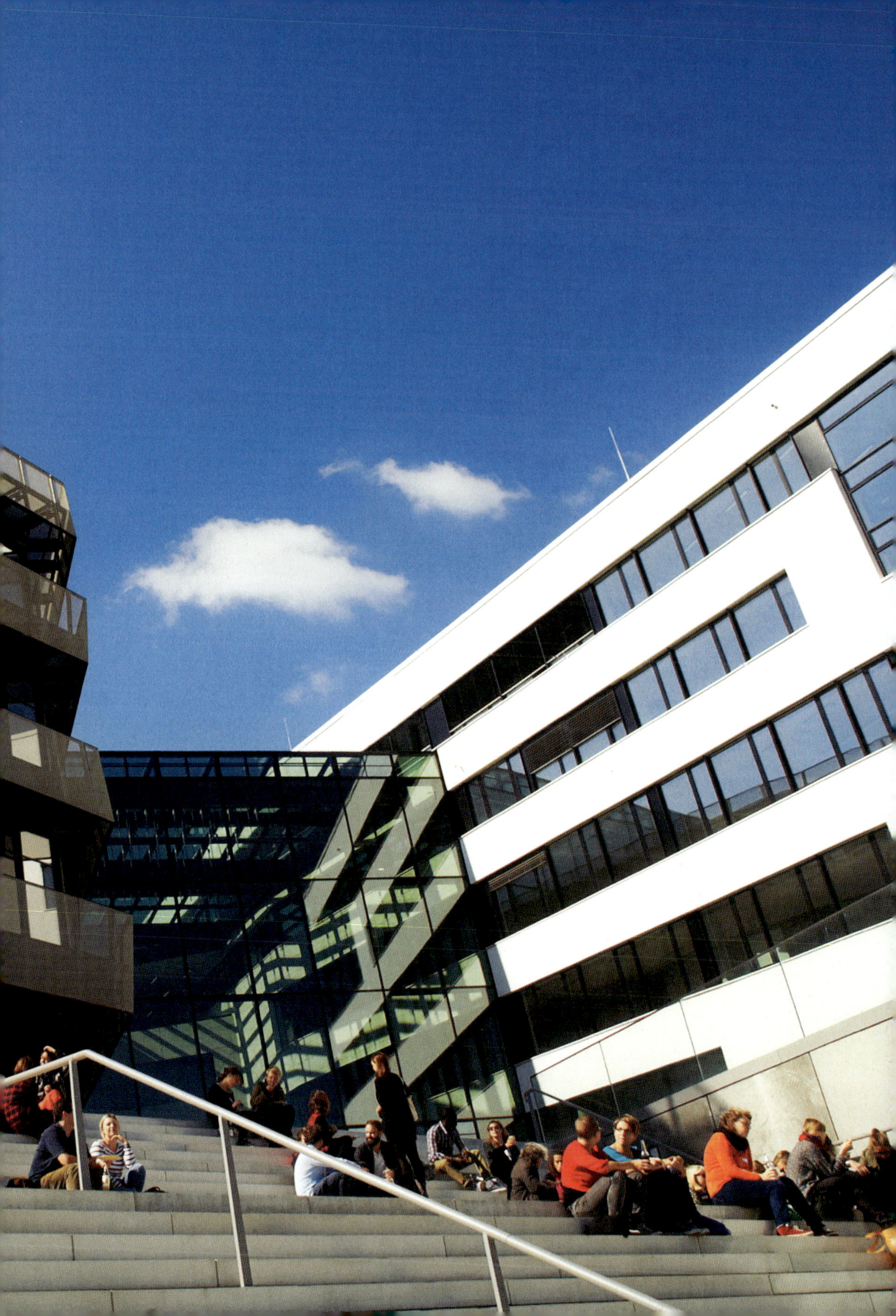

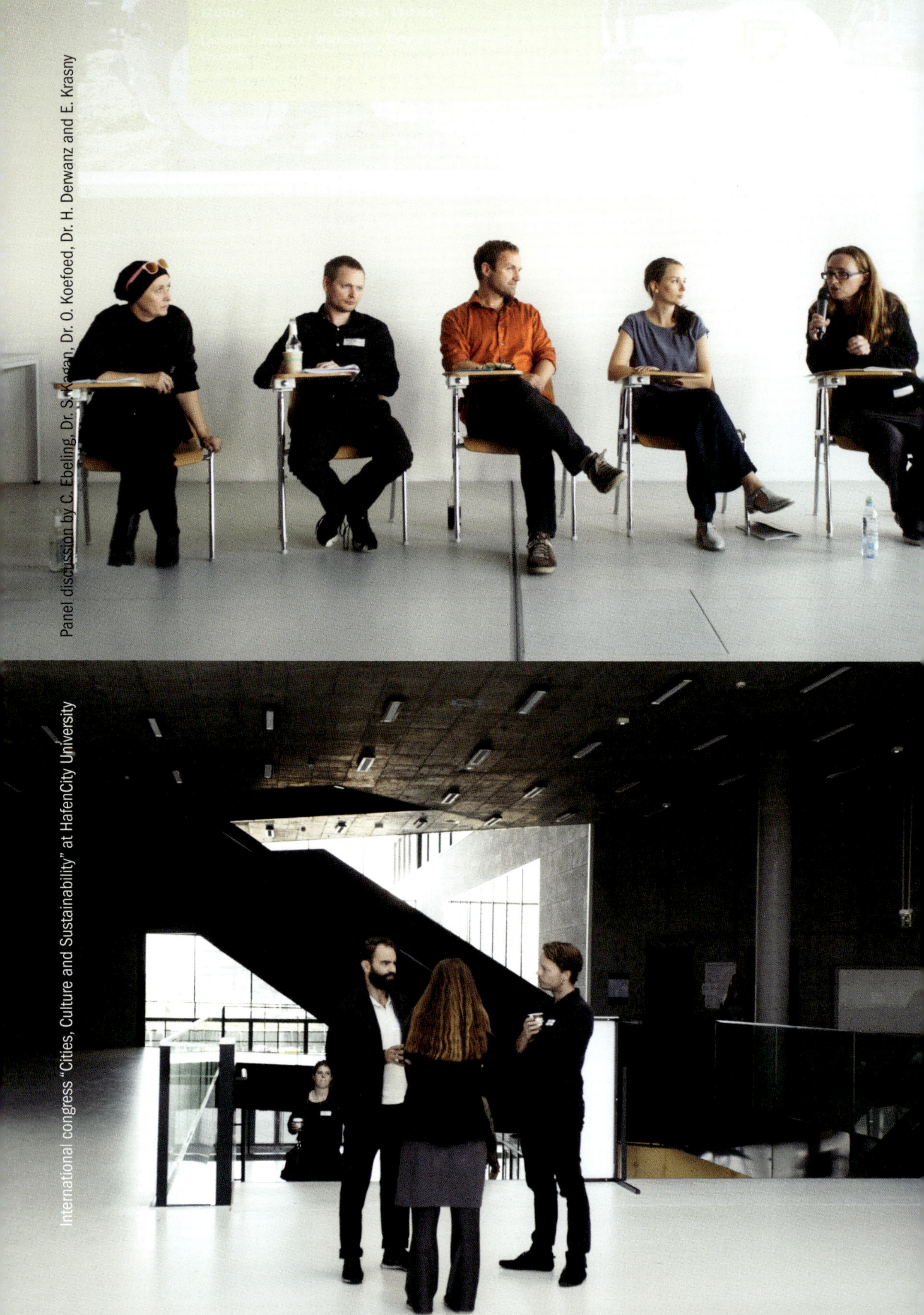

Panel discussion by C. Ebeling, Dr. S. Kagan, Dr. O. Koefoed, Dr. H. Derwanz and E. Krasny

International congress "Cities, Culture and Sustainability" at HafenCity University

Curricula Vitae

Steen Andersen

Steen Andersen is a cultural entrepreneur, editor and writer based in Copenhagen and Berlin. He is trained in urban geography, organizational and developmental psychology, and international marketing. He also studied philosophy and film in London and computer art at Aarhus School of Art. From 2011 to 2015 he was the coordinator of the cultural and entrepreneurial platform PB43 in Copenhagen. He is the co-initiator of The Working Community PB43 Nordhavn, Culture Hall Building 5, The International Summer School "Urban Culture in Theory and Action" and the award-winning projects PB43 Publishing and Prague's Garden (Prags Have). From 2014 to 2015 he had a seat in the Local Council of Amager Øst, Copenhagen and was a member of the editorial team for the Amager local newspaper. In recent years he has worked on cultural exchange between Copenhagen and Germany, and has been editor and author of various books and articles about city development, social activism, urban culture, and sustainable architecture. Recently he has been writing a series of articles called "Poor, But Sexy" for the German Urbanist Magazine.

Till Haupt

Since 2009, the Hamburg-based artist and activist Till Γ.Ε. Haupt has been involved at the Gängeviertel and in the Recht auf Stadt network. Trained as a marketing and communication specialist, he studied graphic design and fine arts in Darmstadt and Hamburg. From that time on, he has been occupied with the concept of usable artworks known as *Handlungskunst*. Based on those ideas he has developed a concept of Real Life Art, which he dubs *subsoziale performance*. In 2012, he became one of the project managers of City Link in Hamburg. He holds a seat on the board of directors at the cooperative Gängeviertel Genossenschaft 2010 eG as well as the local association of fine artists BBK Hamburg.

Sacha Kagan

Since 2005, Sacha Kagan has been a research associate at the Leuphana University Lueneburg, ISCO (Institute of Sociology and Cultural Organization). He coordinates the research area "creative and artistic praxis for a sustainable urban development" in the research project "The City as Space of Possibility." His activities lie in the transdisciplinary field of arts and (un-)sustainability. He is a founding member of Cultura21 e.V., founding coordinator of Cultura21 International, and the chair of the Research Network Sociology of the Arts at the European Sociological Association.

Oleg Koefoed

Oleg Koefoed works as an action-philosopher who is based in Copenhagen and co-directs the "thinkery" Growing Pathways—creating culturally anchored strategies for sustainable futures. He develops new methods for bringing in cultural mindsets to sustainability strategies within e.g. urban change, strategies for cities, and links between the implementation of policies and street-level practices of sustainable urban innovation. He has co-developed a method for the development of social and sustainable innovation, which is currently being used to teach, advise, and inspire individuals and organizations. He regularly assists the Nordic Council of Ministers in developing strategies for culture and sustainability, and works with a.o. the European Commission and the Maltese Ministry of Culture in regional and urban cultural strategies for sustainable development. He is co-founder and board member of Cultura21 Nordic and part of Cultura21 International's core group and collaborates with a number of higher education institutions in Denmark and around the world. He is a father of four and lives on the island of Amager in Copenhagen.

Elke Krasny

Elke Krasny is curator, cultural theorist, urban researcher, writer and Professor of Art and Education at the Academy of Fine Arts Vienna; 2016 she taught at the Postgraduate Program on Postindustrial Design at the University of Thessaly, Volos; 2014 City of Vienna Visiting Professor at the Vienna University of Technology; Visiting Scholar at the Canadian Centre for Architecture in Montréal in 2012; Visiting Curator at the Hong Kong Community Museum Project in 2011. Krasny holds a Ph.D. in Fine Arts from the University of Reading, Department of Art, Research Platform for Curatorial and Cross-disciplinary Cultural Studies, Practice-Based Doctoral Programme. Recent curatorial works include *On the Art of Housekeeping and Budgeting in the 21st Century*, curated together with Regina Bittner and presented at Bauhaus Dessau, *Hands-On Urbanism 1850-2012. The Right to Green* which was shown at the Architecture Centre Vienna, the Museum for Contemporary Art Leipzig, the 2012 Venice Architecture Biennale and at Moravská Gallery Brno 2016-2017, *Suzanne Lacy's International Dinner Party in Feminist Curatorial Thought* at Zurich University of the Arts in 2015 and *Mapping the Everyday. Neighborhood Claims for the Future* at Simon Fraser Gallery in 2011-2012. Her 2015 essay *Growing the Seeds of Change* was included in Jordan Geiger's volume Entr'Acte, Performing Publics, Pervasive Media, and Architecture. She co-edited the 2012 volume *Hands-On Urbanism. The Right to Green* and the 2013 volume *Women's:Museum. Curatorial Politics in Feminism, Education, History, and Art.*

Michael Lingner

Michael Lingner is professor of art theory at the Academy of Fine Arts in Hamburg. Since 2004 he has headed the "Labor: Art & Science"; Previously, he has held teaching positions at several universities, among others as Head of the Theory Department of the Jan van Eyck Academy, Maastricht. He studied art, philosophy, sociology and art history. As a practicing artist, he participated in several exhibitions, among others at the Documenta VI; as art theorist, he has published numerous articles and books.

Levente Polyák

Levente Polyák is an urban planner, researcher and policy adviser. He studied architecture, urbanism, sociology, and art theory in Budapest and Paris, and worked on urban regeneration projects for the New York, Paris, Rome, Vienna, and Budapest municipalities. He is Managing Director of Eutropian Planning and Research, and board member of both the Hungarian Contemporary Architecture Centre and the Wonderland Platform for European Architecture. He specializes in urban regeneration, cultural development, community participation, local economic development, and social innovation, with a special focus on building development, scenarios on existing resources. In the past years, he has been researching new organizational and economic models of community-led urban development projects, including the temporary use of vacant properties and community-run social services. Based on this research, he has been helping public administrations as well as professional and community organizations of various sizes and geographic locations across Europe.

Carsten Rabe

Carsten Rabe is a curator and fine-art photographer living in Hamburg. He has exhibited his photographs in national and international solo and group shows since 2000. For the past fifteen years he has been based at Westwerk Hamburg, where he works as curator and coordinator of the exhibition program, and is closely linked to the Gängeviertel initiative. Since 2010 he has curated several larger group and concept exhibitions in Paris, Copenhagen and Hamburg. He is one of the main coordinators behind the City Link Artist Exchange between Hamburg and Copenhagen and was responsible for the exhibition program of the City Link Festival.

Christoph Schäfer

Christoph Schäfer is an artist, activist, and author living in Hamburg. Since the early 1990s, he has worked on everyday urban life and the production of spaces for collective desires. This interest is reflected in a wide range of work that often reflects and sometimes intervenes: Christoph is decisively involved in Park Fiction, the park at St. Pauli's Hafenrand, based on the "collective production of desires." As a member of the group

"Park Fiction," as well as the "PlanBude"-Team, Schäfer is interested in the exchange between different subjectivities and the collective redefinition of public space. With Park Fiction, Schäfer was part of documenta 11. His first book, *The City is Our Factory*, was published by Spector Books in 2010. His drawing series "Bostanorama" was shown at the 13th Istanbul Biennial in 2013.

Annabel Trautwein

Annabel Trautwein works as a freelance journalist in Hamburg. She graduated in cultural studies, religious studies, and history and took up her profession at the editorial desks of a local newspaper. She lived, worked and studied in France and Syria. Today she publishes her own hyperlocal online magazine WilhelmsburgOnline.de and writes for the street paper Hinz&Kunzt and the weekly DIE ZEIT. The question that haunts her is: how can socially disadvantaged people seize the chances and opportunities that urbanity has to offer?

Michael Ziehl

Michael Ziehl lives in Hamburg where he is running Urban Upcycling—Agency for Urban Resources. He holds a Master of Science in the field of urban planning and is a graduate engineer in the field of Architecture. He is the chairman of the supervisory board of the Gängeviertel Genossenschaft 2010 eG (Gängeviertel Cooperative) and is currently working on his Ph.D. in the research training group "Performing Citizenship" at the HafenCity University Hamburg. His current interest focuses on cooperation between citizens' initiatives and municipalities with a contribution to more resilient cities. Within the frame of City Link Festival he organized the Congress "Cities, Culture & Sustainability."

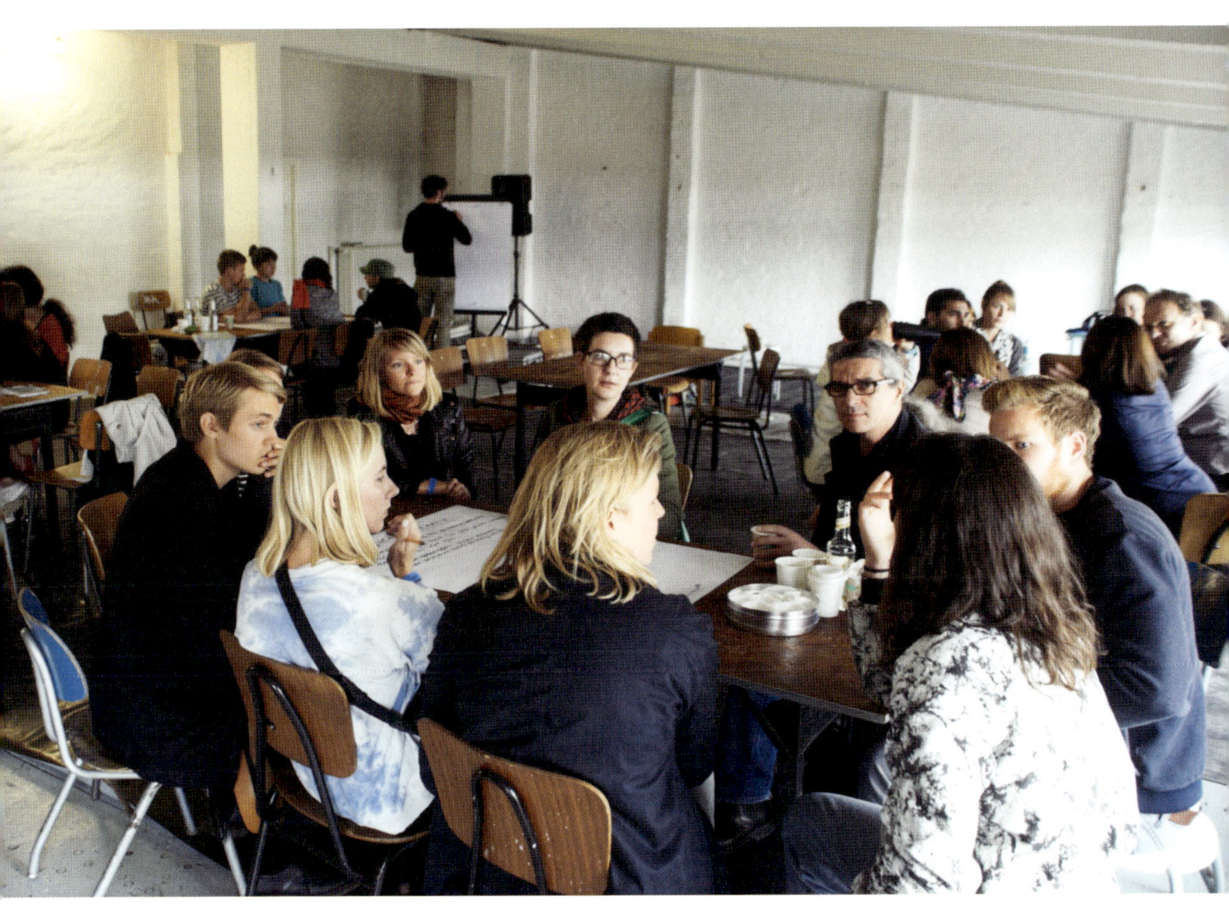

City Link Workshop at ABM

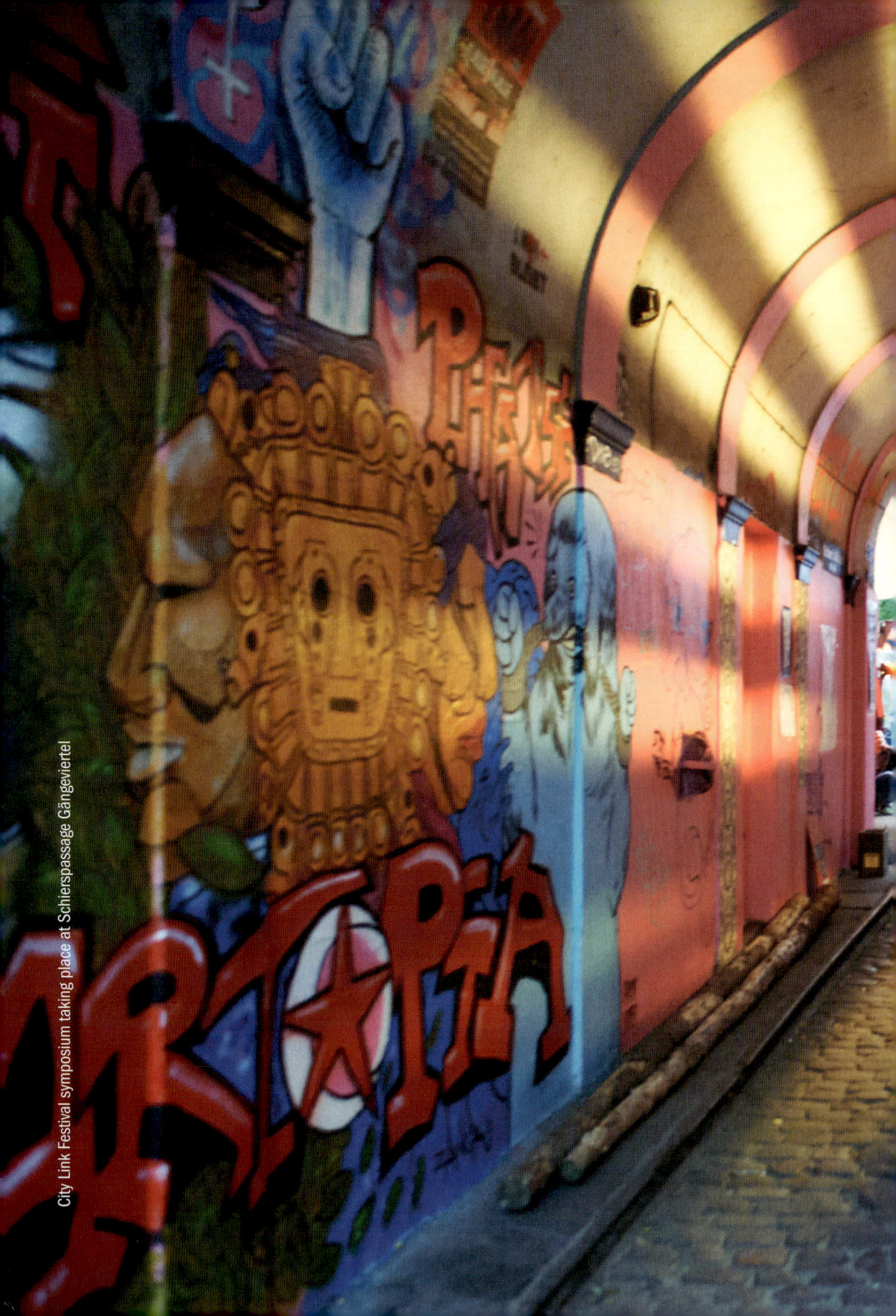

City Link Festival symposium taking place at Schierspassage Gängeviertel

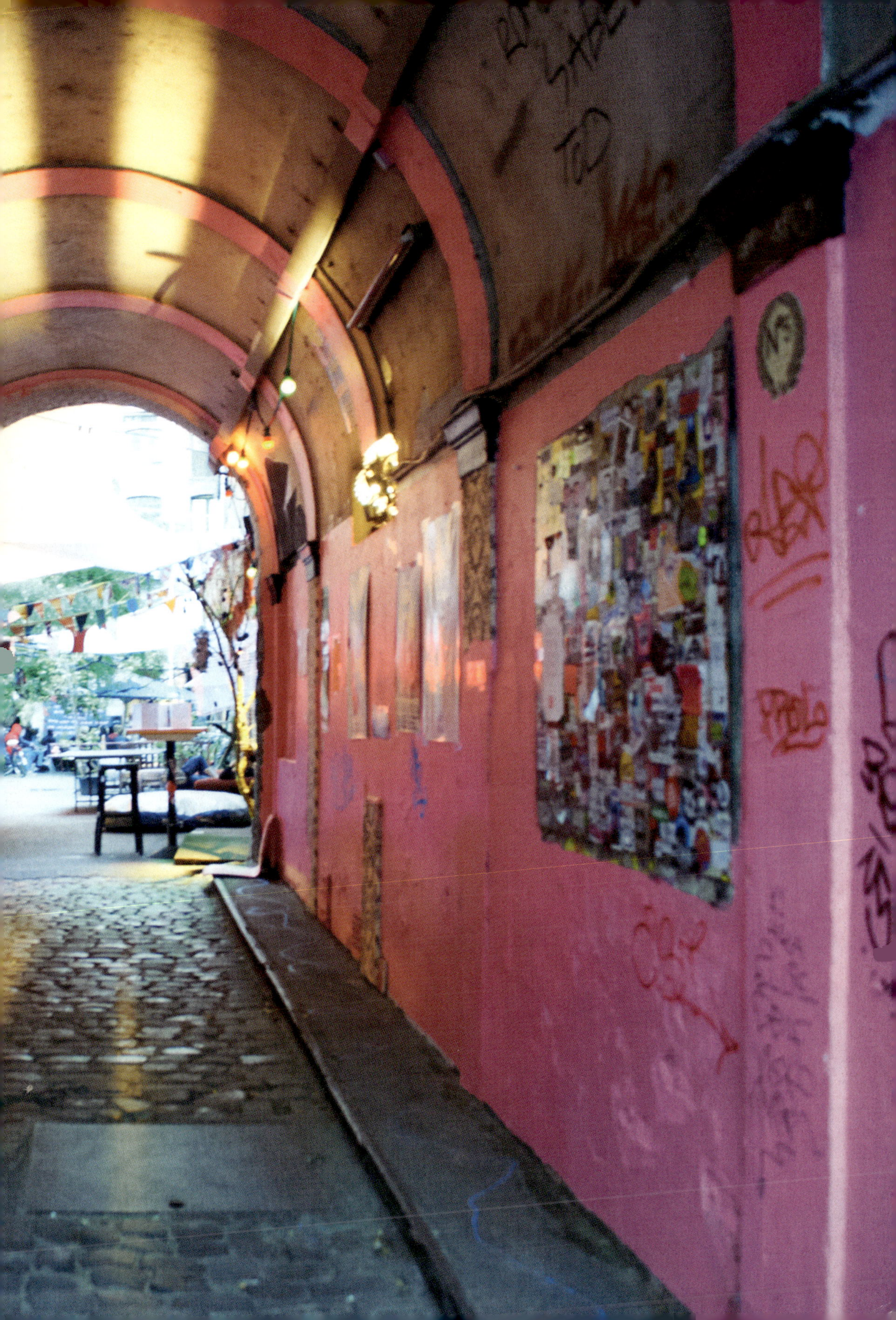

Imprint

© 2016 by jovis Verlag GmbH
Texts by kind permission of the authors.
Pictures by kind permission of the photographers/holders of the picture rights.
All rights reserved.

Editors: Michael Ziehl, Carsten Rabe, Till Haupt
Contact: kontakt@urban-upcycling.de

Design: Carsten Rabe

City Link Festival photos: Franziska Holz, Till Haupt, Carsten Rabe
Photos page 52: Elke Krasny; 53: Chi-Ho Chung; 54: Shu-Mei Huang, Becky Au; 55: Ho-Man Au, Elke Krasny; 56: Elke Krasny; 76–81: Franziska Holz; 90: Ingrid Bugge, Antonin Matejovsky; 92: Anders Find; 98 Maria Dembek

Cover front: Video still *Balancing Act* by Nina Mangalanayagam at Galerie Speckstraße
Cover back: *Diorama* by David Stjernholm at Hinterconti

Translation: Daniel Caleb Thompson
Proofreading: Justin Ross, Berlin
Printing and Binding: GRASPO CZ a. s., Zlín

Bibliographic information published by the Deutsche Nationalbibliothek
The Deutsche Nationalbibliothek lists this publication in the Deutsche Nationalbibliografie; detailed bibliographic data are available on the Internet at http://dnb.d-nb.de

jovis Verlag GmbH
Kurfürstenstrasse 15/16
10785 Berlin
www.jovis.de

jovis books are available worldwide in selected bookstores. Please contact your nearest bookseller or visit www.jovis.de for information concerning your local distribution.

ISBN 978-3-86859-416-4